A SEASON OF WEATHERING

BOOKS BY WILLIAM A. OWENS

Tales From The Derrick Floor
with Mody C. Boatright
Three Friends: Ray Bedichek, J. Frank Dobie, Walter Prescott Webb
This Stubborn Soil
Look To The River
Fever in The Earth
Walking On Borrowed Land
Slave Mutiny: The Revolt on The Schooner Amistad

A SEASON
OF
WEATHERING

BY WILLIAM A. OWENS

For
The Students of Ector High

William A. Owens

CHARLES SCRIBNER'S SONS

NEW YORK

Printed in the United States of America
Library of Congress Catalog Card Number 72–1196
SBN 684–13022–x (cloth)

A PROLOGUE PROLONGED

When I was sixty I published *This Stubborn Soil*, a book I wrote in search of myself. I hoped that by setting down memories of my East Texas boyhood and opening them to scrutiny the questions I kept asking about myself would be answered. At the time, the sense of place was uppermost in my mind, so much so that I opened the book with the following:

PIN HOOK

If one was born in Paris or London or New York, or even in Dallas, to name a place closer to home, he has, when writing about himself, only to mention the city and the reader pictures place, buildings, people, and he can go ahead to particulars about himself and his family. But since I was born at Pin Hook, Texas, a place whose character has not been made known to the world generally, I must begin by writing all I know or ever heard about it.

For as long as I can remember, Pin Hook has been a local force, like a strong character in a play, more so than any other community I have ever known—much more a byword than Woodland to the east or Novice to the west. As I see it now, the first settlers, the Witherspoons and McLemores, the Halls and Duvalls, who came up the Red River—the Rio Roxo of the Spaniards—from Arkansas, and leaving behind them the comparative safety of Pecan Point back on the river, settled along Little Pine Creek in spite of the danger of wild animals and wilder Indians, brought with them an attitude toward living that is still felt there—an attitude that makes the fiddle as useful as the plow and the Bible more to be treasured than all the libraries in the world.

English, Welsh, Scotch-Irish, a little French Huguenot, they were the trickle of a flow that for two hundred years had been moving slowly westward from the first settlements in Virginia, North Carolina, South Carolina. In their wagons and oxcarts, on horseback or as they said "foot-back and walking," these settlers came to a wilderness of oak and sweet gum made denser by huckleberry thickets on the uplands, by canebrakes in the creek bottoms. On grants from the Territory of Arkansas, sometimes with no grants at all, they staked out land for themselves which, when Texas became a republic in 1836, they were able to claim, as deeds in the General Land Office in Austin show. In those days, in that place, land was easy to come by. Holding it was not so easy. With no better tools than a poleax and a crosscut saw they cut away some of the timber—enough for patches of corn and cotton and black-eyed peas. With the help of a few Negro slaves they built log cabins for themselves, the timbers hand-hewn with a broadax, the boards for the roof hand-split with a froe and a wooden maul. They cleared the land and worked it and found in a few years that, sand on the surface, red clay underneath, it was "too pore to sprout peas"—as worn out as the land they had left behind in Tennessee and Arkansas.

It was a lonely land they had come to. From time unknown, Indians had passed through it, leaving woodland trails, leaving camping sites where the white man's plow turned up arrowheads and bits of broken pottery. The first settlers had only these trails and the trail they had made themselves up from Pecan Point. Then there was the trail coming on a more direct route for the settlers who crossed the Red River at Fulton, Arkansas, and moved west over the land. In time, the trail up from Pecan Point extended southwest through what is now the county seat, Paris. With the establishment of a steamboat landing at Pine Bluff, where Big Pine Creek empties into the river, the settlers cut a road north to it and south toward new settlements on Blossom Prairie. Where these roads crossed, Pin Hook came into being, named by persons unknown, with a name given in derision or despair to countless other places by settlers who had found the reality less than the dream.

It was a land tortured by weather. There were wet springs when days of pouring rain put creeks out of banks and washed away cotton and corn. At times, before the water could drain off, dust storms blew down from the western plains, clouding the sky and making mouths gritty. Summers were long, hot, dry—worst in the dog days of August, when creeks ran low and scummy and the earth cracked in the sun. The people learned to be grateful for the first cool days of fall, and to bundle up in hard winters when blue northers swept down across Kansas and Oklahoma. They shivered in their shacks and said there was "nothing between them and the North Pole but a bobbed-wire fence."

During the thirty years between the coming of the Witherspoons to Pin Hook and the outbreak locally called the "war between the sections," only a few new settlers arrived, and those who had already claimed the land were struggling hard to set up plantations like those they had known in Mississippi and other states of "the Old Southwest." Such plantations had proved possible in the rich red earth of the Red River bottoms. At Pin Hook the land was against them. The log houses of the owners were larger but in other ways no better than the log huts of the slaves, and the fare for both showed up as a laugh in a song: "hog and hominy and poke for greens."

Wars came and went, each leaving its mark: the Texas Revolution, the Mexican War, the Civil War. Men and boys from Pin Hook must have gone off to at least one of these, but they left no record that could be carved on a tombstone. Nevertheless the effects were there, especially after the Civil War, when the slaves took themselves and their freedom to the woods northwest of Pin Hook, where the Negroes still live. They were willing enough to come back and work by the day chopping or picking cotton, but the white men, with little money for hired hands, worked themselves, their wives, their children.

After the Civil War a great number of settlers, displaced persons, came in from Tennessee, Arkansas, Missouri, and Mississippi. Needing land, they bought small farms from the people who had been granted the land but could no longer hold it. This was a second move toward poverty, the Civil War having been the first. Worn out, saddled with what they saw was not hope but despair, they cleared their twenty-five or fifty acres, built shacks of logs or boxing planks, and settled down to a cotton and corn and black-eyed peas existence, a living submarginal, exhausting to mind and body. The living was added to with what could be brought from the woods and creek—the game and fish—and the pigs and cows and chickens kept by barefoot wives and barefoot daughters. It was taken from, drained away, by malaria, hookworm, and a short-rations disease called by Pin Hookers "pellegrisy."

The will of at least some of the people was to have a living better than this. They did what they could for church and school. From the beginning, homes were opened for meetings any time a preacher passed through. They were also opened for a kind of subscription school that was better than no school at all.

It took them fifty years to get a schoolhouse—a one-room building on land that now belongs to the graveyard, like many of the homes built of logs and chinked and daubed with clay. This school, called Pin Hook and open three months each winter, was good enough for more than twenty years. Then a new one-room frame building was built between the cross-roads and graveyard, on land deeded to Pin Hook by my father.

Pin Hook, a name good enough for the old school, was not good enough for the new. In tribute to a man of some prominence in the county, the new school was named Faulkner. The tribute proved small. The name Faulkner appears in school and election records, but it is rarely used in other ways. The name never did fit the temperament or way of living of the people in Pin Hook. In time the school was absorbed by a county system. Faulkner seems likely to be forgotten, but never Pin Hook.

In winter it was school by day, debating club by night, where men met in all seriousness to debate such subjects as whether a Negro has a soul. In one of these debates the referee, to stop a fist fight, ruled that, in view of the strong arguments on both sides, a Negro could be judged to have half a soul. In summer, with the addition of brush arbor under the oaks, it was a meeting house of church and singing school. It took them a hundred years to get a church building, and then it was secondhand, built from the lumber of the schoolhouse when, no longer needed, it was torn down.

Mostly Methodists and Baptists, Pin Hookers were religious in their own way—fervent in summer, cool in winter—and industrious when they had to be. Those who could, made music. Those who could not, listened. In meetings and Sunday-night singings they sang hymns with a whang that gave a minor cast to every tune. At Saturday-night parties they sang English and Scottish ballads, long and doleful tales of lords and ladies, of unrequited love, of murders as violent as anything on the frontier—and the people of the ballads were as real to Pin Hook as the singers of the songs. The language they sang or spoke, having existed some two hundred years with little benefit of writing or printing, was to anyone who had been outside "no end quare."

The Pin Hook I was born in was still a part of the frontier. The last Indian raid in Texas was only twenty years back and as fresh as yesterday in the minds of the people. Tales of the frontier were a part of daily life. So were the tales of the war between the sections and of that greatest of all heroes, Jesse James.

So I am from Pin Hook and Pin Hook is a part of me. All of my life has been a flight from it, but now, after many returnings I see that it has overtaken me at last.

Who am I? fretted me as much the day after the book was published as the day before, or in all the days I had spent recalling emotions and experiences and forming them into words. Help I had hoped for from others did not come. Many who read *This Stubborn Soil* wrote to ask what happened next, as if what I had written was a first volume designed to whet the appetite for the next. Whether I liked the task or not, I found myself again thrust into searching through emotions and experiences of succeeding years, again to expose them to scrutiny, my own and others'.

The search was infinitely harder. Within the simpler limits of Pin Hook, or even of my job at Sears Roebuck, reactions to experience could be defined in terms of the physical or emotional. From the first day I forced myself into school at Commerce, the intellectual had to be added, and a new complexity entered in. I had been swinging from country to town, uncertain as to where I was going —with doubts if indeed I could ever find a way. Entering training to be a teacher was still no guarantee. Neither was the day-to-day, hand-to-mouth existence I had during the training.

Nor could I be as internal or as alone. The account had to reflect, if at times tangentially, as clearly as possible the times I lived through and the people who lived through them with me, including my family.

When I arrived in Commerce June 3, 1924, I regarded myself as almost entirely shut off from my family. They had gone their ways; I had gone my own. Within a few months I knew I was wrong. My family, spread now to East Texas, West Texas, Chicago, with the barest communication among us, still marched through time as I did, chronologically abreast, perhaps emotionally abreast, as we were in our own ways reaching out to each other, but our feet were set on different treads. To examine my own experience fully, I soon saw, I had to examine theirs that touched mine.

The result may be the second part of an extended telling, with me at the center as I was at the center of the first. If so, the part that is mine is more symbolic because I became so much more the creature of a time than of a place. Pin Hook was still there, a magnet drawing me, a condition gnawing at me, so strongly that I never got over the feeling of wanting to go back. As awareness grew, I began to know that I was part not only of a time but of a special time. Perspectives began to change. I began to understand how much sway time has over place.

Almost daily some teacher reminded me that we were in a

time of remarkable change, especially in education, especially in education in Texas. Occasionally a teacher singled me out—me and my country language, my Pin Hook schooling—as an example of the need for change. These were moments of embarrassment, eased only when the teacher pointed out that I was there to take part in the change, in one of the most difficult ways, that of country schoolteacher.

No teacher brought out one thing that I knew: I was going to be a country schoolteacher at Pin Hook. It was a way, I told myself, to bring time and place together.

A SEASON OF WEATHERING

I

The excitement of being in school again lasted while I was alone, but when I got back to the boarding house, among students who could look at my class schedule and tell me what it meant, I began to feel doubt and then fear and then a craving to escape. What had been laid out for me was more than anybody eighteen years old could do. The adviser had assigned me to the eleventh grade—the last year of high school—because Commerce had discontinued all the other high school grades, even though I told her I had completed only a part of the eighth grade at Pin Hook. I now understood what she had been saying: I would be expected to keep up with the work of the eleventh grade while I made up on my own the two or more I had missed. All I could see at the moment was that I wanted my money back, ten dollars for tuition, four for the use of books. I could get it back, they told me, but I would have to ask the adviser.

The adviser, looking gray, tired, was at her desk, taking one by one the students waiting to see her, most of them older men and women, country schoolteachers forced to take summer courses to qualify for certification under the new state regulations. Some of them had been teaching for years on certificates earned by taking examinations at county courthouses; some had completed only the elementary grades. Now, because times had changed, to keep on teaching they had to take high school courses. She sympathized with them for the extra burden forced upon them and explained again and again that state teachers colleges like Commerce had been set up to help them. One by one she worked out schedules with them. When they left they looked apprehensive but resigned.

Seeing the looks on their faces I was glad I had decided to give up before getting started.

When my turn came the adviser took my schedule and looked surprised when I told her I had come to get my money back. I told her that I had come to Commerce expecting to get an elementary certificate at the end of the summer. Gently but firmly she repeated what I had heard her say to others: counties could no longer issue teaching certificates, only the state. Under the new state regulations I would have to go three terms to qualify for the lowest grade. That meant staying in school from June through the middle of March. I could not see how. I might stretch my money to the end of the summer term, but no farther.

Unwilling for me to take my money and leave, she kept a line of people waiting while she tried to show me why I should not go. I had already accomplished too much. She reminded me again of the grade I had made on the entrance examination. I was in. It would be a shame to leave without trying. One term, she pointed out, and I would be a third through. Three terms and I would have both an elementary teaching certificate and a high school diploma. She smiled. I could then begin working on my college degree. I knew now what she meant but kept silent. Stay at least for the summer, she urged. Then, if I had to, I could stay out a term and make enough money to come back.

"We are here to help you."

I did not doubt her sincerity, and I began to feel that I should stay if I could.

There was still the problem of the sequence of courses called "Plane Geometry and Academic Algebra," a four-term sequence. The first term was not being offered that summer. To complete the sequence in three terms, I would have to start with Book II of plane geometry. On the basis of part of a year of algebra at Pin Hook she was willing to let me skip the first term of plane geometry. If I could pass the second term, she assured me, they would give me credit for the first. Geometry was by now a frightening word to me, but, if I wanted to stay I had to take it and not from the beginning.

Quietly she talked to me about what Commerce was trying to

4

do for the boys and girls of East Texas. Then she advised me to read the catalogue, especially the descriptions of courses I had been assigned to. Then, or perhaps a little later, I learned that she was Miss Julia Hubbell, Assistant Dean of Women.

My education at Commerce began with plane geometry. At six in the morning I went to Mrs. Carr's boardinghouse, where I set tables, stacked dishes, brought breakfast—platters and dishes of scrambled eggs, soda biscuits, stewed dried apricots for a sweet—to the boarders, mostly country schoolteachers hurrying to get to their classes. In a hot small kitchen I took full dishes from one Negro woman at the stove and returned dirty dishes to another at the sink. By the time the last dirty dish was in and I had crammed down my own breakfast it was time to be on my way to class at a trot.

When I found the room the seats were all taken and boys were standing around the wall, their backs against chalky blackboards. It was school in town but the students were not very different from those at Pin Hook, only older, and the boys wore shirts and pants instead of blue overalls. Most of the girls had gingham dresses, homemade, country style—not at all like the store-bought dresses I was used to on the streets of Dallas. Boys and girls alike, they had come from Pin Hooks all over East Texas, and most of them looked as uncertain as I felt.

The teacher, a slightly stooped, middle-aged man, came a little late, gave his name—H. T. Brown—and the name of the book we would use, and started a review of the work of the first term: the first book of geometry, the book of angles. We had to understand angles before we could begin the book of circles. He drew a triangle on the board and then faced us. I could see his schoolteachery eyes moving around the room, searching out the standees along the wall, and knew they would light on me. He pointed a finger at me and said, "What can you tell me about this triangle?"

I was afraid to say, "Nothing." I was afraid to say anything.

After a moment someone answered for me: "The angles are unequal."

The teacher nodded but he did not give up on me.

"Explain the theorem."

5

I had never seen a geometry book before that day. I had never heard the word *theorem*. I could feel the heat in my body and the blood in my face. I knew everyone was staring at me.

"Yes?" He sounded impatient.

There was no way out. I had to start with a failure.

"I—"

I was going to explain that I was willing to learn from the beginning. He never gave me a chance.

"Who wants to explain it?"

Half a dozen hands went up. At a nod from the teacher a thin-faced town boy standing near me began talking. He sounded sure of himself, talking of unequal angles, but I could not tell. Everything he said was new to me.

"Very good," the teacher said when the boy stopped.

All I wanted was for the class to be over—for a chance to get away. It went on and on, with me shifting from one foot to the other, not understanding anything anybody was saying. New words came at me: axiom, proposition, corollary. I wrote some down and then gave up. There was too much I did not know.

Then the class was over and I was free to ask questions, not of the teacher but of Aaron Parker, my roommate, who had moved in the night before. He was red-headed, older by six or seven years, and a schoolteacher from the black waxy land of Lamar County. I found him in the room, studying, and told him what had happened.

"How much algebra have you had?" he asked.

"About a year at Pin Hook."

I did not have to tell him that a year in school at Pin Hook meant five to seven months. He had gone to a school like it and had contracted to teach in one only a little better.

"It's easier than algebra. All you've got to do is memorize the propositions and how to prove them."

He offered to help me make up the part I had missed and showed me where to begin. After he had gone to class I tried memorizing, sitting on the edge of the bed, going over the first pages of the book. If I could get the words into my head, I could then work on meaning.

6

Before noon I was back at the boardinghouse, putting in my two hours—two for breakfast, two for dinner, two for supper for my meals—hurrying out the bowls of stew and beans and black-eyed peas, the plates of cornbread and light bread, taking out dirty dishes, setting places, nodding to Mrs. Carr that there was more room, hearing her say to someone waiting outside the dining-room door, "You can come in now." Mrs. Carr called it "waiting tables"; the boarders called it "slinging hash"; I knew to leap when someone called, "Hey, hashie." But it was a job and I was glad to have it. With it I could hold out till the end of summer. It left me three hours in the morning, four in the evening, for classes and study, and as long as I could stay awake at night.

It was different from my last job in Dallas, waiting on priests and hearing them talk about religion. Here the talk was of classes and teachers and teaching jobs, at times of affiliation and consolidation—words I had not heard before—and changes taking place in Texas public education. Schools that taught only the three R's were backward. Subjects like shop and home economics had to be added. Some consolidated schools were already hauling pupils in on trucks. In bad weather, especially on roads made bad by red clay or black waxy mud, trucks could not run. Then it was walk or ride horseback. Education was at the center of their talk, and for the first time I learned another meaning for education: the courses that had to be passed to meet the requirements for certification. Every one who wanted to teach had to take courses in education.

My course in education was taught by A. L. Day and called "Teaching the Elementary School Subjects." It was a vague course taught in vague language. Even the course description was vague: ". . . the student is brought to see the significance of the material essential for the elementary subjects, to select the important from matter of less value, and to apply direct methods to his future work." Generally it left me puzzled, except in those moments when the teacher put aside the textbook and talked about the problems and rewards of being a teacher.

Stragglers often came late to meals and I had to wait on them between bites. At times I could talk while I waited for them to finish, about my courses, especially about geometry and why I saw no reason for a country schoolteacher to study it.

"You may need it," they told me. "They teach it in some of the bigger consolidated schools."

That was too far away for me even to consider. I would have to complete two years of college to get that kind of certificate.

The ones who had passed geometry had advice for me: Memorize everything and never let up. The work would get harder and harder, and I would need the first to understand the last.

"Wait till you get to the square root of the hypotenuse," one of them said. "I never seen anything harder to explain than that."

Some courses, I learned, could be slighted for geometry, among them the course in agriculture, listed in the catalogue as "Elementary Farm Crops." The teacher, A. L. Hatcher, was a kind man, known as an easy grader. Even with a little study I could talk well enough to satisfy him on the problems of raising cotton and corn and black-eyed peas.

Pin Hook, it was a relief to discover, had prepared me in one subject, English, which was called "Grammar, Rhetoric, and English Literature." The first term was grammar, and Sarah Garvin, the teacher, demanded only that I be able to conjugate, parse, and diagram accurately. T. F. Jessee had taught me that and more.

The best part of the day came after supper, when the boys at Traughber's rooming house trailed over to the college bathhouse for showers, trailed back in the cooler hour of dusk, and hung around the porch, country boys in town. One game we played almost nightly, a game most of them could not play in their homes or schools. The electric switch box on the porch always stood open. A boy would stand on one side and hold a corner plate between thumb and forefinger. Another boy would grasp the plate on the other side. Then we would join hands in a circle to feel the current race through us. At times we experimented. Enough of us in a circle could absorb the shock and feel only a tingling in our fingers. Too few, the shock knocked us apart. At times we played jokes. A charged hand to a boy's ear could send him winding, while the others laughed till the girls at the boardinghouse next door

came out to see what was happening. When the fun wore off some
of the boys went to sit on steps with girls. Others went to their hot
rooms to study. Only rarely was the wish stated for electricty to
reach houses and schools back home.

Saturday night had a special routine. That was the time when
all of us could lay off from study and walk around town. There was
always a girl at the boardinghouse ready to walk to town, past the
stores, on to the post office, and back—girls with names like Annis
Attaway, Eddiy Thornton, Lala Belle Parker, my roommate's sister. On Saturdays, Commerce was a country town, with wagons
and mules tied along the streets, with country people in the stores
to sell and buy, or standing under store awnings, putting off the
time when they would have to hitch up the mules and start home.
We knew their routine. The boys and girls I walked with were
from towns like Cumby and Pecan Cap and Brashears—not so
much from the towns but from farms close enough to the towns
for them to spend Saturday "e'enings" the way the farmers did in
Commerce. They were in town only to get the printed voucher
that would let them go back to the country.

For me, Sunday nights were different. At dusk, boys and girls
went to church, to singings, prayer meetings, young people's meeting, some singing as they went "Follow, follow, follow the gleam,"
their voices soft in the dusty streets. I went alone to a little Negro
church across the tracks, where I sat on a bench at the back, in the
yellowish glow of coal-oil lanterns, breathing the smell of last-
winter's ashes in an iron stove, of people sweating, pressed against
each other, listening to songs and praying and preaching, watching as a sister or brother, happy for the moment, danced back and
forth on the rough wooden floor. It was a reliving to me, not a new
learning. I had seen the same at Galilee, a Negro church not far
from Novice and Pin Hook. Quietly, almost stealthily I went,
telling myself I was just going to watch. I never did more than
watch, or answer yes when a deacon said to me, "You want to come
in and take a seat, white folks?" I listened and felt, especially the
songs they sang. I had heard them in cotton patches at Pin Hook
and on the Womack farm down in the Red River bottoms: "Clap
yo' hands, chillun, won't you get ready? They's a great camp

9

meeting in the Promised Land." For a time at least I could forget my loneliness.

One night when the singing and dancing ran late I came home to find the boys sitting around on the Traughber porch, their white shirts blotches in the darkness.

"Where you been?" one of them asked me.

I hesitated and then said, "Nigger meeting."

He laughed and said to the others, "He's been to nigger meeting."

There was gentle laughter, but not at me, I felt. They had all been to Negro churches and baptizings, the way town boys might go to the circus—for a show.

"They cut up much?" one of the boys asked.

"Not much. A little dancing and shouting."

"Let's all go some night."

"We could have some fun busting it up some night."

"Let's get us some sheets and go bust it up some night."

"Make 'em think we're ha'nts."

They talked more about it and I was afraid they would. It was not the first time any of us had heard of busting up a nigger meeting. They never did, but I stayed away from meetings the rest of the summer.

My best teacher that summer was my roommate, Aaron Parker, not in the books I studied—he was too far ahead of me for that—but in being what he was and pointing out what we could both be. He was a farm boy from the Clardy community in Lamar County, the oldest boy in a hard-working family. He was determined not to be a farmer, but he did not want to leave the farm. He wanted to spend his life in places like Clardy teaching boys and girls not how to leave the farm but how to have better lives on the farm. Nights when the heat hung heavy and we sweated in our double bed, unable to sleep, he talked about Miss Mysie Lee Robinson, the teacher who had been the one great inspiration of his life. She had taught him books; she had taught him a purpose in life. He wanted to be for others the great teacher she had been for him.

His plan was fully laid out. He would teach in the winter, go to school in the summer, teach in the winter. He would rise from principal of a two-teacher school to a three-teacher school, and, when he had his permanent certificate, he could become principal of a consolidated school. Miss Mysie was then county superintendent of Lamar County. He expected to follow her and do for hundreds of boys and girls what she had done for him. He talked about the thousands of white boys and girls in Texas who could not read or write. They needed more than anything better schools, better teachers. He appealed to me as Miss Mysie must have appealed to him.

"You can do it, too," he would urge in a low voice in the dead of the night. "Get your first certificate and you can work up in the same way."

I worried about ever getting the first certificate. I was having trouble keeping up in history and geometry, and there were two more terms to go. He had one word of advice to give, and he gave it often: "Study."

I studied all right, or at least put in the hours over the books, often with no idea of what I was expected to learn, at times obstinate over something I had halfway learned or not learned at all. In the course in ancient and medieval history I argued vehemently and stupidly that there had never been a split of the Greek Orthodox from the Roman Catholic Church. If there had been, I reasoned out loud in class, the priests I waited on at table would have told me. Forced at last to admit my error, I turned to the one thing I knew I could do: I memorized.

Days and weeks passed. I began to feel more at home in my classes, but even more worried about my future. A day came when I knew I could pass all my courses, including geometry, a day when I knew I had to go on to the next term and the next. The question was, how? In the early days of August I tried for jobs in Commerce but there were none, not even a board job once the term was over and the summer students went home. When there was no other way to turn I wrote to my brother Monroe, asking for a job picking cotton. Almost by return mail I had a letter. I could live with him and his wife at Brookston, ten miles west of

11

Paris, and pick cotton for her father, Dock Farmer. I knew I had to go.

The term ended and I had survived all my courses, including geometry, with something to spare—A's on elementary field crops and class-long ramblings on how to teach country school. Of the five teachers, only one had been tough-minded, Charles Tennyson, for whom memory work was good but not good enough if a student wanted to comprehend the vast reaches of ancient and medieval history.

2

I was a little over a year going from cotton patch to cotton patch, from hired hand to hired hand, from the country of Pin Hook to the country of Brookston. I left Commerce in the heat of noon, not the only one among the boys and girls in my classes going back to pick cotton before school started again. There was no train from Commerce to Paris, and the bus was an old seven-passenger touring car, with a driver who stopped at farmhouses along the way to buy butter and eggs. Fields of cotton were turning white and the picking looked good. I could make pretty good money picking.

From Paris to Brookston, I walked or caught rides, carrying in one suitcase everything I owned. At sundown I walked past hay-brown meadows sweet with the smell of prairie-grass hay. After sundown I walked through Brookston and up a slope to Monroe's house, a two-room plank house furnished by the landowner. Monroe was farming on shares, tenant farming, for a man who owned hundreds of acres of rich black land.

When I got to the door Mae was cooking supper on a wood stove in the light of a coal-oil lamp. Monroe was just coming in from feeding stock at the barn. I shook hands and said, "Howdy." I had not seen them for a year but that was about as much greeting as we ever gave. It was the way of my family.

The house was too small for them and their two children, but they took me in. There were two iron bedsteads in one room. They slept in one; I could sleep in the other and put my suitcase under the bed.

Then we were eating supper and talking about crops. Picking had started and good pickers were getting as much as three hundred pounds a day, at a dollar a hundred. I could begin at daylight. Mae had made a new cotton sack for me. I could pay for it out of picking money.

I tried to tell them about Commerce and going to school, but there was not much I could tell them. He was twenty-six. Ten years earlier he had left school to become a farmhand. She was twenty and had been married five years. School to them meant mostly the three R's, not memorizing geometry or reading ancient history. They took one thing for granted: I had been good in my books at Pin Hook; I would be good in my books at Commerce.

Soon after dark all talk ended. Monroe and I had to be in the field by daylight. Mae had to be up earlier to build a fire in the cookstove and bake biscuits. The room became quiet. I felt at home.

While the stars were still out in a whitening sky Monroe sent me along a turnrow to find the other pickers. They would be at the edge of the new picking, waiting for daylight. I had on blue duckings and shirt and a wool cap I had bought on Elm Street in Dallas. I had my cotton sack over my shoulder, and a pair of old leather knee pads swung from my galluses, ready for use when my back got too tired from stooping. As I walked I stirred up the smell of dew-wet cotton leaves and dew on blackland dust.

I heard the low voices of the pickers and then came to where they waited, sitting on their cotton sacks, each at the end of the row he had taken, like rounded inkballs lined up. I knew the Farmer boys and girls—Mae's brothers and sisters—even in the half-light. Four of them were near my age and they looked about the way they looked the last time we played "Wolf over the River" at Pin Hook. They howdyed me and told me that the picking was good. I would have to find a row for myself a little farther over, "on the other side of the niggers." I went past some other white hands and then half a dozen Negro men and women, the women

13

with faces half hidden by rags tied over their heads and under their chins.

By the time I was stooping over my row I could see cotton bolls pale white among the green leaves, and tell the difference between today's white blossom and yesterday's blossom turned pink. Daylight enough for picking. Once learned, the knack of cotton picking is not easily forgotten. My hands went in and out among the stalks, my fingers pushing deep into the hulls of the dried bolls to bring out the locks, my left hand moving toward my right, my right hand moving on to the mouth of the sack, leaving wads of cotton to sink slowly down the sack. The opened hulls ended in sharp points like dried thorns. Skilled fingers got jabbed from time to time; unskilled fingers could come to the end of the day pricked and bleeding.

Early morning is the best cotton-picking time, and the lonesomest. A picker wants to get on down the row as fast as he can, to get an early weighing. He can just about tell by the first weighing the kind of day it's going to be. If it's fifty pounds and he's picking at a dollar a hundred, it's going to be close to three dollars for the day—maybe more. Fingers can go fast for three dollars a day.

I picked fast, but I was not used to the sun, the sweat, the dust that rose under my feet or knees. At the end of the first row, everybody was ahead of me, even the Negroes.

"You got to snatch fast to keep ahead of them niggers," the whites told me.

I took a new row, jounced my sack down again, and, already tired, sank to my knees. It was a long way back, and slow going. The sack was getting heavy and the strap rubbed my left shoulder raw. Soon I was yanking it along with my hand, losing picking time each time I did. Dock Farmer had brought the wagon to the turnrow, propped up the tongue, and hung the scales from it. Pickers ahead of me came to the end of their rows, swung their sacks over their shoulders, and went to get weighed up, and for a few minutes of rest.

They were back picking before I came to the end of my row. Then at last I could swing my sack up, stagger a little under the weight, and, for the first time since daylight, look up, not down. We were in the middle of a wide blackland prairie, with cotton and corn fields stretching as far as the eye could see, a flat, green expanse with here and there a farmhouse, a barn, a clump of shade trees shimmering in the hot sun.

Weighing up was simple. Monroe had put a green boll in a bottom corner of the sack and tied a baling-wire hook around it. I hooked that to the hook of the scales and then brought the rest of the sack up with the shoulder strap. Dock Farmer clicked a pea along the notches of the scale until there was a balance.

"Forty-two pounds," he said, "less three for the sack."

He wrote thirty-nine pounds in his daybook.

I hooked the sack strap over my arm and climbed up over the high sideboards into a wagon bed already knee deep in cotton. Dock boosted the sack up to me, I shook out the cotton in fluffy wads, and climbed back down. At last I could take a little rest.

I took a dipper of water from the bucket and sat down under the wagon, the only shade for a mile in any direction. A dry breeze blew on my wet clothes and cooled me a little.

Dock Farmer hunkered down in the shade by me and talked to me about school and getting enough money to go back. He was friendly and encouraging, but Commerce had never seemed so far away. I had trouble remembering much about it. He was sure that if I picked that hard every day I would have a pocketful of money. I only wanted enough to go back.

My next weighing came when the sun was straight over head. Some of the pickers were already straggling along the turnrow, on their way home for something to eat. The Negroes, who had farther to walk, were sitting on their sacks, eating in the broiling sun. I saw a gaunt old auntie gumming a piece of whitish cornbread. She saw me looking at her and spoke.

"I ain't wanting me nothing but a piece o' cornbread till I's thu picking. I ain't no good picking with something heavy in my stomach."

I didn't mind having cornbread, but I wanted something with it, like black-eyed peas, tomatoes, Bermuda onions, and a goblet of iced tea or buttermilk.

Mae saw me come in and stop to wash in the wash pan at the back steps.

"You blistered," she said. "You're blistered to the backs of your ears."

I hurt enough to cry.

"Look at the backs of my hands," I said.

They were red and beginning to puff. If they got too bad I would not be able to pick. She slipped a rag off a milk jar in the safe.

"I'll dip you some cream."

I soothed my face and neck and hands with cool fresh cream, but I felt too feverish from the sun to eat much. It was better to drink over-sweetened iced tea.

Monroe came and they both talked to me.

"You know how sunburn is. You blister and peel. Then you toughen up and get used to it. It'll hurt but you can stand it if you don't get sun poisoning."

I knew what that meant. I had to watch out for festering in the blisters.

When my shadow was barely long enough to be seen I was back in the field, and the heat was worse. Sweat stung my eyes and the taste of salt edged my lips. I inched along on my knees, feeling dirt in every part of me. Pickers passed and repassed me. They were used to sun and work, and they were racing each other. At sundown, one of them would be able to say, "I picked the most in the whole field today." I envied them their unworried faces. The money they made was theirs, and they had no need to spend it to pay for school.

It was late before I had a weighing and a rest in the shade of the wagon. When I went back to my row I could feel a change. The sun was lower, the air a little cooler. Quitting time would soon be coming. White pickers passed me, whistling little tunes, or picking two or three together, talking in low voices. Negro pickers sang songs that were a kind of humming, with no words except "Oh, Lawd" for a beginning or an ending.

When the sun was half lost behind an edge of black we were

called in for the last weighing. Our sacks empty again, we slung them over our shoulders and walked home in a bluish saffron glow, the Farmer boys and girls walking and talking with me. Picking had been good. The best had weighed up over three hundred, and I had got more than half as much.

I knew I had worked for it. My muscles were sore, my left shoulder rubbed raw from the sack strap, my face and hands stinging and feverish from sunburn. Supper was ready at dark, but I was too feverish to stay long at the table. I put cream on my sunburn and went to bed, to lie in burning heat until I had to sleep. It had been bad that day; it would be worse the next, and maybe the next. Then I would begin to toughen up.

Every day was like another until quitting time Saturday night. Then we were paid, the amount figured out to the last copper, the paper and metal pieces hoarded in a round pocketbook with a snap fastener, the pocketbook dropped to the bottom of a duckings pocket, where it could be fingered and rattled. Saturday night there was time to go to Brookston, to walk along the line of stores on a boardwalk, to lay down a nickel for a red and white peppermint stick or some chewing wax.

After supper we played forty-two at Dock Farmer's, boys and girls clustered around a bare table in the yellowish light of a coal-oil lamp, four playing, the others watching, waiting their turns to take on the losers, with a mingling of sounds: low voices talking, the shuffling of wooden dominoes on the wooden table, a domino slapped down in glee or disgust. Sometimes there was a cackling laugh over a trick taken, or a groan over a trick lost. Six hands won and the game was over. Six hands lost and a pair had to give up their places.

Talk between hands was of good luck or bad luck at forty-two, the good days of cotton picking, money in the pocket, money to be hauled out and counted. "You gonna wear your money plumb out just counting it." At Commerce the talk was of teaching; at Brookston it was farming. No one wanted to hear what I had learned at Commerce; hours at a time I forgot about Commerce and slipped back into Pin Hook ways of talking.

Sunday mornings we could lie in bed till sunup. Then I could walk to Brookston with Monroe to buy a steak for breakfast, a middle-of-the morning breakfast of steak in flour gravy, fried potatoes, sliced tomatoes, and hot biscuits. Before the heat of the middle of the day we walked to the fields to see how good the picking would be.

The skin on my face and hands turned blotched brown and pink from the peeling. The tops of my ears hardened to a dark brown scale. My muscles toughened and the soreness faded away. I could stoop from daylight till dark day after day and snatch cotton, not with the best but close to the best. When I was stooping down a row alone I could think of Commerce and replace in my mind the reality of the cotton patch with the reality of a classroom. I could count the days to September 29, the first day of school.

Then on a Sunday walk even I could see that the picking was getting thin and I would have to go faster and get less. I had saved all the money I could, but it was not enough, and I could not make enough in thin cotton. Count as I would, I was twenty-five dollars short. I figured it over with Monroe and Mae. Even if every day the next week I led the field I still would be short. We talked of other things I could do. Cotton picking would not last much longer, but there would be other work if I would take a job as a hired hand and not go back to school. I could go down to the barns and the man who owned the land would give me a job cutting stalks, getting ready for fall plowing.

All week I drove myself as hard as I could, but on Thursday I knew I could not make it. That night I wrote Mrs. Carr giving up my job at the boardinghouse. Saturday I would go down to the barns, not in despair but in frustration at the time I would lose before I would get back to Commerce. A new term would start after Christmas. By then, I told myself, I would have the money.

That night in the dark, after we had gone to bed, Monroe and Mae talked to me across the room. They had decided that they could lend me twenty-five dollars to get me through to the end of the term in March. When I got out of Commerce I could work and pay them back. They did not have the money to spare, I knew, but they offered and I knew they wanted me to take it.

The next morning I wrote another letter to Mrs. Carr, asking her to hold my job for me, and Dock Farmer bought me a fountain pen for good luck.

3

Saturday I was in the cotton patch. Monday I was back at Mrs. Carr's boardinghouse, up before daylight, setting tables, serving, clearing off and setting again after the last stragglers had left. Then I went the half-block to the campus—a Bermuda grass square with three red brick buildings left over from the years when it was the East Texas Normal College, buildings still revered as monuments to W. L. Mayo, the founder, monuments more effective than the granite blocks near the Administration Building that marked his grave. The campus was as I had left it except for the walls of the new Education Building that were beginning to rise.

In the summer term Commerce was a place for country schoolteachers and boys and girls studying to become country schoolteachers. On campus and streets most of the people looked country. In winter, it was different. Some of the country people were still there, but most of the students were from Commerce and other East Texas towns. They were younger and less serious. The ones who talked about teaching wanted to teach in town. They might be willing, they said, to take a country school for a year or two, but only to get the experience required for teaching in town. Some of them had no intention of becoming teachers. They would get their degrees and marry or make their livings some other way. This was a disturbing thought for me. I had believed that everyone went to Commerce to become a teacher, a belief I found justified by a statement in the catalogue: "All energies and activities of the East Texas State Teachers College are bent to the single proposition of preparing teachers for the public school of Texas and for dignifying the profession." For "public schools" I had read "country schools." Two days out of the cotton patch, I could not understand the ones who looked down on country people and country ways, or on teaching as a way of life.

At the Administration Building I began picking up where I had left off at the end of the summer term. Lines of students waited for advisers. There was time to read and reread the catalogue and talk to other students about courses and teachers. They debated about choices. When I reached an adviser I found that my courses had been selected for me: geometry, rhetoric, music appreciation, European history, and reading. At registration each was given a set of rules for conduct and we were sent to the auditorium, where the Dean of Men and Dean of Women held up to us the Christian ideals of the Y.M. and Y.W.C.A. and pointed out the punishments that would come for those not punctual in class attendance or those who in any way resisted efforts of the college and faculty in character-building. They charged us as future teachers to be moral as well as intellectual leaders of the pupils placed in our care.

The meeting over, we left quietly and I went to the boarding-house to sling hash, not to country schoolteachers but to construction workers on the new building: bricklayers, plasterers, an Italian terrazzo worker and his Italian wife. A tall, thin plasterer from Oklahoma, old enough to be my father, gave me a dollar when he found out I was working my way through school, and promised me a dollar every Saturday night if I worked hard and kept my grades up. Others talked to me about the things I could do and see if I would go on to college. I listened and told them I had to finish high school first. Then I would think about college. I knew that I would be lucky if I could hang on till March and get my elementary teaching certificate.

Again I relied on memorizing, not only names and dates in history, propositions and proofs in geometry, rules of grammar and syntax, but also long passages of any kind of text or teachers' notes I could expect to use on examinations. I had to pass. I had picked too much cotton to fail now. For most of the teachers, memorizing and quoting back was enough, but not for all.

Moselle Schaff, my music-appreciation teacher, wanted memory work all right but she wanted a great deal more. Young, talented, enthusiastic, she took a class whose musical experience was for the most part limited to country fiddling, guitar picking, and singing school songs, who, if they read music at all, read shaped notes, and led them into the unknown world of round-note music, which she called "classical." We were going out as elementary-school teachers, she reminded us, as she gave us demonstrations on what to teach and how to teach it. With a Graphophone and records we could teach the best music in the world to boys and girls all over East Texas.

She played it through till we could hum it. Then she took it part by part to show us effects of melody, harmony, rhythm. When she put it together again she had us gallop around the room to show how it could be turned into a rhythmic game or adapted for a rhythm band.

The demonstration over, she knew that we needed music more than method. She talked about pieces we should know and then played them over and over until they were familiar. She let us know one thing without ever saying it: Any teacher could wind a Graphophone.

At times there was learning outside school. Once a week in the warm fall nights I went to the main part of town to watch the Ku Klux Klan assemble in their white sheet robes and hoods and march around the stores and through the streets. At times there would be forty or fifty Kluxers, indistinguishable from each other except by height or breadth or the backs of their heels. Polished black heels belonged to merchant or doctor or teacher; rough brogans belonged to farmers. White people sat on porches to watch the marchers pass, or stood on street corners to hear what they had to say. Negroes kept inside with their doors shut and their windows shaded. After the march there were speeches in the middle of town, mainly repetitions and enlargements on slogans I had lived with all my life: "Keep the niggers in their place," "Give them a inch, they'll take a mile," "You watch out, they'll take the bread right out o' yo' mouths." I listened and was inclined to believe them. I had watched black hands snatch cotton ahead of white hands.

After the speeches the marchers swung around toward nigger town and slipped off their robes in the dark. Then there were clusters of men on street corners talking in low voices, with now and then a laugh. I hung around one group or another, listening. In one I heard a man saying, "You want to change yo' luck, you just go over in nigger town. You git you the biggest, blackest gal you can find. You git her down and you jist bury your nose in the stink under her arm and jounce her up and down as hard as you can. If that don't change yo' luck, nothing's about to."

Days afterward there was talk about the Ku Klux Klan. "We need them," Commerce people said. "The Lord knows we need them. You never know." I heard nothing from the Negroes. Silently they went through the streets in the early mornings to their work in white kitchens; silently they went back at night, the lucky ones with paper sacks of "totin's"—leftovers from white folks' tables.

Late on winter afternoons I went to a classroom in the Industrial Building to hear Professor W.H. Warmington talk about words. He was not impressive in appearance; he was impressive when he talked in an English accent strange to East Texas ears. Aware of the poverty of our language, he came once a week on his own time and talked about words to any who wanted to come. He understood his audience. Few had studied Latin; perhaps not one had studied Greek. Yet he used those languages and others and made words come alive to me as I had never known them. He took a common English word like horse and traced its forms through half a dozen languages, including Latin, Spanish, German, and French. Then, using lines from verse or fiction, he showed the word in as many associations. Skillfully he moved from dictionary definition to

22

slang and back again. He never spoke to me directly once, nor
I to him, but, after him, a horse could still be an East Texas
nag. It had also to be a symbol of chivalry.

Before the end of the term I came to what I feared most: the
Pythagorean proposition, "in a right triangle the square of the
hypotenuse equals the sum of the squares of the other sides." I
memorized the proposition, the proof, the drawings that illus-
trated the proof, and reproduced them fully on the final examination with no understanding of what had been asked of me or of
what I had given. The teacher, a football player, wrote B on the
paper and asked no questions. I had passed. The term was over and
I had only one more to go.

In advanced algebra I had the good fortune to encounter a fine
teacher. She was Miss Georgia Gantt and she was from Blossom,
Texas. Our paths had come close to crossing at Blossom. She had
never been to Pin Hook but she knew what a two-teacher school
in Lamar County was like. She saw at once that I was not ready
for advanced algebra, but, instead of sending me out of her class,
she gave me extra review work and stayed with me often in the
afternoon to explain what I had not understood. At times she
paced behind her desk, tall, thin, intense, and talked about what
she wanted to do. She had a long way to go in school, but her plans
were made. She would study and teach at Commerce as long as she
could—in high school if she had to—adding credits and credits till
she got her degree. But she would not stop there. She would go on
and on, earning and learning, taking degree after degree and at last
be a teacher in college.

At times she talked not about equations but about words—the
magic of words. It was then I learned that she liked literature and
wanted to teach literature. Teaching algebra was her bread and
butter while she waited for an opening in English. For the rest of
the term she slaved over algebra with me and then took time to
open up to me her own world of books.

In literature class we read English ballads that I had known before but had not seen written down except in "ballet books" at Pin Hook. I knew some of the tunes and offered to sing them, but the teacher was interested in teaching them only as literature—only as examples of an inferior kind of literature. The other students looked on them as country and not worth spending time on. For me they were recollections of Saturday nights when singers without organ or guitar, because "ballet" music did not chord well, sang the long sad stories of "Barbara Allen" and "Fair Ellender." I did not know enough to understand that for them literature was one thing, life another, and that, consciously or unconsciously, they were separating the two.

Then Edgar Lee Masters, in a visit to the campus, showed me how the two belonged together. Never had I seen a live writer, much less heard one speak. The admission price, six bits, seemed high, but I bought my ticket and went to the balcony in the dark old auditorium. I suppose I expected him to look more like a god than a man, or at least like the bearded pictures of Whittier and Longfellow. He did not. He looked like a farmer in a hand-me-down suit that did not fit well and needed pressing. He began reading and his voice was a flat monotone: "Seeds in a dry pod, tick, tick, tick." A boy behind me snickered and then there was a sound of soft laughter around me. They were laughing at him for calling this literature—or poems. I laughed a little with them. Then he read from *Spoon River Anthology*:

> *Where are Elmer, Herman, Bert, Tom and*
> *   Charley,*
> *The weak of will, the strong of arm,*
> *   the clown,*
> *the boozer, the fighter?*
> *All, all, are sleeping on the hill.*

I began to see the people and hear them talking from the graveyard. They sounded right out of life. When he came to "Lucinda Matlock" he was touching my life. There were Matlock girls at Pin Hook and at many a party I had played snap and found the girl I wanted to walk home with. What he was saying was true, but it

was not like any poetry I had heard or read. It was like talking—
like Edgar Lee Masters talking for people lying in graves unable
to talk for themselves.

I never knew what Edgar Lee Masters thought about Commerce. I knew very well what Commerce thought of Edgar Lee
Masters. He was rough and uncouth. What he read as poems could
hardly be called poems—no rhyme, no lilt, no words that sounded
like poetry. At the next English class there was general rejection
of it as poetry, and certainly not worth six bits. Houdini had been
there before Masters, and I had not spent the money for a ticket,
though I had watched Houdini himself carrying props from a car
and setting them up in the auditorium. In a way I felt that I should
have spent my money on Houdini. He was dark and handsome and
looked like a magician. I was not ready to understand that what
touched me in Masters was also magic.

One afternoon I went to the auditorium for a free lecture by
Ruth Cross, a Lamar County farm girl from south of Paris who
was to speak about her novel, *The Golden Cocoon*. She did not look
like a farm girl. Her clothes were too fine, and her skin looked as
if it had never felt the Texas sun. But when she talked about the
book, about the struggle of a girl to get away from the farm and
go to college, I knew she had lived through just such an experience.
I wanted her to talk more about writing and what it meant to be
a writer. She turned her talk into a sales pitch, directed not at the
students but at the club women who made up most of the audience.
She ended with a plea: "Don't borrow my book. Buy it and tell
others to buy it."

Then it was March and my work at Commerce was coming
to an end. So was my money. I would have a high school diploma
and an elementary school teaching certificate, but no job and no
prospect of one. Country schools were beginning to close down for
the year; I would not meet requirements to teach in town.

A letter from my mother offered a solution: I could go to the
Panhandle and work on a ranch. She was sure I could get a job at
one of the big places along the Canadian River. It was a solution
that appealed to me. For six months I had been in Commerce, long

enough to be tired of paved streets and boarding houses. The feel of spring was in the air, and I felt good at the prospect of being on the land when spring arrived.

On my last day in Commerce, after all my records were approved, I paid for my teaching certificate but not for my diploma. A dollar was too much to pay for one. The teaching certificate would come in handy if I could find a teaching job out west.

I packed my suitcase and walked alone to the railroad station. Nine months in Commerce, and I was leaving as I had come.

4

It was a long ride, first by train and interurban to Dallas and Fort Worth, and then on the Fort Worth and Denver all day long to Amarillo, the train moving from town to town, at first across prairies where fence rows and creeks were lined with trees, and then out onto the open plains where the land stretched out and out, reddish brown meeting bright blue on a far horizon, with here and there a bare cottonwood where dry washes marked the earth. A strong wind seeped cold around the windows, rolled windrows of tumbleweed along the banked right-of-way, and trailed the lonesome whistle back over the train at every road crossing. After Wichita Falls there were towns I had never heard of before— Quanah, Childress, Memphis, and others before we got to Amarillo, with here and there a place too small for a stop, or for the conductor to call the name. Away from the tracks there were houses and barns, far apart, some with trees, some with none, built low, hugging the earth against the wind.

My mother had written me: Stay at a hotel in Amarillo, take the morning train to Canadian, catch a ride to Gem with the star-route carrier, who would be looking for me at the post office. It was dark when we got to Amarillo and I stepped from the train into wind and cold and the dryness of dust. The feeling of spring had come to Commerce; it would be a long time coming to Amarillo. I found an old hotel near the station and slept cold under a pile of quilts.

In the morning I was on the train again, crossing land flat, dry, carved by the wind. There were new towns—Panhandle, White Deer, Pampa—and miles of land that seemed to have no use at all. From Fort Worth on the feeling had been growing on me that I was getting farther and farther away from the known; when I got off the train at Canadian I felt I had come to the last bluff of the world, and still had twenty miles to go.

The star-route carrier was waiting for me at the post office. He cranked his Ford and we were headed toward low-lying hills on a dirt road outlined only by a barbed-wire fence on either side. There were a few houses and mailboxes along the way, but he did not stop. He was a star-route carrier and his job was to get the mail to Gem. He did not talk much until I asked him what it was like where I was going.

"It's a good farm," he said. "Lank Smith's a good farmer, and a good man. I've knowed him a good many years. I've seen yo' mammy since they been married, but I ain't to say know her."

He had touched on a part of the unknown. I was going to the home of a man I had never seen, to stay in that home till I could get out on my own, to see my mother for the first time in eighteen months, not at Pin Hook but in his home, called by a different name. It was like going to Deport, to begin life again with a new stepfather. We had brought Roy home with us from Deport, twelve years before. Lank Smith had brought him with my mother to West Texas, to make a household of three. I felt strange about becoming a part of it even for a little time.

At a place in the road only the tops of fence posts stuck out of the sand.

"Wind," the mail carrier said to my question.

Farther on, a stretch of posts swung above the ground.

"Wind," the mail carrier said again. "Sandstorm last week."

At times our wheels were on hard pan, at times in deep sand. One minute we were passing jutting bluffs of wind-cut gullies; the next, rounded mounds with the sand laid on in wavy ridges—all done by the same wind that sometimes colored East Texas skies with a yellow haze.

Absent-mindedly the mail carrier whistled a tune I had never heard before, not with a sharp whistle through rounded lips but with a flat whistle between his teeth, the sounds shaped by the pushing out and pulling in of his breath. It was a loping kind of tune, easy to remember, hard to keep off the mind, and I found myself going over it, though I did not make a sound.

We passed some hills that in East Texas would have been called mountains. I asked about some higher hills on the far horizon.

"Antelope Hills," he said. "Oklahoma. Clear on the other side of the Canadian River. You can see them plainer from over close to Lank's house."

We passed a three-room schoolhouse with the painted white walls scoured by sandstorms. Gem, when we came to it, was a cluster of weather-beaten houses around a general store with a gasoline pump on the porch and a two-story hotel and boarding house. A wagon and team had been hitched close to the store.

"Lank's waiting," the mail carrier said.

I got down with my suitcase and a man came out of the store and out to meet me. He was a large man with gray hair under a gray western hat. His voice was friendly, his handshake an awkward farmer's.

"Your mammy stayed home. Pile in the wagon. We've got a ways to go yet."

He hitched the team and took one side of the springseat. I took the other. Then we were moving and there was a sound of iron wagon tires cutting into the sand of the road. Out of town, everything looked square. Fields had been laid out in squares. Roads ran straight; cross roads came at square corners. We traveled a back road where there were curves around hills and then across ranches on sandy roads at times no more than trails. The earth, close up, was not in squares. The wind, as if in wild fancy, had scooped and piled till man-made squares could not be seen. After three miles and an hour of traveling we came in sight of a small house and barn at the edge of a square pasture.

"We had a right smart of a sandstorm the other day," Mr. Smith said. "You'll see when we get to the barn. It blew in the stable till I had to shovel it out to get the horses down low enough to come out the door. They tromped and tromped and got higher and higher."

I laughed, but I did not believe him. It would take a heap of wind and sand to do that.

We rounded a curve and went slowly toward the house, an unpainted house with a front porch the length of the two front rooms and one room attached to the back, a house no bigger than the one we had lived in at Pin Hook. Beyond the house there was a shed and a windmill. These were all the buildings on the farm.

"Dewey got here ahead of you," Mr. Smith said when we pulled up to the barn.

"Dewey? I thought he was still at Pin Hook."

"He come out to look around. He might settle out here. Get him a job." He gave me a sideways glance. "I think I got you a job over on the Canadian—"

"What kind of job?"

"Ranch. They call it cowboying."

Smoke was coming from the chimney and there was an acrid smell on the wind.

"What's the smell?" I asked.

"Cow chips. We're burning cow chips in the stove. You'll soon get used to it so you don't notice it."

The same acrid smell was in the house when we went in: cow chips burning in a heater in the front room, cow chips burning in the kitchen. Roy was by the heater. Dewey got up from the piano, the one we bought while we were still at Novice.

It was an awkward meeting. We had never been a family for hugging and kissing. My mother said, "Well, hello there," and came up to me. She laid her left hand on my shoulder and kissed me on the cheek. Close up, I could see that the West Texas wind and sun had left the backs of her hands dark brown, her face a lighter brown but roughened by tiny dried-out wrinkles. Roy was nearer the size of a man. There was a limp handshake from him and then one from Dewey, who looked tall and thin and out of place.

The sandstorm was something everybody could talk about.

"Sand seeped in everywhere," my mother said. "It got so deep on the floor I had to rake it out with a hoe when the wind died down."

They took me out to the stable to show how the horses had to be dug out. Mr. Smith brought the horses from the wagon to stable them.

"See the piles of sand," he said to me. "They come out of the stable. It just piled up and the horses tromped on it till they was up higher than the door. I've seen lots of sandstorms but this is the first time I ever had to shovel out the horses."

Back in the house I began to know what it was to live with sand: grit ground by my shoes on the floor, grit wherever I sat down, grit in the victuals when we went to the table for supper.

"I'll never get used to the wind and sand," my mother said, and her voice was too quiet. "I'd like it better out here if we just had trees in the yard."

There was one tree, a bare-limbed apricot. She meant big oaks like the ones that shaded the house at Pin Hook. Lank Smith reassured her in a half-joking way that she would get used to it, that the day would come when she would never want to go back.

"I wouldn't go back to Pin Hook," he said, "if they'd give it to me."

After supper Dewey picked out a tune on the piano. It was the mail carrier's tune.

"You know the words?"

Roy did. So did everybody around Gem, I soon learned.

> *I ride an old Paint, I lead an old Dan.*
> *I'm going to Montan' for to throw the hoolian;*
> *My horses is saddled, I'm ready to go,*
> *With my spurs and lasso on a bucking bronce.*
> *Ride around, little dogies,*
> *Ride around so slow,*
> *My horses is saddled, I'm ready to go.*

Soon we were singing, with Dewey seconding on the piano. West Texas had been hard on the piano. Dust had seeped inside the case and the strings vibrated with a gritty sound. We went over the words enough times for me to have them in my mind.

They said the wind was quiet that night, but it kept me awake, rattling the windows, whistling at the corners, leaving grit on my sheets and pillow. Late in the night I was still awake and I knew it was more than the wind. I was beginning to worry whether I had done the right thing coming. I had expected West Texas to be different, but not so hard on people, or so lonesome. It took a lot of this land to keep a family going, and houses had to be far apart. A part of getting used to the land was getting used to being lonesome. Words kept running through my mind: "They feed in the coulee, They water in the draw, Their tails are all matted, Their backs are all raw." It was a lonesome tune and it went through my mind over and over like a slow lope. I began to feel lonesome, thinking of going over on the Canadian to cowboy it on a ranch. Lank hadn't said when, but it would be soon. I would find out at daylight.

First came the burning-grass smell of cow chips and then the yellow-orange light of sun through dust. Hearing the others up and stirring, I put on enough clothes to keep warm and went to the kitchen, where my mother moved slowly from stove to table, putting on the biscuits and middling meat she had saved for me. It was like breakfast at Pin Hook, with a molasses pitcher and a bottle of pepper sauce in the middle of the table. We might have been at Pin Hook, the way my mother talked about having us all together again, but both of us knew that was not possible. Monroe and Mae were living at Brookston. Cleaver was in Chicago, putting himself through an electrical school, learning how to be an electrician. They would never come to Gem, and Dewey was beginning to talk of going to Fort Worth, where he had a chance to work his way through a business school.

"I hope you're aiming to stay a while," my mother said to me. "You'll get to liking it out here. I've got used to about everything but the wind and the sand." She gave a little laugh as if she had

31

just remembered something. "Don't let them give you gyp water."

It was a joke played on newcomers, who would not know the difference between sweet water and gyp. "Till you get used to it," they said, "gyp'll scour you out good."

I felt better about my mother. If she had got used to cow chips and gyp water, she would get used to wind and sand. In a kind of apology she told me that I had come in about the worst time of the year for weather.

After breakfast, Dewey sat at the piano in the front room picking out "I ride and old Paint" with one finger. Roy went to the barn, saddled up his pony, and rode off to school. The sound of a lonesome whistle came back on the wind.

Later I went with Mr. Smith in the wagon to pick up cow chips. In the winter they burned coal, but coal was low in the bin and had to be hauled by wagon from Canadian. It could be stretched by cow chips. He drove slowly across a pasture, turning to right or left to miss prairie-dog holes. A horse can break a leg easy in a prairie-dog hole, he told me. Near the house the cow piles were still damp. Farther away, they had turned to brownish gray chips, hard and rough, easy to pick up by hand, dry enough to rattle in the wagon bed, and with little smell until it was released by fire.

In some of the prairie-dog holes there were signs of goings and comings—fresh dug earth, the beginnings of spring. Other holes looked deserted.

"Rattlesnakes," Mr. Smith said. "Rattlesnakes hole up there for the winter. You won't see none now. It's too cold. When the days get warm they'll come out to sun. Then you got to watch out."

In spite of what he told me, I looked down at the ground more than I looked up at the sky.

It took us most of a day to pile the wagon bed half full of chips. Then, riding on the springseat, we went back across pastures, opening wire gates when we came to fences.

William A. Owens

The next day Mr. Smith took me to a ranch over on the Canadian to see about a job. His house was midway between the Canadian and the Washita. As we went we could see dust rising from the dry flats of both. We turned to the Canadian and followed the edge of a river bed that was mostly dry washes with a few cottonwood trees to mark the banks. Then we came to a ranch with house and barn and sheds set close to the earth, with barbed-wire fences and plank corrals rising out of fields of sand. Herds of cattle strayed across sod pastures with their heads down, in search of tufts of dried grass. Another herd gathered around sheet iron sheds. Men were at work at the sheds.

I cannot recall the name of the man who owned the ranch. I can recall his leathery brown face and whitened blue eyes under a wide-brimmed hat. I have forgotten what he said to me, or at least the words in which he said it. He did have a job for a hand—not a cowboy—the men riding the range for him stayed on year after year—just a hand to pick up and do anything that needed to be done around the place. It was a steady job at fifteen dollars a month, with grub furnished and a bunk in a house down by the barn. He was ready for me to start any time, but I might as well come the next Monday. There would always be a horse for me to ride when I was not working, if I would be careful with him and watch out for prairie-dog holes.

I agreed to come the next Monday and Mr. Smith and I went to the wagon.

"You stick by him, he'll stick by you," Mr. Smith said.

We passed a man patching a corral fence. He looked up to watch us pass but he did not stop the tune he was humming. It sounded like "I Ride an Old Paint."

Before we were out of sight of the house and barns Mr. Smith stopped the wagon and climbed down to the road.

"Distance is decency," he said. "That's how we have to look at it in West Texas. We don't have bushes."

We went back by Gem and stopped at the store. Mr. Smith bought groceries and talked a while with the men sitting around a coal stove, chewing and spitting.

33

That night we huddled close to our cow-chip fire and talked. They were glad I had a job and would be close to them. Now if only Dewey could get a job there. But he did not want to. He had made up his mind to go on to Fort Worth and go to business school. My mother, as always, took his decision quietly, but I knew from the look on her face how hurt she felt.

Late in a sleepless night I knew I was going with him, and I knew why. It was in part the low pay. It was more that I had seen Gem in West Texas and knew I would never be happy there. All it had to offer as far as I could see in music, literature, drama was "I Ride an Old Paint." For humor there was another stanza about the man who had two daughters and a song: "One went to Denver, the other went wrong." The tune kept running through my head and I had to get away from it.

My mother was taking up biscuits when I told them that I was not going to take the job. She set the plate down and began shaking her right hand as she always did when she was upset.

"What're you aiming to do?"

My mind was made up.

"Go back and stay with Monroe and Mae. Maybe I can get a teaching job for the fall."

"You could work here and maybe get a teaching job. Mr. Smith'll help you. He knows the trustees."

Not anger but sadness was in their voices as they tried to talk me into staying.

"I get so lonesome out here," my mother said. "It'd be a heap o' company if you got a job close enough to visit."

It was no use. No matter how much I wanted to stay for her sake, I had to go. I hated to leave her there. I hated to leave Roy. I had seen enough to know that Mr. Smith was good to them in his own blunt, undemonstrative way, but she was beginning to look like the other women I had seen around Gem, pinch-faced and bent from work and weather. For Roy, the life was good. He had his own horse and rifle and was free to live out any boy fantasies of life in the West. But schooling would stop with the seventh grade and he would have to get a job on a ranch or stay there on the farm. His mind, it seemed to me, was too good for that.

34

5

A week later, in the gray of dawn, Mr. Smith hitched the team to the wagon to take Dewey and me to the train. My mother said an awkward goodbye and then, "You come again when you can." Mr. Smith turned the wagon toward the Canadian road. I looked back to see my mother, a gray figure against a gray wall, and knew how much she was grieving to see us go. I knew also that there was no turning back for either of us, and especially for Dewey. Of all my brothers, he was the one who needed most to find a place where there was security for himself and ways to use his emotional energy.

From the back of the wagon bed I could see him on the spring-seat, tall and thin of body, held in, barely swaying with the movement of the wagon; so unlike me that we might not be taken for brothers. His hair was straight and brown, mine light and curly; his eyes brown, mine blue. Some of our ambitions were the same.

In his suitcase he had a tablet in which he was writing in pencil a kind of Western love story. It was not good writing, but he had been working on it at least two years and would keep on working on it not knowing how bad it was unless someone could tell him. He said he wanted to learn penmanship at business school, but he had other things in mind as well. At business school someone might help him with his story, though he was afraid too much time had passed him by. He was twenty-four and had not gone past the fifth grade. I knew why he had quit school and the knowledge made me uncomfortable. He had become a farm laborer to help take care of the family, to give the younger brothers a chance. Now that he could make it on his own he was afraid he was too old.

At the railroad station Mr. Smith did some bargaining with the ticket agent for lower fares to Fort Worth. It meant going up to Kiowa, Kansas, and all the way back across Oklahoma and a part of Texas to Forth Worth, but it would save us a couple of dollars apiece and money was worth more than time. The train came. Mr. Smith shook hands with us and turned away. Through a smoke and sand fogged window I watched him walk toward the wagon, the lines of his face hidden by the brim of his hat.

All day long we traveled over land at times hilly, at times flat, but always desolate with a look of dry sod, dry sand. We sat together but talked very little. Dewey was by nature silent. I was gloomy because, after nine months of work and study, I had no prospect for the future. At times he whistled "I Ride an Old Paint" under his breath, almost soundlessly. I tried to put the tune out of my mind but it stayed with me mile after mile, tune and words louder than the clack of wheels on rails:

> *Now when I die, don't bury me a-tall,*
> *Put my saddle on my pony, lead him out of his stall,*
> *Tie my bones to the saddle, head our faces to the west,*
> *And we'll ride the prairies that we love the best.*

It was dark when we got off the train in Fort Worth and went to a little hotel near the station. Rooms were cheap, and should have been. They were dimly lighted and smelled of old carpets and musty bedding. We had a double bed in our room and the bathroom was down the hall. We looked at each other. It was not good but it would do for one night.

We ate in a grimy restaurant near the station, at a long counter with men in greasy overalls from the railroad shops. I wanted to walk around the streets and see a little of Fort Worth but Dewey was afraid. We did not know our way around and no telling the trouble we might get into. Infected with his fear, I followed him back to the hotel and up to our room, to sit and worry in silence.

When bed time came I went down the hall to the bathroom and saw no one. Dewey went down and was back in less than a minute, his face white, his hands trembling.

"This is a bad place," he said.

"What did you see?"

"A naked woman, coming down the hall this way. She'd a

come right on in if I hadn't a shut the door. It's one of them places."

He locked the door and worried out loud about the evil we were in. He worried because we had to stay in it for the night. The woman downstairs had made us pay in advance, and we did not have enough money left to walk out and find another place. It was wrong, morally wrong, religiously wrong, we both knew, but we ended up staying there for the night, making use of a pitcher and bowl on a washstand and scratching at bedbugs that came out of the walls when the light was turned off. Dewey went to bed with the key in his pocketbook buttoned inside his long underwear.

We got up before daylight, and each with his suitcase, crept down the stairs and out the front door. There was no one to see us go. Standing on a street corner in the graying light, he talked to me earnestly about the evil of cities, and warned me to watch out for bad women. He had been a help to me this time, but I was going off on my own. I would have to do my own watching out for trouble. Without so much as a handshake he went to hunt for the business school and I went to the interurban station.

As I looked back on it, the night had brought me nothing worse than bedbug bites, but the evil had been there, close enough to touch. It was always there in the city. I was glad to be leaving Forth Worth, going back to the country.

6

I had last seen Brookston at gathering time. Now it was planting time, with a warm sun and soft winds blowing up from the Gulf, and a sheen of new green on trees and turnrow grass. Straw-hatted men were in the fields with teams and plows, turning the moist black earth, or with planters planting corn. I crossed a new-plowed field to talk to Monroe and another to get to the house. Mae saw me in the field and had started making a homecoming supper by the time I got to the house. I was glad to be there.

The day I came back, a Thursday, I went down to the barns and got a job, starting the next Monday, at a dollar a day and board myself, plowing, hoeing, chopping—anything that came up. I would stay with Monroe and Mae and walk to the barns at daylight, back at dusk. I could see nothing else to do at the time. In early April I could begin applying for jobs for the fall in country schools.

Again Monroe and Mae crowded up to make room for me. That night, after supper, Monroe talked to me about new plans. When the crops were laid by, or when they were gathered, he wanted to move to town and get a job carpentering. Times were getting hard on the farm; a tenant farmer didn't have a chance, no matter how many hours a day he and his family worked. People were moving to town, working shorter hours, drawing better pay, sending their children to school instead of the cotton patch. Houses were being left vacant to rot and run down in the weather. I went to sleep with them still talking about what they would do when they moved to town.

Friday morning, with nothing else to do, I hitched a ride on a truck to Paris, to walk around the square and down to the wagon yard, looking for anybody from Pin Hook or Novice. I did not find anyone I knew but I did walk through many streets. Paris was clean and beautiful in the bright warm sunlight, and friendly enough for men and women to speak to me as I passed.

Midmorning I was idling through the Kress store when I met Mrs. Farmer, Mae's mother. We talked about my trip to West Texas and I told her about my job on the farm. I expected her to be pleased but she was not pleased at all. It was a comedown, after all the work I had done to get through Commerce.

"You won't get anywhere working by the day," she told me. "You ought to get a job in town till schools open up. Be somebody." She looked around the store. "You might get a job right here."

Before I had time to answer she had asked a girl at a counter for the boss man and he was coming down the aisle toward us, a young man in a white shirt and dark tie. He turned from the girl to me. It was too late to back down when he asked what I wanted.

"I'm looking for a job."

Mrs. Farmer moved on down the aisle away from us.

"Are you the man I see about a job?"

"I'm the store manager. Harold G. Watkins."

He waited for me to say something else.

"I've got a farm job, but I wouldn't mind working in town. I've worked in town before."

A beginning of interest showed in his gray brown eyes.

"What kind of work?"

"Stockroom."

I did not tell him I had been fired.

"Do you have a high school diploma?"

"I don't have it with me, but I could get it and my teaching certificate. I hold a first-class elementary."

"They won't care about the teaching certificate, but you have to be a high school graduate. District office won't let me hire you if you aren't."

He looked at me and there was a firmness around his mouth.

"You afraid of hard work?"

I told him about working at Sears Roebuck and working my way through a year at Commerce.

He left me waiting while he went to answer a bell at a counter. The long counters full of things to be sold were clean and bright under rows of lights. There was a hum of customers and clerks and jobs being done. A few minutes before I had never thought of working there. Now I was worrying that he would not give me a job. He answered two or three other bells and then came back to toilet goods, where I was standing.

He came close and looked at me earnestly.

"What is your aim in life?"

Cowboy? Farmer? Country schoolteacher? At the moment I wanted very much to get a job with S. H. Kress and Company. There was only one way for me to answer him honestly.

"I want to get ahead."

"You sound like you mean it. I'll give you a job, starting Monday."

Before I could ask how much he would pay he said, "Eighteen dollars a week. Is that all right?"

It was three times as much as much as I would get as a farmhand.

"Yes, sir. I'm sure much obliged."

He shook my hand and I felt that I had both a boss and a friend. He walked down a long aisle with me, pointing out counters filled with men's hose, hardware, glassware, buttons, each thing separated neatly by glass dividers. Girls behind the counters were polishing, dusting, rearranging.

"I like to see it looking good," he said. "I like to imagine I'm a customer walking through. I like to feel interested just walking through."

At the back of the store we went up to a balcony office from which the cashier could look down and watch customers and sales girls while she counted money.

"I hired us a new boy," he said to her.

She barely glanced at me and picked up a card.

"What's your name?"

"W. A. Owens."

"When do you start?"

"Owens starts next Monday," Mr. Watkins said. "We'll give him a try. I'll finish making out his time card later."

He went with me toward the front of the store as far as the jewelry counter.

"There are just two of us men," he said. "We have to be in before eight. I get here about seven-thirty. The girls come at eight-thirty. We open at nine and stay open till six. You come to the Lamar Avenue door and knock."

"Yes, sir."

I looked around for Mrs. Farmer but could not find her. Then I went out and walked around the square, past two banks, a picture show, drugstore, jewelry store, and a dozen or more clothing stores. People spoke to me and I felt at home. I walked out Lamar Avenue, almost to the place where I had first seen Paris from a load of peanuts. It was still the prettiest street I had ever seen. Then I went back out Bonham Street, past secondhand stores and grocery

40

stores, and rows of homes. At the edge of town I caught a ride from Brookston, to tell Monroe and Mae that I would be staying in town, and to thank Mrs. Farmer for pushing me into the job.

That night, when the men came in from the fields, I went down to the barns and told the man I was not coming to work for him Monday.

7

Paris was quiet and full of spring when I got off a truck on Bonham Street. Too early to go to the store, I walked around the square on Main Street as far as the Hotel Gibraltar, glad that I was going to live in Paris. It was a city of railroads: the Santa Fe and Texas and Pacific crossed there; the Paris and Mt. Pleasant connected the two towns. It was also a city of churches. In my short walk I saw the First Methodist, First Baptist, Episcopal, and Cumberland Presbyterian. It was a good business town. A little farther out South Main and I could see the cotton compresses and smell the vinegar and cotton-oil mills.

At seven-thirty Mr. Watkins met me at the Lamar Avenue door and let us in. Without lights, the store looked gloomy, and the counters were covered with long strips of blue chambray, cut in half-bolt lengths. The air smelled closed-in and heavy with a mixture from cotton cloth, candy, and racket-store perfume. Mr. Watkins opened doors and hooked chains across to keep people from coming in before opening time. He turned on lights and looked up and down the counters from the balcony. It was pre-Easter in the store calendar, a time for yellow and purple flowers, for pink chenille rabbits and yellow cotton chickens, for jelly beans and hollow chocolate eggs. Easter seemed to be all over the store in one form or another.

"Looks good," Mr. Watkins said. "It pays to stay late Saturday night. That's the only way you can make it look good Monday morning."

He got an application and a pencil from the cashier's desk. "You'd better fill this out for the cashier."

I stood at a counter and filled in the blanks I could. Date: March 30, 1925. Name: W. A. Owens. Date of birth: November 2, 1905. Address: I/C Monroe Owens, Brookston, Texas. I still had to find a place in town to stay that night. Education: high school diploma, East Texas State Teachers College, Sub-college Department, Commerce, Texas. Employment: Sears Roebuck and Company, Dallas, Texas, August–November, 1921; August–December, 1923.

Mr. Watkins read what I had written and said, "That's enough for now." He took me down stairs to the alley door.

"Your first job's to get the freight up. Deliveries are heavy Monday morning. You ever worked an armstrong elevator?"

"No, sir."

He raised a wide wooden door and we stepped inside on a square wooden platform. "Here's how you release the brake." He moved a lever and took hold of a large rope that looped over a wheel at the top of the shaft and another wheel fastened to the elevator floor. "Now all you have to do is pull. That's why they call it armstrong." He pulled us up a few feet and then let me take it the rest of the way. Hand over hand I pulled till the elevator came even with the second floor. "Don't forget to set your brake. It could fall hard."

I set the brake and he lifted the door. We were in a stockroom that was dark except for streaks of light from front windows. He turned on the lights in an aisle and I could see row after row of bins with merchandise neatly stacked and labeled with hanging tags. It was smaller than a stockroom at Sears Roebuck, and neater. He stopped at a large table.

"You unpack everything here and number and price it before you put it in stock. That way nobody can make a mistake. I'll show you how after you get the freight up."

He walked down the stairs and left me to bring the elevator down. Empty, going down, it moved with a light pull on the rope. Full, going up, it would be back-breaking, but no worse than geeing and hawing a team of mules hitched to a cultivator.

Salesgirls came in, punched the time clock, and went to their counters. They took off the cloth coverings and the whole store came to life while they waited for the chains to be unhooked, the customers to come in. Then I was at the alley door, receiving freight, signing bills of lading, stacking cartons on the elevator. Mr. Watkins came by to check on me.

"Don't load too heavy," he told me. "Just stack the freight inside when you receive it. You can take all day to get it up to the stockroom if you need it."

That first morning everything was fine about the job except the elevator. The first trip up I loaded it too heavily. Three-quarters of the way to the top, when I was sweating and out of breath, the elevator stopped and I could not budge it. Nothing to do but work with the brake lever and ease it back down. I expected someone to laugh at me when I began to unload some of the cartons, but no one noticed. With what I had thought was half a load I took the elevator up and with aching arms unloaded it.

Deliveries stopped coming and before noon I had all the boxes and cartons and packages stacked by the table on the second floor, ready for opening. Mr. Watkins sent me to a boardinghouse on Kaufman Street where I rented a room and arranged for supper every night for fifty cents a meal. For breakfast I could get coffee and a doughnut for a nickel at a place near the square. At a stand on Bonham Street I could buy a hamburger and coke for a dime. It would cost me half my pay to eat and sleep.

After lunch Mr. Watkins came up to show me how to open packages, check invoices, mark and shelve merchandise. The first he opened was from Perth Amboy and packed with rolls and folds of ribbon. I had never heard of Perth Amboy and had never thought much about ribbon. Kress had a whole counter of ribbon. It was part of my job to think about it. Mr. Watkins marked and shelved the ribbon. Then he handed me a carton and watched as I went step by step through the procedure.

"You are a good observer," he said. "One of the best things in business is to be a good observer."

The hundreds of things for sale on the dime-store counters

43

had to be taken out of their wrappings by me, priced by me, arranged by me on the shelves. My hands had to feel the texture of every item; fragrances of far-off places lingered around me. I forgot about farming, teaching, everything else but my job of getting things out to sell. Coming and going through the store, I heard the sound of cash registers as girls rang up sales. I knew what the sound meant and liked it.

Later in the afternoon counters had to be restocked. Some of the girls gave me orders to fill. Others came to the stockroom, and pulling a basket along the aisle with a rope, picked out the things they needed. My job was to take the baskets down the elevator and pull them through the aisles to the counters.

Mr. Kress, in New York, I soon learned, had worked out the system. Everything had to be done the way he said in New York.

At first the girls called me the new stockboy and asked for help only when the baskets were too heavy. Then they learned my name and I could hear them calling. "Owens, come to candy," or "Owens, you got some empty shelves in stationery." They were friendly girls, mostly from the country, from families that had moved to town so the girls could work at the dime store for seven dollars a week while they waited for husbands.

Mr. Watkins warned me about being too friendly with them.

"It's against rules to date girls in the store. It could cause you to lose your job."

Then he told me that Mr. Kress did not hire married girls. If a girl got married, she had to leave. Then I understood why there were two types of girls in the store: the young and pretty behind the counters, the older, more serious working as supervisors—they called them floor girls. Everyone had to get along with the floor girls.

Late in the afternoon, when there were not many customers in the store, I sprinkled cedar dust on the oiled floors and swept them down with a wide hair broom. At six Mr. Watkins closed the doors; the girls covered their counters and punched the time clock on the way out. Again Mr. Watkins and I were alone in the store and he wanted to talk.

"You like it?"

"Yes, sir."

"Good. It looks like we can get along. I can see you're not afraid of work."

"No, sir."

He talked to me about education and assured me that I had had enough schooling to get ahead in business. What I needed to concentrate on, he quoted from the Kress training rules, included a willingness to work hard, a set goal, and a pleasing personality. With these, there was no limit to what I could accomplish. He left me time to think these over and then changed the subject.

"You want to see a good selling window?"

He took me to the front of the store and showed me the window he had worked on in his spare minutes all day. It was for a special sale on glassware and crockery. There were plates and cups and dishes on glass shelves balanced on interlocking glass vases, with one-vase stands in the front, three-vase stands in the back. He had strips of fluted red and white crepe paper crisscrossed at the back and running to each shelf, the red strips ending at price tags.

It was a good selling window, I could see, and I told him so.

"Trick is to keep it from falling in on you. One shelf gets off balance and the whole thing goes. A window like this could fall in and ruin your profits for a week."

At ten o'clock he called to me.

"You about ready to close up?"

"It won't be long. I've got to sweep the part back by the elevator."

"I'll get us a coke."

He brought bottles from the corner drugstore and we leaned against a counter and talked. He was taking a course in Pelmanism—a course designed to help a man get ahead in business and at the same time become a man of good character. Mr. Kress had given him the opportunity. He was determined to make the best of it.

"I know I can make it pay off," he said.

Not only in salary, he let me know in an earnest voice. At the end of the year he would get a bonus, a percentage of the profit made by the store. I knew without being told that he was counting on me to help turn a bigger profit.

Saturday was a long day. The store was open from nine to nine. After the store closed Mr. Watkins and I had to see that everything was ready for Monday. For us, the day could last from seven to eleven. There were always people waiting for the store to open, country people who had come in with a wagon load of firewood or with eggs and butter in the back of a buggy—women in ankle-length dresses, some of them in starched sunbonnets, the men in duckings and wide-brimmed hats. The doors open, they moved slowly down the aisles, fingering the goods on the counters, spending their money carefully, talking in low voices.

People from Novice and Pin Hook stopped me.

"You working here? I didn't know you was aiming to work in a racket store."

"I wasn't aiming to, but they gave me a job."

"I heered you was aiming to teach school. You applied yet?"

"Not yet."

Then I had to be on the run. There was freight to take up, baskets to bring down, with bells ringing from the counters, a telephone ringing upstairs, girls calling to me, "Owens, I've got a customer waiting." Mr. Watkins expected me to run and I ran, upstairs, downstairs, till I could feel the sweat galling.

In the middle of the day I took time to go to the stand on Bonham Street for a hamburger. The square was crowded with country people who, their buying done, had nothing to do but stand around and look and talk till it was time to hitch up and go home again. Some crowded around the hamburger stand; others bought a dime's worth of cheese and crackers at Pete Humphries', watching the clerk whack off a piece of cheese and dig into a barrel for a handful of crackers.

By late afternoon the country people had gone home. The customers were now town people, most of them in a hurry. The girls had time to reorder for their counters. The orders filled, I had time to eat supper at the boardinghouse.

At night, when the town lights were on, Negroes congregated

46

in the store. For them, Saturday was "Sa'day night." They hung around the candy counter and the perfume counter. The women bought jars of Polly Peachtree Hair Pomade and aluminum combs that could be heated over a fire and pulled through kinky hair to make it straight. Mr. Watkins was always polite to them. Some of the girls were not. He did not hesitate to remind a girl: "Their money's as good as anybody else's."

After the girls were gone I swept once more while Mr. Watkins read cash-register totals and compared them with totals of the Saturday night before. He came down to the floor and there was a look of worry on his face. I soon learned why. It had been a good week except for cash-register shortages. They were charged against him, against his bonus. They might be mistakes or they might be thievery. Unexplained, they were charged against him.

"I've got to watch hardware," he said. "She could drain me dry."

We closed the doors at eleven and I was free until seven-thirty Monday morning.

8

By the end of my second week I saw that I could not afford the boardinghouse and that I would have to find a different place. The place I found was in the home of an automobile mechanic who lived on an unpaved street out past the water tower. He and his wife were country people who had moved to town so that they could be closer to his work. The house they rented was a four-room frame bungalow. For five dollars a week I could share the front room and double bed with their son, a boy still in high school. The father and son, I soon learned, had little to say. The mother talked constantly, of her daughters who lived in the country, of the neighbors around her, of girls she knew who worked in the Kress store.

She talked to me about David Phillips, a boy preacher who lived with his mother on another unpaved street a few blocks away. He was licensed, not yet ordained, but people looked on him as a regular preacher.

"You ought to get acquainted with him," she told me. "He does good for nearly everybody he meets. He passes by here a lot. Some night when you're not working I'll get him to stop."

She told me what religion had done for him. Before he got religion he was just one of the neighborhood boys, out of school more than in, running around with boys who could not keep out of trouble. Then he got converted and his whole life changed. He went back to high school, started preaching anywhere he could get a congregation, and people were beginning to look up to him. She was sure that we would be friends.

The Easter rush was about over and we were working most nights in the week, Mr. Watkins in the office or on the floor, I in the stockroom, cleaning shelves, arranging merchandise. We had to put away spring, get out summer. We could also expect the district manager on one of his visits. Everything had to be in order for him.

Certain nights, I learned, I could count on not working. They were the nights when his wife met him at closing time, to take him home to an early supper and then the picture show. Those nights I stood at the corner of the square, watching them swing along Lamar Avenue, young, well dressed, happy.

Other nights he stayed home to study Pelmanism. I knew now that it was a series of twelve lessons put out by the Pelman Institute of America and required of store managers. He had been through most of the lessons and was proud of the changes they had made in him. At times when he stopped me to talk I knew he was reviewing a lessor or clarifying his own thinking on an idea he had encountered. Other times, he was the teacher, I the pupil, the subjects taught the principles set forth by Pelman, the one to be kept uppermost: "Success must first exist in the mind." An average man, Mr. Watkins explained, can be a success in business if he is self-confident and energetic.

He often came back to the question of my aim in life. As often, I could not answer to his satisfaction, or mine. Then he would review basic principles. To get ahead, I had to have an aim in life and I had to have interest in what I was doing. People without an aim become drifters. Interest develops self-confidence and increases will power. My problem was clear to me, if not to him: My aim in life kept shifting; I was interested in almost any kind of work I laid my hand to.

One night when we had worked later than usual he stopped me in a stockroom aisle.

"I've been thinking," he said. "You might be a good learner. You interested in being a learner?"

I knew what he meant. From the day I started to work salesgirls had asked if I was a learner, or was going to be a learner. From then I knew the steps up were from stockboy to floorwalker to assistant manager and, someday, manager of a store. Mr. Watkins was offering me a chance to advance.

"I've been watching you, Owens," he said. "You're like me. We've never known anything but hard work."

He leaned against a bin, the darkness of the aisle behind him, the light of a bulb on his face. I thought I could detect Pelmanism in his manner. There was more than a measure of Pelmanism in the intense honesty in his eyes.

"Here's how I look at it for me," he continued. "When I started to work for Mr. Kress, I didn't have anything but a wife and daughter. Now I'm manager of a store. If the store makes good, I make good. I set my aim when I became a learner and I have lived up to it. They're giving me a chance to set a higher aim. They're training me to be a buyer. Notions buyer. If I make good, they'll take me in to the New York office. That's where you make the money."

I did not understand his law of compensation or how he was making it work for himself. I could see that he was getting ahead, and he had started out as a learner. If I was interested, he assured me, he would speak to the district manager on his next visit. In the meantime, he would begin teaching me the business.

We went to the notions aisle and turned on the lights. There were rows and rows of bins stacked neatly with boxes of needles

49

and thread, ribbons, and binding tape. They were small boxes and there was a kind of symmetry about the stacks.

"You like notions?" he asked.

I had not thought one way or the other. He did not wait for me to answer.

"I know more about notions than any other department. I'll start you off on notions."

For half an hour he talked of ordering and inventory, of being stocked but not overstocked. A lot of money can be tied up in needles and thread.

That night, after we had turned out the lights and locked the door, I walked all the way around the square before turning north on my street, seeing Paris as I had not seen it before, asking myself whether I could ever be satisfied living and working in town.

On a Saturday when I came back from lunch one of the girls stopped me on my way to the stockroom.

"David Phillips just came through the store. Did you see him?"

"I don't know him."

"You will. He comes through the store talking to everybody he sees." Her voice became tremulous. "He's so young to be a preacher. He's about as old as you are, and his hair is coal black. I never heard him preach but once. Everybody said it was a good sermon for anybody as young as he is. There's something about him. I don't know what it is. I'm going to hear him every chance I get even if I have to walk."

From the stockroom window I saw David Phillips on the northeast corner of the square, walking slowly, stopping to shake hands with farmers and their wives and children, like somebody running for office except he was not handing out cards. He was wearing white duck pants, a white shirt, and a black bowtie. His hair was blue-black and curly and trained back from a high forehead. I could not hear what he was saying, but I could see the vigor in his steps, in the outthrust of his hand as he came up to groups of people. Men pushed their hats back on their foreheads, women wiped their hands on their dresses when he came up to shake hands with them.

I watched him nearly halfway around the square. Then I had to go back to work. Full baskets were lined up at the elevator, ready to be taken to the counters. The aisles were full of people. I had to work my way through, basket at a time, holding the basket above the heads of customers.

When I got back to the stockroom window again a Salvation Army group was beginning to rattle their tambourines on the far side of the square. I could see David Phillips, moving slowly toward the Salvation Army corner. A man in Salvation Army uniform stood on the curb and lifted a trumpet. There was the sound of the trumpet and then a bass drum. The song was one I had known at Pin Hook, "Power in the Blood." Words came back to me from brush arbor meetings:

> *Would you be free from your burden of sin,*
> *There's power in the blood, power in the blood;*
> *Would you o'er evil a victory win,*
> *There's wonderful power in the blood . . .*

The sound of trumpet and drum echoed through the stockroom, and then the sound of singing, too far away for me to hear the words, but they were running through my head:

> *There is power, power, wonder working power*
> *In the precious blood of the Lamb.*

Another load of baskets down, the empties back up, and I could catch my breath again at the window. The crowd had closed in and formed a circle with two in the middle: David in his white clothes and a woman who was singing in a high clear voice:

> *I sing because I'm happy,*
> *I sing because I'm free,*
> *For His eye is on the sparrow*
> *And I know He watches me.*

Her song ended, there was a flourish of the drum, and David lifted his hand for silence. He began speaking but his voice did not carry across the square.

When I went out to supper the Salvation Army group had gone. So had David, or at least I could not see him on the square. But I had seen him and knew that, no older than I was, he was confident, positive, different.

That night I heard from my landlady that there was a vacancy at the Hopewell school for the next year. If I could go out the next day there was an all-day singing with dinner on the ground, and I could see all the trustees at once. It was not too far to walk.

Early Sunday morning I walked the six or seven miles to Hopewell, first on gravel and then on sand, on a road I had never traveled before. The sun was hot, dust rose from the road, stirred by cars on the way to Hopewell. Cars and wagons and teams were parked at the edge of the school ground and along the road. By middle of the morning the school house was full of people and the singing had started, with a leader beating out the time, a woman seconding on a piano, the voices rising and falling in four-part harmony. They went from song to song, barely catching breath in between, paying no attention to an old man who kept saying, "Amen, that's a good'un." Longer pauses came only when a new leader took over. There was nothing for me to do but wait and listen to songs like "Will the circle be unbroken" and "When I take my vacation in Heaven."

Dinner time came and the people moved outside, to the long plank tables set up under trees. Women spread tablecloths. Men brought trunks and boxes and tubs of food. After a long blessing the people moved up to the tables, the men quietly filling plates, the women urging them to help themselves. It was like dinner on the ground at any of the country places I had been. Hopewell could easily be home to me.

I found a school trustee and told him why I was there. It was my first time to apply for a school, and my first trustee was a tough one. He sat on a wagon tongue with a plate of grub. I haunched down in front of him. His doubts about me, between bites, were strong. I looked "purty" young to be trying to teach school. I might be all right and then again I might not. You never can tell about a teacher who has had no experience teaching. Big boys might want to run me off. Nobody knowed me in Hopewell.

He asked me about my certificate. I answered confidently, "Elementary, first class, good for two years. I got it going to school at Commerce."

It did not seem good enough for him. I could teach through the seventh grade all right, but at Hopewell older scholars sometimes wanted to go to school, some of them about my age. What if a scholar wanted higher work? I had no answer.

Women began passing pie and cake. He said he would bring my application up with the other trustees, but he could not promise anything. The trustees had been elected to see that Hopewell had a good teacher. He was sure they would have a lot of applications.

The singing started again. I listened for a while and then walked back to Paris, slowly, discouraged. A whole year at Commerce and I still was not good enough for Hopewell.

At dusk, because I had taken longer than I needed to walk from Hopewell, I came to the edge of Paris. Then, because I needed to, I went past both doors to the Kress store. The day had made two things clear to me: the trustee at Hopewell did not want me; Mr. Watkins did. I could go to work the next morning and never tell Mr. Watkins I had been turned down.

On the way to my room, after the sidewalks ended, I heard someone walking on the gravel behind me, walking faster than I was and singing a song from church. It was David Phillips in his white shirt and white pants. He came up beside me and put out his hand.

"Shake hands, brother." His clasp was firm, his voice friendly. "What's your name?"

I told him and we walked side by side.

"You new in Paris? I never heard your name before."

"I've been here a little while. I work at the Kress store. I've seen you before. You must know everybody in town."

"Nearly everybody. I'm a preacher, through God's will, and I have to go among the people and talk to them about God's work. It is the task laid on me. You go to church?"

He sounded so concerned that I hated to say no, but I had to. All the time I had been in Paris I had not thought once of going to church.

I told him that I had lived at Pin Hook and that my family were Baptist. He took my hand again.

"I'm Baptist, licensed to preach in the Missionary Baptist Church. I go to Immanuel Baptist in West Paris, when I'm not out preaching somewhere. The pastor is one of the finest men I ever knew. When I was on the road to ruin he found me and converted me. My father's dead and he got to be like a father to me."

I had to tell him about my family, my mother in West Texas, my brothers scattered.

"I want you to go to church with me," he said. "Church has been so good to me that I want everybody to know what it can do for them. People at Immanuel are common folks, most of them just moved into town from the country, but they know the old-time religion. Can you go with me next Sunday night? I've got to preach out in the country at Glory Sunday morning."

We stopped at my corner, facing each other in the dim light of stars and far-off street lamps.

"I'm reaching for you, brother," he said.

I knew he meant it, but I could not respond in the same way. I was not used to talking about the things inside of me. I shook his hand and he went on down the dark street, singing another church song in a voice not smooth but strong for leading.

9

The next Saturday, while I was hustling baskets through crowded aisles, David Phillips came to the store looking for me. He asked for me by name and the word went along counters till it came to me by the elevator, "David Phillips is looking for you." The girl

who gave me the message made me feel that I had been singled out
for something special. I went through the store almost to the front,
where he stood with his back to a counter, with people lined up
waiting to shake his hand. For the first time I was seeing him close
up in daylight. His hair was black and curly and shiny with bril-
liantine, his eyes black-brown with fleeting areas of light, his face
ruddy dark above his white shirt and black bowtie. The line moved
forward as he said, "Glad to see you, brother." "Glad to see you,
sister," "The Lord bless you." He paused with each one long
enough for eyes to meet, for hand to touch hand. Worn country
faces brightened at his words. Trembling voices said, "I heered tell
o' you. I'm pleased to meet you. You coming to preach out our way
sometime? We're Missionary Baptist, too. I get so hungry for some
good preaching." He took time to get the name of the person and
the church and encouraged them: "You tell me the Sunday, I'll
come if I can."

He saw me and I thought his face became different, perhaps
from the pleasure of seeing a friend. He stepped out from among
the others and took my hand. "I've been looking for you. I want
to make sure you will go with me tomorrow night—out to Immanuel Baptist. I want to talk to you some more." He lowered his
voice. "I'm still reaching out for you, brother."

My face must have showed how glad I felt to be noticed by him,
to be singled out from the crowd, to be made something special.
I was afraid to show how much I wanted to go with him.

"I reckon I can."

"Then, the Lord willing, we'll go. I'm preaching out in the
country in the morning, and they'll bring me back to town after
dinner. We can meet about sundown. You be at the bank on the
Bonham Street corner of the square."

I felt the grip of his hand on mine and said, "I'll meet you." I
wanted to say "brother," but it did not sound right, coming from
me. It sounded better just to say, "I've got to get back to work."

I went back to carrying baskets and answering bells. At times
I could see him slowly working his way through the store, being
a friend to everyone who put out a hand to him. For each there was
a light in his eyes, and the blood in his cheeks seemed close enough

to touch. He went out the back door, with people following after. Later I heard that he was down at the wagon yard, and did not like what was said about him: He's bad about shaking hands.

On my lunch hour I went past the courthouse as far as the wagon yard, but he had gone on, some thought with someone in a car. At supper time I took my pay envelope and went around the square to where the Salvation Army people were singing and preaching. A woman not quite old enough to be my mother was preaching to a small crowd. David was not there. He had not been there that day they told me. I bought a white shirt, white duck pants, and a black bowtie and went back to the store.

Sunday I spent killing time, waiting for Sunday night. I walked out the streets leading from the square—north, east, south—and back again in a Sunday town with most of the businesses closed, most of the people in their best clothes going to church. Paris claimed to be a town of high mental and moral standards. If going to church was any proof, the standards were about out of reach.

An hour before sundown I was in front of the bank where Bonham Street runs west from the square, waiting, the waiting itself giving rise to excitement. David came while the sun was still in the sky, while there was still enough to shine on the gold KRESS over the front of the store and the red background of the letters. He came along the north side of the square, the white of his shirt and pants reflected, moving, in the glass of show windows. He crossed the street and, with a quick glance at my clothes, shook my hand.

"White's good to wear to church. You ready to go?"

He had dropped the "brother" and seemed less like a preacher, more like a friend as we fell into step and started out Bonham Street. The bus ride out was only a nickel, but he wanted to walk and talk, to tell me the things that had made him what he was. Life had not been easy for him—not much easier, I soon saw, than it had been for me. His father, a small storekeeper, had died a year or so before, poor, broke, with nothing to leave to his family.

"They say he was a Jew," David said quietly. "I don't know for sure. I got my black hair from his. He was good to me but he died."

His mother was a country girl from out around Tigertown. David was living with her but his sympathy had been with his father. There had been trouble between them and he had gone from one to the other—at times on his own, playing hookey from school, hanging around poolhalls and domino parlors, learning things a boy his age should not know. He was getting tough, and on his way to trouble. "I started going to Immanuel Baptist Church and it changed my life. I was converted and it made all the difference. I had been dirty and I was washed clean. The love of Christ flowed through me. I got so I wanted to tell everybody about it. Then I knew I had been called to preach the Gospel."

We crossed the Santa Fe tracks, close to the station, where four years before, I had first taken the train to Dallas. I told him about working in Dallas and going to school in Commerce.

"You finished high school?" he asked.

"Yes, at Commerce."

"I've just got a little over a year to go for a diploma. I had missed so much I didn't think I would ever finish, but when I got the call I knew I had to finish high school. They're letting me make up my work any way I can."

God's work then, he explained, would be to preach, not to get an education. The heart matters more than the head. In the Missionary Baptists, God sometimes calls a man who can not read or write, and there is nothing for him to do but answer the call and depend on God to put the words in his mouth when he gets up to preach. David wanted to finish high school. He might go to school after that, but his main mission was to preach Christ and Him crucified to all people no matter how poor, how ignorant, how low he had to stoop to reach them. Some good preachers had been ruined by too much education, by the vanity of words.

On the way, David stopped to shake hands with the people we met and give them God's blessing. We came to the Bonham Street Methodist Church, where people were standing around outside, waiting for night services to begin. He shook hands with the ones near the sidewalk and we went on.

"If only God could make them see the error of their way," he said when we were out of their hearing.

I asked what he meant.

"They have not been baptized in water and in blood. A little water sprinkled on their heads, and they call it baptized. They've got to go down in that stream and be put all the way under. Then they'll be baptized. Only then will the redemption of Christ's blood be won. That's a sermon I've preached two or three times this spring. I'll keep on preaching it to anybody that'll listen. It's the Baptists that have the only true baptism."

Infant baptism, he explained, could be more than an error. It could be a sin. A Methodist might go through life believing he had been baptized and in the end go down to hell, unredeemed.

He knew I had not been baptized, though I had gone years beyond the age of accountability. He made me know I had delayed long—too long was the danger.

We came to Immanuel Baptist Church, a low white frame building with neither bell nor steeple, with nothing to make it look like a church except that it was larger than the frame dwellings around it. It was dusk and there was a smell of dew on sand. The young people's meeting was over and boys and girls, shadowy figures, stood outside the entrance waiting for preaching to begin. Men and women, some with children at their feet, babies in their arms, walked through the dusk and entered into the light.

David was at home with these people. He was their boy preacher and they were proud to see him, to shake his hand, to ask God's blessings on him. I was with David and they welcomed me as gladly.

"We want you to feel at home," they said.

The pastor, the man who had converted David, met us at the steps and put his arms around us. He was short, heavy-set, ruddy-faced. His voice was rich and full.

"My son," he said to David, "I am glad you can be with us, and your young friend. Welcome. Welcome to the house of the Lord. My favorite Scripture is, 'I was glad when they said unto me, let us go into the house of the Lord.' " He took my hand. "I hope you can make it yours. Brother David, there is time before the singing. Take him around and let him meet some of the faithful."

David took me down the aisle on one side, past the pulpit, and back the other. I shook hands with men in shirtsleeves, some of them deacons already in the amen corner, and with women in lawn and gingham dresses. The room was warm and women fanned themselves with cardboard fans from the funeral home, and with handkerchiefs wiped away the powder and sweat from their faces.

Among the women I met was Mrs. Crockett, the church secretary, a strong-faced, strong-bodied woman, perhaps in her early forties. When she found out that I worked for Kress she told me that she worked in a tailor shop just off the southwest corner of the square and asked me to come around when I needed some tailoring. She let us go and then came up to us again.

"You look like a team," she said. "David and Bill. A good team, but I like Billy better than Bill. I'm going to call you Billy. It's a friendlier name."

David started calling me Billy and giving that name to the people we met. In a few minutes it had become my Immanuel Baptist name.

The preacher took his place in the pulpit, a song book open in his right hand, a Bible under his left arm.

"Let us open our worship by singing a song."

He called out a number. A tall girl took her place at the piano and looked up at him. She gave a toss of her gold-red hair and played the last part of the song for the introduction. It may have been "Count Your Blessings," or "The Old Rugged Cross." There were three or four songs, some as competitions, with one side of the church singing a stanza, the other side another, with the old against the young, the women against the men—anything to get the people loosened up, the meeting going. The singing got louder; the preacher moved back and forth in the pulpit saying, "Amen, and again amen."

At the end of a song the preacher looked out over the congregation.

"Let us continue the worship by bowing our heads in prayer," he said. "Brother David, will you lead us? Let us stand."

David stood beside me and prayed in a voice that was strong, confident, and personal enough to make me feel that he did have

59

a special kind of relationship with God. It was a prayer of thanksgiving that God had seen him, wicked and unbelieving, on the road to hell, and had taken him out of the miry clay and set his feet on solid ground. He was a Saul on the road to Damascus, a persecutor, before God called him to preach the Gospel. He prayed to be allowed to walk in the footsteps of Paul. He turned from himself to the congregation and prayed that God would soften the hard-hearted, the stiff-necked, and open the way for the love of Jesus Christ to enter their hearts. He did not call my name but when he prayed for the hard-hearted and stiff-necked I knew he was praying for me. The prayer ended, we sat down and I could feel his hand resting lightly on my shoulder.

The preacher, when he came to his sermon, seemed to be preaching to me alone. He reminded us all of the miserable lives of the poor, the lonely, the lost, the widows and orphans. His voice, low-pitched, was sad when he talked about the weary in sin. It became loud and angry when he talked about those who crucified Christ with their sins. At the end of the sermon it became joyful when he talked about the saints of God who had prepared to enter the pearly gates.

He stopped preaching and stretched his arms out to the congregation.

"The doors of the church are open," he said. "Jesus is calling you to come. Is there a man or woman, a boy or girl who will heed his call?"

The pianist played some soft, familiar chords and then the congregation began singing:

> *Softly and tenderly Jesus is calling,*
> *Calling for you and me;*
> *See, on the portals he's waiting and watching,*
> *Watching for you and for me.*

I started singing but had to stop when the memories brought by the song tightened my throat. I had not thought in a long time of the nights at Pin Hook when my mother read the Bible and prayed and led us in song. Or of the nights under a brush arbor with the smell of sawdust and drying willow leaves and the sound of words reaching out into blackness beyond the light of coal oil torches:

> *Come home, come home,*
> *Ye who are weary, come home;*
> *Earnestly, tenderly, Jesus is calling,*
> *Calling, O, sinner, come home.*

The preacher, with his eyes on me, spoke in a voice softer than the singing but the words came sharp on my ears: "Come. Jesus bids you come. Come home to Christ. Oh, lonely one, come, and be no more alone." The loneliness. He seemed to know where life was hurting me most.

With only a few chords the pianist shifted to another song and the congregation shifted with her:

> *Come, ev'ry soul by sin oppressed,*
> *There's mercy with the Lord,*
> *And He will surely give you rest*
> *By trusting in His word.*

The preacher called in a commanding voice, "Only trust Him." The people had turned and were singing to me:

> *Only trust him, only trust Him,*
> *Only trust him now;*
> *He will save you, He will save you,*
> *He will save you now.*

David held my arm and talked to me softly. "Don't you want to cast off the burden of sin? Don't you want to accept Jesus as your personal Savior? Won't you trust him? Can't you hear Him pleading with you to come?"

I felt him step toward the aisle and then the pressure of his hand guiding me ahead of him. I saw the preacher move to the edge of the pulpit.

"Come, brother," he said to me. "Come forward to the mourner's bench. Let us pray for you."

Then I was in the aisle with David, moving slowly forward,

relieved to be going, uncertain about what I would do or say. There was a bench at the front and I knelt with David beside it. I could not see people coming but I could feel them touching my shoulders and crowding around me. "It is time," a man prayed, "oh, Lord, it is time."

The song changed and the voices were barely above a whisper:

> *Why do you wait, dear brother,*
> *Oh, why do you tarry so long?*
> *Your Savior is waiting to give you*
> *A place is His sanctified throng.*
> *Why not? why not?*
> *Why not come to Him now?*
> *Why not? Why not?*
> *Why not come to Him now?*

Now there were people praying softly all around me. The preacher was down in front of the pulpit, pacing back and forth, exhorting, crying, "Why not? Why not? Why not cross over to the Kingdom now?"

David was talking to me, "He shed his blood for you. He wants you to believe in Him. You'll never live to regret it." He put his face close and I could feel the heat of his blood. "Why are you holding back?"

I could not tell him, but I knew. I was now waiting for some feeling, some word inside that would make me know that my election was sure: God would belong to me, I would belong to God. I knew I wanted relief from loneliness. I knew I needed help to overcome the burden of sin, the Adam in me. What I waited for was a sign, something more than people sobbing around me.

The singing changed and I could hear a voice, a woman's voice, high and clear above the soft humming of other voices:

> *Come home, come home,*
> *Ye who are weary come home. . . .*

The preacher stood over me and laid his hand gently on the back of my head.

"My son, where is your mother tonight?"

I could see her in the house on the West Texas prairie. I could also see her as I had seen her at Novice or Pin Hook at a revival meeting, talking with sinners, pleading with them. Before I could answer, he spoke again.

"What would she want you to do tonight?"

This I knew. She had talked many times of what she would expect of me when I reached the age of accountability. I had reached it and passed it. My duty was clear. There was no flash of light to let me know I had crossed a barrier, but the woman's singing was more than I could stand:

> *Earnestly, tenderly, Jesus is calling,*
> *Calling, O, sinner, come home!*

Guided by memory, hardly knowing what I was doing, I braced myself with a hand on David's shoulder and stood up. The preacher came toward me, saying, "Give me your right hand." My hand went from David to him. He took it and put an arm around my shoulder. "Do you publicly profess Christ your Savior?"

I said yes but could not hear my voice above the jubilation.

"Thank God. Thank God."

He turned me to face the congregation.

"Do you want to join the church?"

"Yes, sir."

There was a motion to extend membership and the congregation voted me in. The preacher again took my hand.

"We will now extend the right hand of fellowship to our new brother in Christ."

The pianist started a new song. The voices sounded louder, fresher:

> *On Jordan's stormy banks I stand,*
> *And cast a wishful eye*

To Canaan's fair and happy land,
Where my possessions lie.
I am bound for the Promised Land.
O, who will come and go with me?
I am bound for the Promised Land.

Men and women left their seats and crowded into the aisles.
They moved toward me with outstretched hands, the men solemn-
faced, some of the women with tears on their cheeks. Their voices
trembled when they spoke: "Welcome, brother," "One more tri-
umph over Satan," "Thank God, the lost has found the way."

When the last of the people had come by and the singing had
stopped, Mrs. Crockett wrote my name and address in a notebook.
"God bless you, Billy," she said, and there was comfort in the way
she said it.

The preacher stood gripping the lectern and bowed his head for
the benediction. After a short prayer of thanksgiving he let the
words roll out, "The Lord bless you and keep you. . . ."

David and I lingered until the lights were turned out. Then we
walked home slowly through the dark streets, with only a little talk
between us. I was still wishing there had been some kind of a sign,
even after he said, "Before time was you were elect. Now you have
made your election sure."

IO

Work the next day was no heavier than usual on a Monday but I
was slower, so much slower that packages and cartons piled up at
the alley door and the stockroom was lined with full baskets for
me to take down to the counters. The burden was in my mind, and
it grew with the daylight hours, the perplexing burden of living
up to the commitment I had made. I knew I had made it quickly
and under emotional stress—a stress of the moment, and a cumula-
tive stress of nightly prayers and summer revivals, of sermons and

songs ingrained in my mind. Long before I reached the age of accountability two choices and only two had been held out to me: salvation or perdition. Now that the emotion of the night before had passed, I had to confront myself honestly, intellectually, spiritually, or be a hypocrite. Confront myself I did while I pulled the elevator up and down, while I walked through dark stockroom aisles, and the burden seemed more than I could stand. Evil permeated my mind; evil crowded around me. Bible verses called up from the past failed to comfort me. "Blessed are the pure in heart for they shall see God." Girls in summer dresses passed between me and light. How could I be pure in heart when all around me there were girls in summer dresses?

It was not too late to turn back, I began to tell myself. I had taken only the first step. The second was baptism, the ordinance that would seal my commitment eternally. The preacher had said I would be baptized the next Sunday night. I could stay away. I could refuse ever again to go back to Immanuel Baptist Church. No one could hold me to anything. No one but myself.

Mr. Watkins came by while I was opening packages and stacking merchandise on the table for marking.

"Something bothering you?" he asked.

I was tempted to say no, or to make up some kind of excuse for not keeping up with my work—to make up a lie.

Before I could answer, he said, "There must be something wrong, the way you look."

I had to tell the truth.

"I'm thinking about being baptized."

He sat on the edge of the table and I knew he had decided work could wait. He listened thoughtfully while I told him what had happened the night before, and my fears over the step I had taken. I asked his advice and he gave it. He considered himself a moral man but not a pious man. For him, at the time, being baptized or not being baptized made little difference, or belonging to a church. It was the man inside that counted, the willingness of the man to meet life as it comes, the good and the bad, without being either pessimistic or fatalistic. On these matters he expected every man to make up his own mind and not let anybody scare him into anything.

He changed the subject abruptly.

"Mr. Brown's coming next week to inspect. We've got to work hard to get ready. Not tonight but every other night this week."

"Yes, sir."

"Miss Merz is coming with him. Miss Millicent Merz. She works in personnel training and will want to talk to you."

He took me through the stockroom showing me things that had to be put in order. Then he left me to work and think and worry over the doubts that grew stronger and stronger, but not strong enough yet to make me turn my back on the chance to belong. I needed to belong and knew nothing better than Immanuel Baptist Church.

That night I found David Phillips at home, sitting in the front room with his mother. She nodded and said "Howdy" when he introduced me. Then she sat, large and silent, on one side of the room. I wondered how two people so unlike could be mother and son, and, more important, how I could talk to him with her sitting there, making me feel unwelcome. David looked at her and then at me.

"I feel like going out," he said. "You want to walk?"

When we were outside and walking toward the edge of town, going away from lighted streets, he put his hand on my arm.

"I could see you had something you didn't want to say in front of her. What is it?"

"I'm worrying about being baptized."

"How come?"

I talked to him about my confusion, my doubts, my fear from the night before, my feelings of unworthiness all day long. I was glad, I confessed, that I had been extended the right hand of fellowship. It made me feel among friends, and not as alone as I had been. It also made me feel that I was in danger of living a lie. Nothing that I could define had happened inside me, nothing that would make me better than I was before. No voice. No nothing.

I stopped and faced him in the dark.

"How did it feel to you?" I could hear the tension in my voice. "How did you know? What was it like?"

"Like a hot flame in my heart, all at once. I felt it and knew what it meant. I've never had a doubt since."

Such an experience, such assurance only increased my doubt.

"I'd better go back on what I said last night. If that's what it's like, it did not come to me. I'd rather wait till I feel it more."

He was against waiting.

"You've got to give it a chance. In some it's a slow growing. Don't worry about how you get to the mountain top of glory. Let God take care of that. Just be willing to put yourself in His nail-scarred hands. You are of the elect."

"How do you know?"

"You came toward Him when He reached out. You had the yearning. It was His pleasure to elect you before the world was. You gave your hand. You can't turn back."

He was persuasive and I began to feel that I might be of the kind who grow slowly into belief.

"Being baptized will help," he said. "Going down into that chilly water of death and rising to a newness of life will help you. I've seen it work many a time."

Toward midnight, in the seclusion of darkness, he prayed aloud to God to show me the right way—to a God palpable to him, to me something mysterious out somewhere beyond the milky way. His prayer repeated two things: that God through His Son would speak, that I would yield. I heard only David's voice but I felt a strong need to yield.

Then he talked about blasphemy, a sin that had long terrified me, since a preacher at Pin Hook had told me that I was guilty of blasphemy for saying that I did not believe in the church or trust preachers. I had stopped short of what I had first thought—"chicken-eating preachers"—but the weight of guilt was no less. Now, if I was elect of God, damnation would be complete if I rejected Him.

"I'll be baptized," I said in a voice I could barely hear.

He took my hand and asked God to let the morning stars sing together.

As we walked back toward his house he talked of the peace that passeth understanding. I felt a kind of peace, chiefly because I had made up my mind not to worry so much about the contradictions still inside me.

I I

The next Sunday night the preacher met me at the church door.

"You got some other clothes to put on?"

I held out the bundle that I carried under my arm. He took it and led me up to the pulpit. A part of the floor had been removed and I could see the zinc-lined baptistry, filled with clear water, and steps leading down into it from either end. He took me to a small room back of the pulpit and put my bundle on a table.

"You're the only one tonight," he said. "You sit down close front. When the time comes, I'll call you to come up."

He showed me how to enter from the side and where to wait for him.

"They'll be singing a song. You come down the steps on one side, I'll come down the other. We'll meet like this in the water."

He took my hands and folded them on my chest.

"Hold them like this. Lean back easy when I tell you. Don't thrash around trying to get up. I'll lift you and hold you till you're steady on your feet. You'll have enough to do thinking of the sacredness of the moment." Gently he leaned me backward and raised me again. "It's easier in the water. You ready?"

No sermon. No encouragement.

"Yes, sir."

He looked me over.

"I'm glad you've got on white. It'll make a pretty ceremony."

He went to the pulpit to begin the service. I went back into the church and, feeling alone, sat close to the front. There was an hour of singing, praying, preaching, and then the call to the mourner's bench. I was relieved when no one came.

The pianist started a different song and the preacher left the pulpit. When he returned he had changed to a worn black suit, one that looked as if it had gone down into the water many times. He beckoned me with a finger and I went around and up toward the baptistry. He slipped off his shoes. He started down from his side and I matched him, step for step, feeling the water first on my sock feet and then rising up slowly until it was more than waist deep and chilly.

The preacher reminded them of how Jesus had gone down into the river Jordan to be baptized by John. He reminded them that baptism is a cleansing, when all the sins of the past are put aside, when a newness of life is opened up. Then he turned me around and folded my hands on my chest. With his right hand on my hands, he raised his left. The singing stopped and his voice sounded out from the baptistry: "I baptize you in the name of the Father, the Son, and the Holy Ghost." He braced his left hand at the back of my neck and lowered me far under the water. There was a sensation of falling and then of being lifted. When I came out of the water he put a handkerchief over my face and said "Amen!" Then he released me and raised his arms to the congregation, the sign for thanksgiving and singing.

He started me up the steps and followed close behind me. He handed me my dry clothes and pointed me to a side room. "Hurry and get dressed so people can shake hands with you." I expected something more from him, I was not sure what, but he only said, "You had a good baptizing."

I hurried getting out of my wet clothes and then took a long time getting dressed. The heavens had not opened and there had been no sign. It may have been a good baptizing for the preacher. For me, it was another time when I had not measured up.

When I came down from the pulpit most of the people had left. The ones still waiting shook my hand and asked God's blessings on me. The preacher went with me to the sidewalk.

"Be sure to come to the Lord's Supper," he said. "Next Sunday. It's our ordinance of renewal."

I promised and then walked back Bonham Street alone. I belonged to Immanuel Baptist Church; the clerk had entered my name. From earliest memory I had known that sometime I would have to join the church. It was relief to know it was done, though I still worried at not being able to enjoy a special feeling of mystery. Only the words of an old song were in my ears:

> *Baptist, Baptist is my cry;*
> *I'll be a Baptist till the day I die,*

12

Mr. Brown and Miss Merz came to the store early one morning, before the doors were opened. When I came across the square they were studying the display in a front window; he was talking, she was taking notes. I passed close enough to see that he was short, squarish, blue-eyed, sandy-haired. She had black hair and eyes and her dark skin was touched lightly with rouge and powder. I had never seen them before but I knew who they were, why they were there, and that they had become important in my life. I went around to the side and found Mr. Watkins unlocking the back door.

"They're at the front windows."

I was excited. He sounded calm.

"I was expecting them, but not so early."

As he did every morning, he hooked the chain across the back door and turned on the lights. He took time to see that all the counters were covered.

"Everything ready in the stockroom?" he asked me. "You'd better go check. They might want to start there."

I paused at the balcony long enough to watch him walk deliberately through the store, looking right and left as he went, making sure he was ready for the inspection, for the grading that would mark his progress in the company. He had worked hard to get ready and appeared sure of himself. He opened the doors, shook hands with the two, brought them inside, and hooked the chain across the door. It was a meeting of friends, I could see, as they moved along an aisle talking, laughing.

Reassured, I went to the stockroom and checked bin after bin. Then I dusted again the places where Mr. Brown might lay a hand and find a patch of dust. The girls came in, not as talkative as usual, stopped briefly in their coatroom, and went on to their counters. Everyone but Mr. Watkins seemed to be going on tiptoe.

The freight bell rang and I knew they were not going to start with the stockroom. When I took the elevator down Mr. Watkins and Mr. Brown were in the office going over books. Miss Merz was at a counter with a floor girl comparing the layout with plans sent out from New York. Her look was exacting and I knew why: Mr. Kress did not like for his stores to look like junky racket stores.

Soon after lunch Mr. Brown came to inspect the stockroom. Mr. Watkins introduced me to him and then had to answer a call on the floor, leaving me with the man who could with a word or a frown take my job away. With a clipboard in one hand, a pencil in the other, Mr. Brown went down the aisles, comparing numbers on bins with numbers on printed sheets on the clipboard, checking for both accuracy and neatness. Boxed merchandise fitted neatly into bin spaces, but not merchandise like rag rugs and cotton batting. They had to be stacked so that from one end of the aisle to the other nothing but bin edges showed. He took time to show me that coffee cups and stewing kettles looked better stacked with the handles to the right. Mr. Kress, he told me, liked to see everything in good order. On that and on hard work and sound principles he had built his business.

When we were at the front of the stockroom, by a window that looked out on the square, Mr. Brown stopped to talk.

"Watkins says you're a good worker."

"Yes, sir."

Mr. Watkins had told him a great deal about me, I soon learned. Mr. Brown knew that I was a farm boy and that I had worked my way through a year of school at Commerce. Mr. Brown thought himself from observing my work in the stockroom that I had a well-ordered mind. He was much friendlier than I had expected and he soon let me know why. S.H. Kress and Company was looking for men willing to learn the system and keep to it.

He told me of men near the top in the company who had started out with handicaps as great as mine. Some of their stories sounded as if they had come out of Horatio Alger. He was certain a way would open up for me if I was willing to work and learn.

Mr. Watkins came back.

"I've seen all I need to see," Mr. Brown said.

He had found only one serious fault. I had failed to date the cartons in which I had stored the Easter leftovers.

They went down stairs and I began filling orders and hustling baskets to the elevator. My part of the inspection was over and I was relieved. My job was still mine.

When I took a load of baskets down Mr. Watkins called me over to a counter where Miss Merz was demonstrating counter layouts to the floor girls.

"This is our stock boy, Owens," he told her.

She shook hands and then sent me up to the display stock for trays and glass dividers—six-inch trays, twelve-inch dividers.

"You might as well stay and watch," she said when I brought the order down.

The counter had been stripped down to a bare tray, thirty-six inches by forty-eight, and the wood polished a deep cherry. She began rebuilding the counter, fitting in six-by-six trays and clean glass dividers. Expertly she measured glass, ran a glass cutter along the line, and tapped lightly to make a break with an even edge.

"Save glass when you can," she said. "Broken pieces can be cut if they're long enough." To me she said, "You can learn to cut them with a little practice."

When the trays were in place she clipped on price-card holders and showed the girls how to lay in the merchandise for the best effect. She talked to us about taking pride in our displays. The best ones would be photographed for the New York office. A display created in Paris, Texas, might be selected for circulation to stores all over the country.

She also talked to us as employees. Good people made good workers. She had her own philosophy to live by: "As a man thinketh in his heart, so is he." It was a philosophy she wanted us to think about.

When inspection was over and they were on their way to the regional office in Dallas, Mr. Watkins came to the stockroom to let me know they were beginning to count on me. Both Mr. Brown and Miss Merz wanted him to teach me everything about the business he could. On busy Saturdays he would expect me to wear a white shirt and tie and work on the floor. Other times, he would teach me about making displays and trimming windows, and how to watch for the shoplifters who worked through the crowds with their big pockets and shopping bags.

13

At nineteen I had a steady job, with a chance to move up step by step in the company. At nineteen, almost without warning, I became the mainstay of a household. There was a letter from my mother, a short letter, to the point: She was leaving West Texas and coming home. It was not anything against Lank Smith; he was a good man and a good provider. She could not get used to the wind and the loneliness. She could not see how she could stand another winter of snow and wind. She was also worried about Roy. He had come almost to the end of schooling there. If he was to have more, something had to be done for him at once. Feeling that I had no alternative, I wrote that if she was willing to live in Paris I would get a place for us. We could get by on what I was making.

By the time I had found a house for us, a four-room bungalow on First Street, at the farthest edge of town, they were on their way. The house was in walking distance of Immanuel Baptist Church and the West Paris elementary school. My mother could go to church when she felt like it. Roy could finish seventh grade and somehow or other we would send him to high school.

Before she arrived the house was well enough furnished to make do. She shipped some things by freight from Canadian. Monroe and Mae bought beds and chairs secondhand from a Negro couple forced to sell out. Mr. Watkins let me have chipped dishes and glasses and enamel ware from the damaged bins for less than he could have got for them on the damaged-goods counter.

My mother arrived in Paris not long after her forty-fifth birthday, a country woman, shy, afraid to raise her voice, afraid of not being able to get used to town ways. She worried that she was overweight and that all her clothes were homemade and looked country. She put powder on her cheeks but could not hide the roughness left by West Texas sun and wind. At church, the few times she went, she sat quietly at one side, speaking only to those who came to speak to her. At home, she spoke to the women on the street only when they spoke to her. She did not go to their houses and was glad our house was the last on the street. She did not have to bother with people passing by, or be laughed at for the kind of clothes she had to hang on the line.

She depended on me as she never had before: to provide money, to buy everything that came into the house, to say when we would go out, where we would go, and when we would come home again. She was like herself again only when my grandmother or Aunt Niece came from Novice for a visit, when there were hours of quiet talk of old times in the country, of quiet complaint about the do-nothing life she had in town, not even a garden or chickens to take up her time or help out. Or when David Phillips came to spend the night or just to eat some country cooking. They talked little but his long prayers were a comfort to her.

Roy also depended on me, but in a different way. At fourteen he was taller and heavier than I was, handsome, athletic, quick in mind, lazy in body, with a laziness heightened by the fact that he had gone from too much to do in the country to too little to do in town. He made friends easily—in a way too easily. I worried about how to keep him off the streets until the opening of school. Under intense persuasion he allowed himself to be baptized into Immanuel Baptist Church but he was not willing to center his life in it.

At times he listened to me; at times he did not. A major problem was the difference in ages. I was taking the role of father in providing a home, but I was too young to take the role in almost any other respect. He was near enough my age to resent from me most forms of discipline. It was never a matter of fights, or even of strong words, but there were tensions strong enough to be felt and to give me anxious hours—to make me wish someone could tell me how to respond when I had to be less than a father, more than a brother.

14

By the middle of summer there were not enough hours in the day, days in the week for me to get done the things I had to do, or wanted to do. I was spending an average of seventy-two hours a week at the store, working, learning, trying in every way to meet Mr. Watkins' approval. Only once, when I had cost him money, was he sternly disapproving. A newly repaired cash register was left on my work table long enough for me to try ringing up combinations of sales. I did not know that it had been preset and that he would be charged cash against his account for the imaginary sales I rang up. He heard the clank and ran up to stop me, but not before I had cost him a week of profit. He was angry and told me so. I had been stupid and knew it. The only way I knew to make amends was to work harder, longer, and that I could do.

At the same time I was spending another nine hours a week at Immanuel Baptist Church: three hours Sunday mornings at Sunday school and church, three hours Sunday nights at young people's meetings and preaching, three hours Wednesday nights at singing and prayer meeting. This was the demand of the church, that the faithful be totally involved in meetings together, in a room stark with the bareness of wood, with no crosses or symbols, no pictures that might suggest idolatry, only a Sunday school calendar and the Ten Commandments in illuminated letters. There were extra meetings called for church business, when every member in good standing had a vote, even on the question of whether another member was in good standing. It was their way of maintaining congregational, democratic control, as well as the "closed communion" they claimed as their right as the elect of God. There was no liturgy, no order of worship, no printed program. The preacher made up his service and prayers as he went along, Bible in hand, the Bible at the center, whatever the kind of meeting, the final source for truth, for doctrine—to be known from cover to cover, to be memorized in the soul-speaking passages. Like the others, when there was time I memorized, my choice verses in red —the sayings of Jesus—in red-letter edition.

Ritual I had experienced in baptism. Ritual I came to know in the Lord's Supper. The preacher preached on the sacredness of each, the first necessary to the last in the steps of making election sure. He set us above the Methodists and others, especially the Methodists, who had not been cleansed by total immersion, who might backslide and repent and backslide all over again. The danger, he reminded us, was that death might come to a Methodist while he was in the backslid state. Then, eternal damnation was sure. Baptists, once they reached the state of grace, could never be totally lost.

The Lord's Supper itself could be a stumbling block, he warned, if it did not adhere strictly to the New Testament, if it became a kind of formalism, if man-made words were treated like Scripture. A preacher had enough words in himself and the New Testament to administer a true Lord's Supper.

Under his words, a hush came over the congregation. Then he read: "Jesus took bread, and blessed it, and brake it, and gave it to the disciples, and said, 'Take, eat; this is my body' "; Deacons started down the aisle with trays of broken crackers. "Take a piece and wait," the preacher said. "We will all break bread together." Trays were passed along rows. Each of the elect took a piece and held it, waiting. Then the preacher said again, "This is my body," and, careful not to elevate the bread above his lips as the Catholics do, led us in eating the tiny piece of saltine.

He took a small glass from a tray held up by a deacon and read: "And he took the cup, and gave thanks, and gave it to them, saying,

'Drink ye all of it; For this is my blood of the new testament, which is shed for many for the remission of sins.' " Deacons passed trays of glasses along the rows and there was a smell of grape juice in the warm air. Grape juice, not wine, because Baptists believed the teaching: "Look not on the wine when it is red in the cup for it biteth like a serpent and stingeth like an adder." The preacher lifted his glass to his lips and said, "Drink ye all of it." There was a moment of silence and then rattle of glasses set on trays.

With hand clasping hand, baptized and unbaptized alike, we stood and sang "Blest Be the Tie That Binds" and remained standing while the preacher dismissed us with a prayer that the ordinance we had observed would renew our strength, that temptation would be withheld, that the pathway would be smoothed for true believers.

On a Saturday when I had a late lunch hour David Phillips came by the store and took me to a Salvation Army meeting on the square. He believed in the Baptist church, Baptist doctrine, but he also believed that the Salvation Army could help poor and lonely that the Baptists could never reach. He was not trying to convert me to the Salvation Army; he only wanted me to see the work they were doing and why he sometimes sent people to them for help instead of to the Baptists.

He led me through a ring of people and almost to the center of the meeting. Between a song for the crowd and a trumpet solo he introduced me to Mrs. Stella Van Dyke, who was head of the Salvation Army in Paris and had a military title, probably captain. I knew who she was. I had often seen her in street meetings in her blue, red-trimmed uniform, her black straw hat shaped like a sunbonnet. She was a friendly, motherly woman with three young daughters, who sometimes beat tambourines in meetings. I had heard her preach, in a voice that echoed across the square. I had heard her hold out comfort to the hungry, the broken, the ones that life had passed by. Before or after her sermons she sang songs that made people sit on the curb and cry— religious songs, or at times tear-making songs like "She's Only a Bird in a Gilded Cage."

She took my hand and held it for a moment. Then she asked, "Will you join our meeting? Give a testimony or a prayer?"

I looked at her and then at the crowd. Her invitation was genuine but I was not ready to stand up and say anything in a street meeting with the Salvation Army. I thought of my own pride, of what Mr. Watkins might say. The excuse I gave her was that I had to get back to the store.

"Come by the house after work," she said. "David's coming."

I moved to the back of the crowd and listened to a trumpet solo. Then, before the testifying and preaching could begin, I went back to work.

After the doors were locked for the night I went out past the courthouse to Mrs. Van Dyke's house. It was a large, run-down place, yellowish-gray and grim on the outside, bright and comfortable inside. Mrs. Van Dyke sat in a large living room, the center of a noisy and friendly crowd whom she introduced simply as "My Family." One was an army sergeant in uniform, her husband, home on furlough from San Antonio, for the moment nonmilitary. At the side were some old men who roosted on the third floor; around the sergeant, boys and girls from the Salvation Army Sunday School. Across from him David sat on a couch with the Van Dyke daughters.

"You'll have to make a place for yourself," Mrs. Van Dyke said to me.

It was more than finding a seat for myself. She liked having all kinds of people and all kinds of religion under her roof. It was an invitation to make a place for myself among people who held loosely to doctrine, if they held to doctrine at all, among people who had hubbed life often enough to know that not the forms but the substance of life mattered.

David had made a place for himself among them, it was clear to see. After a time of food and laughter and song I was still on the outside.

15

Late in the summer, when the season began to change from the heat of dog days to the first cooling breath of fall, shipments of school supplies began to come in. The areas around the unpacking table was heavy with the smell of cedar pencils, chalk, and rough pulp tablets. School opening was almost at hand. The girls worked all day, Mr. Watkins and I worked at night to make the counters and windows carry out school-days themes. We built special displays for every possible school item from painted lunch boxes to hair ribbons. We had, our instructions said, to create in customers the excitement of going back to school. Then they would buy.

In me we created nostalgia. I wanted to go back to school. This feeling had been with me as many falls as I could remember. It was with me again, with a pull stronger now than that of the Baptist Church or the Kress store. Since the day I left Commerce I had been without books except for the Bible. I had to start looking for books again.

Two blocks from the Kress store workmen were transforming an old post-office building into a junior college. On a lunch hour I went to the building and walked through halls and classrooms, breathing the smell of new paint, looking at new blackboards not yet touched by chalk. I sat in a classroom and knew how much I wanted to go to school. But how? How could I support three people and go to school?

I went down to the office that was for both the librarian and registrar and spoke to the only person there, an old lady, older than my mother, who welcomed me and told me about the college. It had been established because too many boys and girls in Paris and Lamar County wanted an education but could not afford to go to Commerce or any other school. After junior college they could get certificates and start teaching. The college was getting ready to open for its second year and new students were invited.

In the catalogue she lent me I turned first to dates and costs. Registration was set for September 13; classes would begin September 14. Tuition was one hundred dollars a year, a third to be paid at the beginning of each term. I read on. The college had two publications for which a student might write: a newspaper, *The Bat*, and a year book, *The Galleon*. More important, a student who completed one year of work would be eligible for a high school teaching certificate good for two years, and the requirements seemed light: one course in Education, another in English. This certificate, I knew, would improve my chances for jobs in country or consolidated schools.

The woman told me the college had been established for people like me and that I could make it through if I would try. They would accept me on my credits from Commerce, and I could arrange to pay my tuition as I got the money. I would not be the only student working my way through. There were country boys and girls coming in from Glory and Cunningham and Bogota. Some would pick cotton when they could; others would be paying with butter-and-egg money. It would not be easy, she assured me, but nothing worth working for was easy.

All that afternoon I worked in the stockroom, keeping what I had learned to myself, dreaming again of school and what it would be like, bolstering myself with the thought that if others could, so could I. One thing I knew: I could not go to school and be a learner for Mr. Kress.

That night I talked to my mother about going back to school. She wanted me to have a better education but she worried that this was not the right time. I had a job; we were getting along all right. She was worried that I could not make enough working after school. But if going back to school was what I wanted, she would not stand in the way. When we talked about money she said to me, as she had said so many times before, "The Lord will provide."

When we were into September I talked to Mr. Watkins, on a night when we worked late in the stockroom. I told him how much I wanted to go to school, and asked him if I could work part-time during the school year. I was not giving up entirely the idea of becoming a learner. It was only that I knew I needed more education. Though he was sure I did not need to go to school any more, he was sympathetic and, as always, willing to help where he could.

"If that's what you want to do, we'll just have to make the best of it." But there was a sadness in his face. "I had looked forward for you to go places in Kress."

He could give me work through Christmas, but he could not speak for the company about the future. He would ask Mr. Brown about my chances and speak a good word for me.

Still I was not decided. Nights when I was not working or at church I walked the streets and worried about the direction I should take. It was a risk for my mother. It was a greater risk for Roy, at a time when he needed all the help he could get.

September passed and I was still working full-time. Classes had started without me. A few more days and I would be too far behind to start.

One morning near the first of October Mr. Watkins had me take the school supplies out of one of the front show windows and get it ready for a new display.

"We'll trim it tonight," he said, when I had washed the glass and polished the wood. He looked at me and there was encouragement in his eyes. "No, you can trim it. It's about time you tried. Do you want to?"

"Yes, sir. What's going in it?"

"Phonograph records at the back, where they won't melt. Whatever you want at the front."

I had watched him lay out a window on paper often enough to know what I wanted to do: at the back, twenty-four-inch vases stacked three high, supporting twenty-four-inch glass shelves, in all three stands to hold records; in the front eighteen-inch vases and eighteen-inch glass shelves to hold iridescent amber gift glassware; for trim, fluted streamers of black and pale gold crepe paper.

"Sounds good," Mr. Watkins said when I showed him the plan. He liked the colors and displaying the gift glassware. A counter might be set up for it alone. "You don't know, though, how a window'll look till it's done," he warned me.

After supper, while Mr. Watkins worked in the office, with the window lights on and people stopping to watch, I covered the back wall with pale gold crepe paper and hung records like great black polka dots from ceiling to floor. Against this backdrop I set the three stands of records, on each shelf two records balanced in plate holders, the records front and back looped together with twisted black and gold streamers. The next step was to fill in the lower front with glassware, iridescent creamers and sugars on glass shelves covered with gold crepe paper.

At times I went out on the sidewalk to see how the window would appear to a passerby. It was an unusual window, good enough, I thought, to be photographed, good enough to make me noticed.

By ten o'clock I closed the window up and started down the aisle to call Mr. Watkins, to show him the window before I turned out the lights. From the middle of the store I heard a crash and then breaking glass. Knowing what was happening I turned and ran toward the front, hearing my own footsteps, hearing Mr. Watkins bounding down the stairs.

By the time we got outside the whole display had caved in and there was nothing left but a pile of broken records, broken shelves and vases, broken gift glass. Only the records hung on the wall were in place, and they would have to come down. Mr. Watkins walked from one side of the window to the other. I thought he was figuring the cost, the loss in commissions he would have to take. I felt a flush in my cheeks and a wetness in my eyes.

"Don't take it so hard," he said quietly. "It may not have been your fault. A shelf might have broken."

We soon found out that I was at fault. One record had melted enough to bend and shift. One shift of weight and the whole thing had fallen in. Mr. Watkins had every right to say harsh words to me but he did not.

"Shovel it all out," he said, "and turn out the lights. Tomorrow we'll do it all over again."

As I shoveled and swept up broken glass and piled it in boxes in the alley I knew I could not do the window again by myself. I was afraid to: Mr. Watkins would not let me. He would not want to risk again so much cost to him and the company.

The feeling was still with me as I walked out Bonham Street on my way home, a feeling that grew until I felt I had never been cut out to be a learner in a Kress store.

The next morning Mr. Watkins and I worked on the window together. He showed me again how delicately glass shelves had to be balanced on glass vases, how even a metal price-card holder placed too far to the right or left could make a shelf tip and a stand fall down. My problem was that my heart was no longer in the window or the store, even when Miss Merz, on a teaching visit, stood with me outside the window and talked to me about tricks for making people stop and look at displays.

During my lunch hour, almost as if there was nothing else I could do, I went to Paris Junior College and enrolled as a freshman, with a promise to pay tuition as I could. With the help of the registrar I arranged for five classes in the mornings, none in the afternoons. From twelve o'clock noon on I was free to work. My first class would be in English composition, of which the catalogue said, "Ability to write accurately, easily, and effectively is the aim of the work in English Composition."

When I had paid down the money I had, when there was no turning back, I stopped Mr. Watkins in the stockroom and told him what I had done. He was not surprised, but he was sad to see me give up the chance to become a learner and unhappy at having to break in a new stockboy.

"Can you keep me on part-time?" I asked. "I've got to work to go to school."

"As long as there is work."

He did not try to persuade me to stay. He did tell Miss Merz, who came at once to talk to me. She sat with me at the stockroom table and told me of men she had watched make successes in the company. She was sure that with the education I had I could expect to get ahead fast. She wanted to talk to Mr. Brown. She was sure that he would place me as a learner in another store, maybe Dallas or Houston, and before long I would be an assistant manager.

"Mr. Watkins believes in you," she said firmly.

He was my friend. She was my friend. He came up and sat with us at the table. Together they made me feel that I could go far if I would stay with Mr. Kress. They also warned me of the problems I faced paying my own way. For all their questions I had only one answer: "I've got to go to school."

That night I told my mother what I had done. It was no more than she had expected and she did not try to stop me, though she knew it meant getting by on less. She had skimped before, she told me, and was willing to skimp again.

Then I went off to prayer meeting with David Phillips. It was a testimonial night, a time when church members, mostly older men and women, stood up and talked about their religious experiences. They talked of how faith had made life bearable through sorrow and adversity, through the pain of the sick bed and the loss of loved ones. Their faces looked worn, their lips trembled when they talked. It was easy to believe their stories of sorrow, hardship, loss, their feeling of resignation in this life because their faith assured them a better time by and by. They could say together "In my Father's house are many mansions" and fully expect to meet each other there when they were called by the trumpets of judgment.

After the meeting, David walked with me on Bonham Street. He did not talk against education. He did try to make me understand that no amount of education could move one as close to the human heart as the simple testimonials we had heard.

The next morning I was in school, in an English class taught by Miss Ruth Hudson, a pale, blonde young woman who knew books and had traveled in Europe. She had a disarming manner of talking about books and authors, not in a gossipy way but in a way that made the writers seem real to us and the writing of books something any one of us might attain. Our writer of the moment was Robert Louis Stevenson; his essays the works we are most concerned with, especially those in *Virginibus Puerisque*. Her technique was to make us compete with each other memorizing her favorite lines—to let the words and rhythms and meanings soak in. Before

84

the class was over two passages had stuck in my mind: "Restfulness is a quality for cattle" and "Extreme busyness is a sign of deficient mentality."

Back in the stockroom I filled baskets and thought about the class. When the chance came I quoted the two Stevenson passages to Mr. Watkins. What had seemed contradictions disappeared, as he applied the principles of Pelmanism to them. Stevenson had stated extremes to make the reader search for a mean. If he was arguing for anything, it was moderation.

Before a month had passed I found myself pulled three different ways by three different people: a Baptist, a Pelmanist, and, though she may not have applied the term to herself, a humanist. With David it was Baptist doctrine—love God and hate the devil—whether he was preaching in a country church or we were walking through the streets of Paris searching for meaning in the Scripture we quoted. Every Sunday he took a different passage for his text. During the week he memorized it and insisted that I memorize it with him. Hoisting freight or sweeping floors I could quote verse after verse under my breath. As easily, because of Mr. Watkins, I could quote a passage from Pelman: "Where a serious decision must be made about your life aims—ponder long and carefully." Then, because of Miss Hudson, I was mixing in passages from Stevenson. Jesus, Pelman, Stevenson—religious, pragmatic, romantic, separate, distinct, yet at times all flowing into each other in my mind. David wanted me to find myself in the Baptist church, Mr. Watkins in business, Miss Hudson in myself.

Miss Hudson was—I found out by asking her—an Episcopalian. She was sure that Baptists were too narrow and that their beliefs kept them from enjoying many of the good things in life. Like dancing, and laughing, and learning. I could not agree with her about dancing. I listened when she tried to show me how to use passages from Stevenson as models for writing English prose. Then she gave me W. H. Hudson's *Green Mansions* and *Far Away and Long Ago*. The latter opened new worlds to me. Stevenson had been too witty for me to imitate with any success. Hudson's voice and words spoke to me about a kind of life I could understand, a kind of people I felt I had known.

Mr. Watkins was less insistent than the others. We were not as close as we had been and there was not much time for lingering talks in the stockroom. He had hired a new stockboy, one he told me would never be good enough to become a learner, and the stockroom was no longer a place where we could talk.

On a night when we worked late Mr. Watkins and I talked toward the end over sodas in the drugstore. He wanted to know what I was learning. I told him as well as I could. Then he asked about my determination to keep going. I saw no way to turn back.

"By God, you'll make it," he said.

Again he talked about the law of compensation. If I was willing to work that hard, he assured me, there would be compensation farther along.

Miss Hudson was also trying to encourage me. On a day when I was worrying about being able to go on I wrote my story in a composition for Miss Hudson, not expecting help from her but feeling that she would better understand in the times when I could not meet her standards. When the paper came back she had written across the top: "Handicaps but make the winning the sweeter."

They both saw better things farther down the road. With a beginning sense of fear I saw the handicaps that were with me then and there.

16

Late in the fall there was trouble at Immanuel Baptist Church, not with the church but with one of the young members. At first there were only rumors and then the evidence seemed strong enough to require a church trial: She had been at a club on a night when there was dancing—not dancing herself but staying on after the dancing had started. Her parents were leaders in the church and the deacons thought they could not overlook in her behavior something that might lead some other member astray. On a Sunday morning, in ominous voices, they announced a trial to be held the following Thursday night. Every member was encouraged to attend; every member in good standing was expected to vote. Her situation was made clear. If the vote went against her, she would be churched. All church privileges would be denied her until she had publicly repented and confessed her fault. It was a testing of the body to discipline one of its members. Every member had laid on him the seriousness of the test.

When I arrived the church was filling up fast and the deacons had already taken seats together at the front, a grim-faced set of judges with responsibility for trying before the jury—the congregation—transgressors of doctrine and conduct alike. Their eyes and faces were hard with the sense of duty. I took a seat at the side, near them and half-facing the congregation. Most of the regular attenders at Immanuel Baptist were there, the families sitting together, fathers and mothers, children of the age of accountability and under wedged between, brought for a lesson in the hard way of the transgressors. Outsiders were there—Methodists, Presbyterians, Christians, some who rarely darkened the door of a church, taking up all the seats and standing along the walls. Clearly they were onlookers. They whispered and nodded and smiled as they looked forward to a good Baptist squabble.

Preachers came in from the back—one from Immanuel Baptist, two from other Baptist churches—and took seats behind the lectern. Silence came over the congregation. One of the preachers went to the pulpit and prayed God's guidance for the girl, that she might see the error of her way and repent publicly; for the members of the church, that they might judge with both righteousness and humility. His prayers ended, the way prepared, he asked the girl to come in from the side door, where she had been waiting with bowed head.

She was a remarkably pretty girl in full-bosomed youth, with dark hair and eyes, a sensuous lift in her lips, and a flush in her cheeks. She walked slowly, looking down, with enough motion in her body to create a hint of feminine defiance. She stood with her back to the pulpit and beneath it so that the preacher was looking down on the top of her head.

"My young sister," the preacher said solemnly, "you have been duly waited on. You know why you have been called before the congregation. You know the transgressions you are charged with?"

For the first time she raised her head and faced the people who would vote for or against her.

"Yes, sir."

Her voice was low but firm.

"You will answer the charges, God being your witness?"

She nodded.

"Did you go the club?"

"Yes, sir."

"Did you know the kind of place it was before you went?"

"No, sir."

"Why did you go?"

"Some friends took me."

"A boy?"

"Boys and girls. They wanted me to go with them and I went. I didn't know I was doing anything wrong."

"Did you see dancing there?"

There was a rustling as people shifted forward to hear her answer.

"Yes, sir."

"Did you dance?"

"No, sir."

"Did you leave when the dancing started?"

"No, sir."

"Why not?"

"I was with my friends. Some of them wanted to stay and dance. They didn't dance long and we left."

I could see the deacons were not satisfied. She had confessed but there was no sorrow, no penitence in her voice. The preacher, knowing the congregation would not be willing to vote on that alone, turned the questioning to the deacons. An old man in whom the juices of life had dried up rose and faced her.

"You admit that you watched them dance?"

"Yes, sir."

"You know dancing is a sin?"

"A sin for Baptists—"

The deacon stopped her.

"You *know* dancing is a sin. You know it is the work of the devil. You've been told how many girls have gone wrong going to dances." He lifted his finger and his voice got louder. "Are you sorry for your sin?"

She looked at him and her eyes were flashing.

"I felt no sin. I—"

"You looked on a sin of the flesh."

She remained silent, looking down, the light on her hair, her face in shadow. Another deacon took up what was no longer a questioning.

"We cain't punish you," he said. "Only God can punish you. All we can do is withdraw the right hand of fellowship. You want us to do that?"

The girl did not answer, but she looked close to crying.

"You cain't be so hard-hearted and stiff-necked," another deacon said to her.

When the deacons had no more to ask or say, the preacher spoke to the congregation.

"You have heard all. Are you ready to vote?"

"Church her," a woman said vehemently, and the women had their turn, harder on her than the men.

The preacher looked at the girl.

"You want that?"

She shook her head and began to cry in hurt whimpers.

"Then you'll have to confess your sin and ask for forgiveness. There is no other way if you want to be a member of Immanuel Baptist Church."

There was a sound of a woman crying at the back of the church —her mother—and then her father at the front saying, "Lord, have mercy." There were some with wet eyes, many with stern unforgiving faces.

Suddenly the girl turned to the altar. "I confess," she said to the

89

preacher and then, "Oh, God, I am sorry that I was caught in the way of sin."

The trial was not yet over. Deacons had to debate among themselves whether she was truly sorry for the blame and shame she had brought on the church. Not till someone reminded them of the words of Jesus, "He among you that is without sin, let him cast the first stone," did they let mercy temper righteousness. Then a deacon moved that her confession should be accepted, another seconded, and the congregation by voice vote returned her to the fold.

When the preacher announced that the congregation would come forward to extend to her the right hand of fellowship the girl took a quick look at the faces and ran out the side door. The congregation, unbelieving, stood still, listening to the sound of a woman's shoes on the sidewalk, fleeing from the church.

"Let us bow our heads in prayer," the preacher said.

It was only a prayer of benediction, and then the people went out, silently or quietly whispering to each other. A woman's voice rose above the others: "If I was her I'd never darken the door of that church agin, the way they treated her."

17

Fall term ended December 4 and I got my grades: three B's, two D's, one of the D's in algebra, a grade achieved by memory work more than by reasoning out principles and problems. At the time, it was enough for me that I had passed and that I could register for the winter term beginning December 6. We were well into the Christmas rush at the store and I was averaging about fifty hours a week on a part-time job, driven, allowing myself to be driven because I needed the job. Between the job and study, I had to favor the job.

The Christmas rush over, we went into inventory and then the pressure of an inventory sale. Crowds came to the store. Work backed up. Then the sale was over and the store turned quiet. Mr.

Watkins stopped me in the stockroom one night, and as gently as he could, told me that he had been ordered to cut down on help. I would have to go. So would all the extra salesgirls and some of the regulars. He knew what it meant to me to be without a job in January, when jobs were hard to find, when I had two people depending on me, when I was far into a new term and needed to save any credit I could. Then he tried to be encouraging by talking about my self-confidence and determination. He was sure I would find a way.

"Any time I can use extra help I will call you," he said. "You have first claim."

I believed him, but I knew he was not likely to need me before Easter, and I could not hold out that long.

All the way out Bonham Street I worried about what to do. I was taking a course called "Value and Exchange in Business" but it was no help. A thought kept returning: to hit the road and keep on traveling till I could find some kind of job. In the dark streets that seemed an easy way out and I planned where to go: Dallas first, and if there was nothing in Dallas, anywhere I could flag a ride. By the time I got home I had convinced myself that I would never be able to finish school anyway and I might as well bum it on the road.

My mother took the news with a nervous shaking of her hand, and then while I ate the cold supper she had saved for me, she talked of what must have been in her mind before. We would move back to our old place at Blossom. She had it all thought out. The house was empty, the land lying out. We were getting nothing from it. We would save our own rent of twenty-five dollars a month living there. We would burn wood instead of buying coal and we would save the light bill by using coal-oil lamps. Roy could go to the Blossom school, and she could have a garden and chickens. I could catch rides to school in Paris and work at farm jobs on my days off. In the fall I could get a school.

Her plans sounded reasonable, but they made me afraid. At twenty, I would be going back to farming and I did not want to. I was afraid of the years that might pass before I could escape again. But to ease her mind, I told her I would go look at the place and see what we could do.

After classes the next Monday I walked almost to Reno and then got a ride the rest of the way to Blossom. Then I walked the mile and a half of sandy road and across the field to the house. It was January and a chill wind was blowing. The house faced bare woods. Not lived in for a long time, it looked neglected, desolate. The last people in the house had papered the walls with newspapers and left piles of old newspapers and bottles in the kitchen. They had left ashes in the fireplace in the other room and wind had blown them in fine dust over the bare floor. I opened the front door and went out on the porch to stare into the woods, and then walked toward the well and barn. A well bucket and rope had been left and I drew water for a drink.

More discouraged than I had been in a long time, I went back to look at the house. There was plenty of wood and water, but the house would need days of work before it could be lived in. At the moment I could see no alternative. We would have to try it at Blossom.

I went back to town and to the stores, asking for work. There were no jobs and would not be any until spring opened up enough for planting. The best I could hope for then would be farm jobs by the day. No matter how much my mother wanted to move to Blossom, I did not see how we could make it.

A mile or so out of Blossom a car stopped beside me.

"Want a ride?"

Two girls from Paris Junior College had been out looking at schools where they might apply for the next year. I lied to them and told them I had hiked out to Blossom just to get away for an afternoon.

Before going home I went to the preacher and some of the deacons at Immanuel Baptist. They could not help with a job, but one of them did find an apartment in a home for fifteen dollars a month. They also assured me that if I looked hard enough I would find some kind of work.

My mother cried when she had to give up hope of moving to

Blossom. She hated the thought of moving into an apartment. It was moving into another woman's house. It did not matter that the woman lived alone and there was a hallway between the two apartments.

"Ain't no house big enough for two women under one roof," my mother said.

When we could see no other way she yielded and we moved.

January and into February. A time of waiting and worry and dread. There were no jobs and our money was slowly running out. So was the coal, and rent had to be paid. The landlady was kind and understanding, but she depended on our rent. I was too shy to ask for help at the college, too afraid people would think I was begging. Better to eat less than appear to be begging. After a time almost the only thing I could feel was fear.

On an icy Saturday afternoon, when I could no longer keep the fear inside, I went to Mrs. Van Dyke's home, not to ask help from the Salvation Army but to get her help in finding work. I knew that week after week she went to business offices, sometimes with her tambourine-taking collection, sometimes not. She knew the businessmen of Paris, the generous, the stingy. She knew the ones who might have work.

Mrs. Van Dyke was at home with her three daughters, in a warm living room heated by an open gas stove. Blue flames flickered up. Bright light from ceiling bulbs shone down on books and games and sewing. She had laid her Salvation Army hat and tunic on a chair near her and held a work basket on her lap. She called for me to come in, and if she was surprised to see me, she made no sign. She told me to sit down and motioned Mike, the oldest daughter, to move over and make room for me on the couch.

Soon we were having tea and cookies and I was telling them about school, which was going well enough except for trigonometry. Sine and cosine were more difficult for me than even the Pythagorean principle.

I tried to sound confident, but Mrs. Van Dyke could see that something was wrong.

"Are you still working at the Kress store?" she asked. "I haven't seen you there since right after Christmas."

She sounded as friendly and encouraging as I had hoped. Little by little I told the whole story, including my trip to the place at Blossom. What I needed now was work. Without it I could not make it till March 5, the end of the term. Mrs. Van Dyke did not know of any work but she began talking to herself aloud about other ways to get help.

"You tried the Rotary Club?" she asked, with a quick look of pleasure in her eyes.

I had not. In fact, before that moment I had never heard of the Rotary Club.

"They have a student loan fund. They might help you get through."

I had to make certain that going to them would not be begging.

"It's not charity," Mrs. Van Dyke reassured me. "You have to pay the money back." She named boys and girls going to school on Rotary Club loans. I would not be different from them. I would not be made to feel ashamed. "You want to try?"

She made it sound easy. I said yes and listened while she talked to Mr. Marvin Carson on the telephone. She told him who I was and explained my needs. In a few minutes she hung up the receiver and turned to me.

"Marvin says for you to come to his office Monday morning. They will let you have fifty dollars—"

She was saying more but I was not listening. I was already seeing what fifty dollars would do. I could make it to the end of the term. With a job I could make it to the end of the year and a high school teaching certificate.

His office, she told me, was in the bank building at the southwest corner of the square. Then she sent me on my way, knowing I wanted to get home with my news. What she did not tell me was that they were letting me have fifty dollars on her word.

Monday morning, before classes, I went to the bank building and up to Mr. Carson's office. The way had been cleared for me, but it was not easy to go into the office of a man who had money,

a stranger, and explain to him the depth of my poverty. In the
outer office there was a wheel of the Rotary; in Mr. Carson's office
there were other symbols of Rotary. Sitting behind a large desk,
in an office handsomer than I had ever seen before, he seemed to
me a living sign of Rotary. He was an unusually handsome man
in a blue suit with white piping on the vest. His black hair was cut
long. His black eyes seemed to look through me when he leaned
toward me over his desk and shook my hand.

His questions were rapid and to the point. In five minutes he
knew the basic facts about me and the fix I was in—except the two
I held back: how low we were on food, and the coal that would not
last till bedtime. He leaned back in his chair and his voice became
friendly.

"So you come from out around Pin Hook?"

"Yes, sir."

He had been to Pin Hook and knew there was not much out
there. He could not blame anybody for trying to get out and make
a better living.

"What do you want to make of yourself?"

"A teacher, when I can get a school."

"Teachers don't make much, but it's all right if that's what you
want to do."

He took out a blank note form and opened a large checkbook on
the desk in front of him. His voice became serious, businesslike.

"Before I give you a check I want to tell you why the Rotary
Club has a loan fund. We want to help young men and women get
an education. We are looking for good students who will work
hard, and will help them. It is a loan fund. We expect them to pay
back every penny they borrow. The money has to be used over and
over. That way we can help more of them. You understand this is
a loan and that you will sign a note for it?"

"Yes, sir."

"When do you expect to pay it back?"

Jobs would open up with spring, I was sure.

"In two or three months, when I can get a job. I'll quit school
when the term ends and make the money—"

"Do you want to quit school?"

95

"No, sir."

He went to a window and stood looking down on the square. I could not see his face but I could hear what he was saying.

"If you make good grades this time, we might help you some more. But you shouldn't go in debt any more than you have to, or any more than you can pay back. Fifty dollars looks like a lot of money to you now. Some day you will know it was a small amount you invested in yourself, and that we invested in you."

He made out the note for me to sign and wrote a check and signed it with his name for the Rotary Club. He gave it to me and shook my hand. Then, with an abrupt turn back to his business, he let me go.

18

On a raw Sunday morning in late February, when a fresh norther had cleared the sky, David Phillips asked me to help him with a funeral that he knew was not going to be easy. It was for the young child of a couple who had no church connections in Paris and knew him only by name. They needed him and he had agreed to help them through their trouble.

We went over to the northwest part of town, near the box factory, to a shotgun house in a row of shotgun houses, on an unpaved block with no fences or sidewalk to separate front yards from the street.

The father of the child, a young man our age, met us at the door. He wiped his hand on his pants leg and asked, "Brother Phillips?"

David nodded and took his hand. "God bless you in your sorrow."

The young man needed comforting. His face was pale and drawn and his lips worked as if he was constantly on the edge of crying. He held the door open and we went inside, where a girl who looked too young to be a mother bent weeping over a tiny casket, so tiny it could rest on a standtable. The casket was open and a tiny face, pinched and white, showed against pink sateen.

The mother looked away from the casket only long enough to shake David's hand. Two other young women came from the kitchen through the bedroom and stood beside the casket.

David nodded to them, lifted his hand, and in a voice soft but firm quoted: "Suffer little children to come unto me and forbid them not, for of such is the kingdom of heaven." As he asked God to comfort and sustain them they wept quietly. Then he talked of what a blessing that this child, elect of God, had entered already into heaven, innocent, untouched by sin, in all her purity to worship and wait for that great day when they would all come together again in the brightness of light.

Quieter now, they told him about the funeral plans. The other young husbands had gone out to dig the grave in a country graveyard toward Shiloh. They had taken the only car and we would have to wait for them to come back.

We waited, standing or sitting, in a circle around the almost bare room, with the casket in the center where we had to see it before we could see each other. Gently David led them to talk about themselves. They were all from the country and having a hard go of it in town. The men worked at the box factory. The women stretched their wages as well as they could but they were always short for groceries and rent. Life was hard enough when they were well. The cost of sickness had left them scared. They had bought the casket on time and were afraid they would not be able to pay for it.

The other young men came, dressed in overalls and suit coats, with mud on their shoes, streaks of mud drying on their clothes. The grave was ready. We closed the casket and set it on the back seat of David's car. He drove. I sat beside him with one hand reached back to steady the casket. The others got in their car—a borrowed one we now knew—and David led the way out the road west from town.

We stopped on the road by the graveyard and carried the casket to the open grave. There was no place to rest it but on the ground, on the opposite side from the pile of wet gray earth. We opened the casket and the face looked even smaller, more fragile in the expanse of earth and sky.

Huddled together on the windswept prairie, we listened while David read, beginning with "The Lord is my shepherd, I shall not want," and talked about the sadness of sin and suffering on earth, the glory of the life on high. He reminded us that according to the Bible there is a time to live, a time to die. It was not ours to question why death had come to one so young; it was ours to accept it as part of a plan beyond the ability of man to comprehend. His voice was confident and his face seemed to glow from more than the wind as he tried to lead them along the pathway to resignation and faith.

He prayed a long prayer for the parents and friends and then stood silent with his head bowed. The time had come to close and lower the casket. Then the young men remembered: They had neither plow lines nor ropes to lower it with. It would have to be done by hand. One young man climbed down into the grave and braced his hips against the wet earth. The other one and I lifted the casket and moved it forward over the grave toward him. Just as he touched it, it slipped from our hands and landed on end, head foremost. The mother began to cry hysterically, and then the father. It was a sign against them. Bad luck was following them. No telling why, or when it would end.

We lay flat on the ground and helped the man in the grave set the casket right. By now we were all crying. Time had to be taken to quiet the parents and ourselves.

Then David took crumbling wet clay and dropped it on the casket.

"Ashes to ashes . . . "

Forlorn weeping rose louder than his words. He ended the quotation and forced himself through a benediction. Then the men took shovels and filled the grave and shaped it into a small mound which, without a marker, would not be different from the earth around it after the spring rains.

When it was over, the weeping all spent, we shook hands and David walked to the car with the father and mother. Then he turned back. He had gone with them as far as he could.

On the way back to town, my own mind struggling with doubt, I asked him, "Do you really believe that baby has gone to heaven?"

"I have no doubt." From the look on his face I knew he meant it. "Today that child is in paradise." He talked of why he believed it: Every man born of woman is elect, and if he elects redemption, is redeemed by the death on the cross. Those who die before the age of accountability are already redeemed and heaven is open to them.

I was not so sure. It was a comforting belief, but wide in concept. How could it, I asked myself, reach out? How could the most devout believer accept life for a child when death seemed the better way?

19

One day Miss Hudson stopped me after class to talk about a paper. Then, when we were alone in the room, she extended an invitation. The young people at the Episcopal Church were having a dance the next Sunday evening and she was going to be a chaperone. Would I like to come? She was sure I would have a good time. I did not tell her that I could not dance, or that I had been brought up against dancing. Any other invitation from her and I would have accepted at once. But dancing? I asked if I could let her know the next day.

After classes I told David Phillips about the invitation and the problems it gave me. Miss Hudson had been too good to me for me to want to hurt her feelings. If I did not go this time she might not ask me to anything else. He talked about the girl who had been brought before the church for dancing. He did not have to remind me. Then he told me that I was on the verge of sin even thinking about going.

That night, disturbed that I had come close to sin, I went to see the preacher and told him about the invitation. I knew he would not like it but I did not expect a show of anger.

His anger was first at the Episcopal church for the errors of their doctrine. They practiced infant baptism and confirmed children as members without a public profession of faith. They baptized by sprinkling, not by total immersion. They countenanced dancing and card playing that was a kind of gambling. Then it was against Miss Hudson for trying to persuade me into evil ways. He did not know her but he thought little of a woman who would go to dances and persuade others to go. And a teacher at that.

His hardest words were for me.

"You are a baptized Christian," he said. "The waters have washed you free from sin and you are a member of the church." He quoted words from a song. " 'It's a glorious church without a spot or wrinkle. Washed in the blood of the lamb.' Do you want to make it unclean? Have you had it in your heart to witness a sin of the flesh? What has happened to your conscience? Don't you know the gateway to hell when you see it?"

He began to sound like a revivalist. A revivalist getting ready to preach against the sins of lust would shout, "Women, cross your legs. I want you to close the gates of hell while I preach."

The preacher knew I had heard this in revival meetings.

He also knew that I had taken to sitting with the same girl at meeting every Sunday night. He named her name and praised her Christian character. Then he went after me again.

"I say to any man, 'You can't hold a woman in your arms without rousing carnal desires.' Dancing rouses carnal desires. It has to." He brought the girl's name in again. "What if you saw her dancing? Some other man with his arms around her? Would you think as much of her? Would you want to marry her after she had been mauled by any man who showed up at the dance?"

By then he had me convinced that I had been close to sin, and that I should not accept an invitation to a dance from Miss Hudson or anyone else. I could not be a Baptist and do otherwise.

The preacher became fatherly.

"All kinds of people will try to entice you into sin. You must never consent. Let them take their own road to hell."

He sent me on my way but he had been alerted to my weakness to sin. It was his responsibility to keep watch on me himself and to alert certain others, especially the deacons. Before long they found something of what they were looking for.

One night between sundown and dark, while we waited outside the church doors for cars to take us to a picnic, we saw the girl who was to be my companion coming along the sidewalk to join us. She was young and pretty with large brown eyes and rounded freckled arms. Some of the boys began ragging me.

"You sure like 'em plump."

I answered the first thing that came into my mind.

"She's just a good armful."

The cars came and the girl and I found ourselves squeezed close together on the back seat of an overcrowded car. Before we reached the picnic place on the lake I sensed something wrong, but I did not know what. Boys and girls seemed to be drawing away from me, at the picnic and on the way home.

The next night I found out. One of the deacons came to tell me that I had been charged with improper language concerning a young woman in good standing in the church. The deacons had witnesses to what I had said. He had been sent to find out why I had said it and what justification, if any, lay behind the words. None, I told him. I had not touched her more than to take her arm to cross the street. What I had said was only a part of a joke.

"It's not a joking matter," the deacon said. "A girl's reputation could be ruined by such a thing. You've got to think what it could do to her."

He leaned close to me and his voice became earnest.

"You've got to think what it means to be a Christian. You've got to learn how to put Satan behind you in times of temptation. Are you willing for me to tell the deacons that you are heartily sorry?"

"Yes, sir."

"Then let us pray together."

We knelt together and he prayed a long prayer begging God to see me as I was, young, weak, prone to sin and to strengthen me in the way that I should go. The prayer was soon over but I was not through. I had to go that night to the preacher for a pastorly talk on the sins of the flesh.

From the pastor I learned that the deacons had also talked to the girl and to her parents. Their minds were made up. There would be no more times when we would sit together in church or walk home at night hand in hand.

He talked to me again about original sin and how hard the fight is for a man against his nature.

He did not have to tell me the battle I was having with myself, a battle that opened up intensely in unexpected moments. On a Saturday night soon after, I went with David Phillips out to a country church where he was holding a meeting. I had been there with him before, enough times to find in the congregation a very pretty young girl who, even kneeling in prayer, showed the curves of a maturing woman.

When we arrived at the church David was sent to one home for supper, I to another——to the home of this girl. From the way she greeted me I suspected she had managed my invitation. By supper time we had with us another young couple from the community, and we were paired off, two by two.

On the way back to church she and I were on the back seat, the other couple huddled close together on the front, taking no notice of our presence. The driver, in no hurry to get to church, drove fast over country roads so rough that the girl and I were thrown against each other and then into each other's arms. At first we were laughing and then, as warmth touched warmth, the laughter stopped and we pressed against each other in close embrace. Only when my hand was inside her blouse did she push me away, and then not firmly. For a time it became a kind of play as I pursued and she resisted. Then, when we had stayed out as late as we dared, we came in sight of lights in the church.

"You've got to stop," she said. "Somebody'll see us."

Then she was pushing me away and laughing.

"If you don't, I'm going to tie your hands with bob-wire."

We came to the church yard and worked our way in between wagons and teams and cars. Singing had started and we quietly took seats at the back of the church. David saw us from the pulpit and smiled. The church was full. It was going to be a good meeting.

The song ended and instead of calling on a deacon he was calling on me.

"Brother Billy, will you lead us in our opening prayer?"

I knew I was not fit to lead a congregation in prayer. Satan had caught me unawares and I had not fought back. Neither did I have presence of mind to say, "Brother, will you pass me this time?" Their heads bowed, they could not see me, but they did not have to. I could see myself all too well. There was no spirit in my prayer and not much voice. I suddenly had to say, "In Jesus' name we ask it, amen," and sit down.

The girl glanced at me curiously and then sat looking straight ahead through more songs and prayers and then the sermon. David had chosen to preach on sin and damnation, especially the sins of the flesh and the meaning of damnation, and its effect on the damned. For the latter he used a text and object lesson popular with Baptist evangelists: "For wherever the carcass is, there will the eagles be gathered."

He described an ice cake floating down the lake toward Niagara Falls and inevitable destruction. On the ice was a pile of carrion and tearing at it a buzzard, a "cyarn" crow. The carrion was the sin of the flesh, the buzzard, mankind—you and me. Slowly the ice approached the roaring falls, close enough for the buzzard to see the danger, but he could not give up yet. There was time for him to enjoy one more bite of rotting flesh, the way men put off salvation thinking there is a little more time before death and eternal judgment. Then for the buzzard it was too late. The ice touched the crest of the falls and went down, taking with it the carrion and the buzzard, his feet still entangled, down and down, under, never to rise again. So, man—"Amen, brother, that's telling them, brother," a man shouted.

David had not finished. He had to tell us how death comes like a thief in the night, and then it is too late to call upon God.

The girl looked at me coolly.

"How do you feel now?" she asked.

She was not asking me to tell her.

David ended his sermon with a plea for the faithful to renew themselves in prayer at the mourners' bench, for the sinners to give up their carrion and eat the bread of life. The people began singing, "Why not? Why not? Why not come to Him now?"

I knew that David was counting on me to be among the first to go to the mourners' bench and renounce all sin, but I could not. Satan had come too close. I was too weak.

"Bow your heads," he called. "Close your eyes. Do not look on a troubled brother wrestling with his sin."

He saw me take a step backward. With eyes on me, a puzzled look on his face, he watched me back quietly to the door and out into the darkness. With the sound of singing and praying in my ears I ran on the dirt road, trying to mortify the flesh, trying to make peace with myself, with God, knowing that within the night I would have to go back to David and make peace with him.

20

While I was still punishing myself with guilt and doubt the church in business meeting elected me as one of the delegates to represent Immanuel Baptist at a convocation at the first Baptist Church, Waco. The other delegate was a deacon, younger than the other deacons, a man who had often been a friend when I needed one. I was certain he had asked that I be a delegate. It would be good for me, they said, when I was nervous about missing classes. I would learn more than I ever could in a week of school and I would be shouldering my responsibility as a Christian.

The college registrar did not agree, but left the choice to me, after reminding me that I had been reported for unsatisfactory work in trigonometry. In my own mind the choice had been made.

Early one morning we loaded the deacon's model-T with bedding for sleeping out and enough food for the first day. It was a long trip: a hundred miles to Dallas and then ninety to Waco. It was spring—bluebonnet time. The weather was warm and cloudy and all along the way there were people working in the fields, plowing, planting. South of Dallas, everything was new to me. The land was the same black waxy, but there were new towns for me to see: Waxahachie, Italy, Hillsboro. We sang hymns as we went and I was content because I thought I was doing right.

After sundown we came in sight of the lone skyscraper that marked the city of Waco. We drove on country roads outside the edge of town until in a pasture we found the roof of a cattle shed that had settled to the earth under wind and rain. It would be shelter to crawl under if the weather turned bad. After a cold supper we spread our bedding on the grass and lay down to sleep close to the earth, close to the sky. Flat on his back the deacon prayed aloud for our spiritual guidance then and in the meetings the next day.

Though I had not been to a conference before, he told me enough for me to know what the meetings would be like. The church would be filled with spiritual leaders, men and women, delegates from all over Texas. It would be a love feast for the ones who had spent their college years at Baylor University and in the First Baptist Church. It would be a time of renewal for the ones who had gone out in missionary work. There would be pleas for all who would to take up the cross of Jesus and follow Him into any part of the world where darkness still lingered. It was an honor, I knew, to be seated among men and women who had proved themselves, but also for me a burden, the burden of the unworthy.

Late at night, when we were lying under a clear sky, with stars hanging low over us, I had to wake him and confess my guilt, though he was not an easy man to confess to. I had heard him at meetings call for churching others who seemed to have done no more sin than I felt. I had watched him gradually break a man or a woman down with questions till there were tears and cries and pleas for forgiveness. Keeping others on the path of righteousness was to him a deaconly duty. Not knowing what he would say to me, knowing only that I had to expose my guilt, I told him about my sin with the girl, the sin of lust. If he wanted me to stand trial before the church, I would stand trial—anything to ease my conscience.

When I finished he lay quietly, his face turned to the sky, the light of stars outlining him against the darkness of the earth.

"You have sinned," he said, in a voice that made me cringe. "The Bible says, 'If a man looketh on a woman to lust he hath sinned in his heart already.'"

I tried to tell him again how it had come on me unexpectedly, how Satan had taken me unaware. This he understood.

"It's the old Adam in us all," he said. "He sinned the sin of the flesh, and we are marked by his sin."

Suddenly his voice was softer.

"Billy, I know how powerful lust can be. Powerful and terrible. I will tell you something I've never told anybody. It's about me and my wife. She put me off before we were married and I had to wait till I just couldn't stand it. It had to be the Adam in me. We got married and when we were by ourselves that night I couldn't wait any longer. I tore her clothes off till she stood there in the room naked, not saying anything. Then I saw her eyes and knew I had done wrong. I touched her flesh and felt her shiver. We went to bed but everything was all wrong. I tried to make it up to her but she wouldn't let me. We've lived with this all these years and there's still a coldness between us. Nobody sees it but it's there."

He sat up and seemed to be talking to the night.

"Oh, God, if I had only been able to hold myself in."

Then he turned to me.

"I can tell you about sin. You can pray for forgiveness and feel that God has forgiven you, but the mark is left, like my wife standing there, afraid of me because of my lust. I wish to God I could make people see what it's like to live with the mark of sin. I'd do anything to head them off."

He touched me gently on the shoulder.

"Your sin has to be between you and God. No one's going to bring you before the church unless the girl does, and I don't think she will. She's waited too long. It'd be easier for you if she brought you before the church and you could open up your heart and clear your conscience. It's harder to have to live with it by yourself. I know."

There was a day of preaching and devotionals and people talking earnestly and openly about the conditions of their souls. My own burden of guilt seemed lighter because I had confessed to another and found him also frail and human. All day there was a building toward the night meeting, when the people would be raised to the mountain top of spirit by singing, praying, preaching.

Then it was night and we had seats in a church packed with people, among them men and women who had waited a year for this outpouring of spirit. I could feel emotion building around me through songs and prayers and the tremolo of the organ. Women yearned toward the altar. Men whispered amen and when the song leader called "Shout amen!" they made a roar of deep male voices.

Before preaching there was a chalk talk, a form of worship I had never heard of before. A woman stood before an easel with her right hand raised. When the organist started a hymn she sketched in quickly with colored chalk a distant range of mountains against a sunset sky, green gold for the mountains, and then a purple valley in the foreground. A woman in the choir rose and started singing:

Close to Thee, Close to Thee . . .

Her voice was high and haunting and soft like a prayer:

Close to Thee, Close to Thee . . .

The woman with the chalk was working quickly, deftly. A brown cross took shape on the highest hill, and the woman glanced at the singer. The words were clear and pleading:

Thou, my everlasting portion,
More than friend or life to me;
All along my pilgrim journey,
Savior, let me walk with Thee.

With the magic of hand and chalk a red rose took shape on the floor of the purple valley and lay there, alive, glowing, for the eye to see as it lifted up, up to the cross.

The song ended, the picture finished, singer and painter, with bowed heads, stood aside. The people sat, tensely quiet, with their faces aglow. The organist played through again, softly, with a sound like human voices crying "Close to Thee, Close to Thee." I looked and listened and, in a way I did not understand, felt the burden of guilt lifted from my shoulders and a sense of peace settle on me. I had come close to what I had searched for and could not feel before. At last I had come close. No matter what happened now, no matter how I might slip and fall, I could never lose what was mine at that moment.

The exaltation lasted until the meeting was over and I was back out on the prairie, flat on my back, searching the stars, the heavens for more understanding of this mystical reality that had come upon me. At the center, I knew, was Jesus Christ, but try as I could I could not focus on Him as tangible in any way—only as a presence brought to me in the flow of poetry, music, and painting—a presence and an elevation of spirit.

21

While I was at Waco, Cleaver came back from Chicago to live with us. He had finished the school for electricians and was looking for a place to settle down. In the two years since I had seen him he had worked on a dragline in the Trinity River Bottoms, learned a trade, and joined the Baptist church. At twenty-three, he seemed much older, more assured. In Chicago he had started calling himself Charles, his first Christian name. *Cleaver* had too often been mistaken for *Cleveland*, or *Cleburne*, and he did not like the nickname *Cleve*. He had given up the name that came down from my great grandmother, Missouri Ann Cleaver, the one we clung to for family pride. I understood why. Changing his name had helped him break away from what he had been at Pin Hook. He looked different because a surgeon had straightened his eyes. He seemed different with a new name. Always of a serious nature, he was now both serious and religious. He had not, however, forgotten how to laugh or to find reason for laughter in what people said and did. He had not forgotten how to work. But there was no work in Paris for him as an electrician, only as a laborer at the box factory. He went to the box factory.

My mother was tearful at having him back. She began to wish out loud that Dewey would come walking in one day and she would again have us all under one roof. At times she talked of how much she needed us. She was going through a period when she felt more and more useless physically and emotionally. In the morning she cried a great deal. In the afternoon she dozed in a chair as if she was trying to escape the things that gave her anxiety. We knew her distress and as much as we could avoided mentioning it, not knowing how to reconcile her to the kind of life we found ourselves in or how to change the way of life.

Certain things had to be lived through first. In a few weeks I would qualify for a high school certificate and Roy would finish the seventh grade. In a few weeks we could try for a new life in a new place. She understood and wanted us to make a way for ourselves but she still fretted. We did not talk about going back to Pin Hook, and for her that was a sadness.

Then, without warning, the job at the box factory ended. The only work Charles could find around Paris was on farms as a day laborer. He had to go on, first to Dallas and then to the oil fields of West Texas. Maybe he could find work; maybe we could find a way to do better. It all depended.

I was sad to see him go. He had been patient and understanding with my mother. He had been a great help with Roy. They had always been closer to each other than I had been to either. It was not a matter of antagonism but of temperament; they were simply closer to each other in temperament. He knew how I felt but he had to go—he had to work.

The effect of the trip to Waco began to show itself in many ways. The sense of guilt was less, so much so that I could stand up in church or Sunday School and testify to the goodness of God without feeling hypocritical. Moreover, my experience at Waco was pushing me toward other forms of religious expression. I tried writing poetry, which Miss Hudson read and discussed with me, and suggested that I put aside. It was too much like Baptist hymns. She thought I should look for models other than Fanny J. Crosby to imitate. Music was a possibility, but piano lessons were more than I could afford. At last I turned to chalk talks, with no more skill than I had absorbed in one evening at Waco. For a dollar I could get colored chalk and newsprint scraps were free at the newspaper. To be good, a chalk talker had to have speed, boldness of line and color, and feeling. What I lacked in the first two, I decided, I could make up in feeling.

On a Sunday night, after a few days of practice, I went with David Phillips to a country church, taking with us a young lady who would sing songs while I developed a lesson in chalk. It was a small church north of town, with a reed organ and coal-oil lanterns for light. After a song and a prayer David asked the people to watch carefully as we demonstrated a new kind of church worship.

While a woman played the organ, the singer, dressed in white, stood beside it and sang in a high, clear voice, "Close to Thee, Close to Thee." For a moment I waited, looking out at the faces in the red-orange light, country faces of men and women. I raised the chalk and their eyes were on my hand. They wanted a message that would speak to them. Feeling what they expected of me, I lined in curtains of light blue tied back with bands of dark blue. Then I put in a dark hill against a darkening sky. To that moment I had not known what the message would be. While my mind was still searching I sketched in a dry road on dry rocky ground. Then a feeling I had not known was in me began to work. A cross took shape under my hand, dark brown, slanted, being carried up the dry road, and then under it a man bent with the burden—not a figure, only a shape that suggested a man. The song ended; with a few strokes the picture was finished. For a moment there was silence and I could see their faces as they searched for meaning.

Then a woman said, "That's the purtiest thing I ever seen."

David took up the woman's fervor and preached on the burdens of sin and sorrow, and on redemption through the cross. While they let him he took them through stories of misery and suffering that brought tears to their eyes. Then, with rejoicing in his voice, he told them of the peace, the quiet, the glory that would be theirs if they truly followed the cross right on through the valley of the shadow of death.

He called for a song and I could feel the lilt, the happiness as they sang:

> *I must needs go home by the way of the cross,*
> *There's no other way but this;*
> *I shall ne'er get sight of the gates of light*
> *If the way of the cross I miss.*
> *The way of the cross leads home,*
> *The way of the cross leads home;*
> *It is sweet to know as we onward go*
> *The way of the cross leads home.*

Then people were around me, shaking my hand, blessing me for giving them something so beautiful, begging for the picture, and, when it was gone, for me to draw more. That night, a half-dozen pictures or more were carried home, to be tacked up on bare walls and left till the chalky color wore away.

Soon David and I were getting calls from country churches to come as a team. The people liked chalk talks almost more than they liked sermons. They liked, I learned from talking to them, the feeling that they were sharing in the creation of the picture; they liked, at times, to ask for pictures that would illustrate a particular Scripture of lesson. We began to follow a pattern: He preached a sermon; I followed it with a chalk talk and music that would help to illuminate the sermon. People came in wagons and on foot to see and hear, and waited after the meeting for a picture to take home.

When there was time I worked out pictures and memorized strokes for quick reproduction but not once did I think of getting lessons or of reading a book of instructions. I was convinced that God would direct my heart, my hand if I could only let Him, if I would answer calls from His people and do His work.

One call I could not accept. It was from Mrs. Van Dyke, who wanted me to join David for a Saturday afternoon Salvation Army service on the square. This I could not do. I was still not ready to testify even with a chalk talk on a street corner in front of all kinds of people. I was not ready to be laughed at, for that and for being with the Salvation Army. I could hear the bass drum beating, calling people to come and listen. I could hear a trumpet playing, the people singing:

> *Hallelujah! Thine the glory;*
> *Hallelujah! amen;*
> *Hallelujah! Thine the glory,*
> *Revive us again.*

I could hear as clearly the parody I had learned long ago in cotton patches at Pin Hook and heard repeated around Salvation Army meetings in Dallas:

> *Hallelujah! I'm a bum;*
> *Hallelujah! bum again;*
> *Hallelujah! give us a handout*
> *And revive us again.*

It was not the religion of the Salvation Army people; it was the company they kept. No matter how much I owed Mrs. Van Dyke, I could not stand on the street corner with her. An excuse came easy: chalk talks needed lamplight; daylight destroyed the illusion.

23

Some of the preachers in town had begun stating publicly their concern over kinds of teaching going on at Paris Junior College. Their concern was heightened when a local businessman announced that he had purchased a marble replica of a Greek statue and was giving it to the college. To make matters worse for the preachers, he offered a five-dollar gold piece to the college student who could guess the name of the statue. This sent the students in search of photographs of Greek statues. There were not many art books in town, but enough for boys and girls to be encouraged to study nakedness. A rich man, people began to say, had little to do with his money if he spent it on things like that.

Rumors got around that though no student had correctly identified the statue, it was "The Wrestlers"—two naked men. Objections began to come from parents as well as preachers. It would be a sin to put such a thing where young people, especially young girls, would have to see it. They had to see and hear enough filth as it was.

The statue arrived and was placed in front of the library, where anyone looking up had to see naked thighs and torsos. There was a presentation ceremony and stories in the paper.

The Immanuel Baptist preacher called me in.

"I'm going to preach on that statue," he said. "I'll burn their hides for this."

He was angry at the man for giving the statue, at the college for accepting it and displaying it. Step by step he went through the sermon he planned to preach. He would remind them that true education comes from the study of the Bible. God has so ordained. Any other can only lead the young into the ways of temptation. Better not to study anything than to be exposed to man in his nakedness.

"You seen the statue?" he asked when he had wound down.

I had, at a time when everybody else was looking.

"Not close enough to see anything."

"I want you to take a good look and come back and tell me."

When there were no people around I did take a long look. The parts were exposed on one figure only, in an almost secret way, and not much more than would show a naked baby boy.

"Is it naked like they say?" he demanded when I went back to the church.

I had to answer both yes and no. The nakedness was there, but it could hardly be seen, and there was no way of covering it. Nobody seemed to notice the statue any more, I told him.

He never preached his sermon. People in time forgot their worry over the effect the statue would have on their boys and girls.

24

Before school was out, still without a teaching job, I went from one country school to another looking for any kind of vacancy. Usually I went with a girl from the college who could borrow her father's car for the day, and who was willing to apply to teach the lower grades while I applied for the upper grades. At times I caught rides on wagons; at times I walked. On Saturday mornings I waited around the courthouses for trustees who had come in to see the county superintendent.

I learned fast that there was no one tougher, harder to talk to than the trustee of a country school, especially a trustee with a job to give out. When I went out I had to ask for the names of the trustees, find their homes, and walk across plowed fields till I found the man I was looking for. School-hunting time was a busy time for farmers, and most of them resented having to stop work long enough to talk to anyone who wanted to be a schoolteacher. One told me scornfully that there were more schoolteachers than

Baptist preachers. He let me know that he had little use for either.

At Tigertown, I got one of my hardest lessons. I went out with a girl a year ahead of me at the college. She needed a job, I needed a ride. Beyond that, we had no connection.

We found a trustee out in a pasture patching fence. He had a barbed wire stretched and held the end wrapped around a post while we told him who we were and what we wanted. He looked at me and than at the wire.

"You know enough to hold this while I steeple?"

I held his stretching boards while he got staples out of his overalls pocket and hammered them into the post. He tested the tautness with a finger and said, "I reckon that'll hold a while."

Then, after he had looked us over like something he might buy, he got down to school business.

"I reckon we might have a place—maybe two. Folks is dissatisfied with the ones we got. It's their first year here and they let the young'uns run over them pretty bad."

These teachers punished the pupils only by keeping them in after school. The trustees thought some good old-fashioned switching would do more good.

"You had any experience?" he asked us.

Both of us had to say no. He wiped wetness from his beard with his sleeve and looked at us as if we had said something ugly.

"No experience? How you gonna keep 'em from running over you? You don't look no older'n some o' our big'uns. How old air you?"

We told him and he was even more displeased.

"You good in your books?"

The girl was on the honor roll. I was far from it and afraid he would ask me my grades. I had barely passed algebra, one of the subjects I would be expected to teach, and was close to failing trigonometry. While I was still thinking how to answer, he dropped the matter of books.

"You two sparking?" he suddenly demanded.

We shook our heads no, too startled to speak. Then he told us the trouble trustees have hiring for a two-teacher school. Two women have trouble controlling the older boys, or get crossways with each other. Husband and wife pay more attention to each other than to the school. A single man and woman are likely to end up courting and making people talk.

"We don't want no sparking," he said.

He began stapling a loose strand of wire to a post and I knew he was ready for us to go. I asked about seeing the other trustees.

"I reckon it ain't no use. I reckon we'll wait and see who else comes along. We might want to keep the ones we got."

Without another word he turned his back on us and began stretching the wire.

We walked back across the fields knowing we had failed, and with little to say to each other. It was not so great a loss for her. Her family could afford to send her to school another year. I was beginning to get desperate. Hiring for the next year was almost over. In his own way the trustee had let me know how many gaps I had against me, in spite of two years in school and the required courses in education. The education teachers had not told me how to get experience when I could not get a job without experience.

25

End of the spring term came. I had passed my work and was eligible for a high school teaching certificate, but I did not have a job. At the county superintendent's office I was told that all contracts for country schools had been signed. My only chance was for someone to resign, and that was not likely. My chances would be better after another year of junior college.

The next week I got a job—the only one I could find—working for Uncle Charlie Kitchens at Novice, chopping cotton at a dollar a day and board. This time I had no feeling of getting ahead, only a feeling that I had to hold things together a little while longer. A dollar a day, six dollars a week, twenty-five a month—better that than nothing, and I was glad Uncle Charlie was willing to take me in, though I knew it was only for cotton-chopping time. Then I would have to find something else.

For that time I had to set my pace to theirs. Unlike most farmers, they were late to bed, late to rise. When neighbors were already in the field , Aunt Niece would still be putting hot biscuits and side meat on the table, and my grandmother would be waiting at her place with her head bowed, her eyes closed for the blessing. It was a slow-moving meal with little talk unless there was a threat in the weather. As slowly, Uncle Charlie and Austin hitched up teams to cultivators and followed a turnrow at the top of the hill. Ruthie— her work a man's work—and I went with our hoes. Trying to keep her youth and beauty, she swathed herself against the sun, her face in the deep shadow of a sunbonnet, her arms wrapped in thick cloth to keep them white, her hands gloved to prevent corns and callouses. Raymond, who slept latest of all, might bring his hoe when the sun was high in the sky.

A hoeing rhythm had to be set, not fast like killing snakes—the hoer burned out too soon—but slow and steady, a pace that could be kept till the sun was down and dark coming on, broken only when it was necessary to lift the head long enough to stare down the row ahead at green leaves in shimmering sunlight. One row done, another waited, rows down a long hill to a creek and back up again. Thirst started halfway down. Halfway back it had turned to cottony spit in mouth and throat. Then it could, at the top of the hill, be slaked with warm water from a stone jug under a bush.

At dinnertime we had to wait for Uncle Charlie to unhitch his mules and start up to the barn. At night it was the same. Shadows came across the field. In the half-light it was easy to leave gappy cotton as we whacked away at Johnson grass and cow itch vines. In the gloom of first dark, with our hoes swung over our shoulders, we went to the house and to supper at a table on the back porch.

It was hard work. Our rest came only when there was rain, and there was too much rain that summer.

"More rain, less work," we said to each other, knowing there had been too much. Cotton grew. So did weeds and crabgrass. Even if we got the cotton hoed and plowed it could go all to stalk with too much rain, and the crop would be thin. Boll weevils would thrive in the wetness. Uncle Charlie had good land and he was a good farmer, but he could not stop the rain and the rain could ruin him.

My grandmother talked to me one night on the front porch.

"Charlie's going to the bank."

I knew what that meant. He had to borrow money against the cotton crop, and pay back with interest at picking time.

"Prospects don't look good," she said.

He went to the bank and another heavy rain fell. I could feel a difference in him and the others. On a Sunday morning we would still pump a few rolls through the player piano—"Over the Waves," "The Maple Leaf Rag," or wind up the Graphophone to play "The Preacher and the Bear," and "Stars and Stripes Forever"—but there was no fiddling or singing. More often we walked in the fields, seeing the work to be done, doing none of it. Times would have to be very hard for them to work on Sunday.

Wet days hung heaviest on me. There were no books in the house except the Bible and an explanation of the Scriptures. I read through the Dallas *Semi-Weekly Farm News* the night it came, and read it two or three times more before another came. At work or on the porch at night, when the others rested without talking, I repeated to myself Stevenson and others I had memorized, and wished that I had been made to memorize more.

We mudded through the first chopping and Uncle Charlie had no more work for me, nor money to pay me. There was no hope for a job anywhere nearer than Dallas, and going there meant abandoning for a time any plans for school or teaching. When there was no other way, I hit the road.

26

The job I got was in the stockroom at Butler Brothers, the Dallas branch of a large wholesale chain. The building, on South Akard Street, was large and square and built of ugly brown brick. My job was in the Christmas toys and ornaments warehouse, where there were bins for items boxed by the dozen, low platforms for the ones sold by the gross. My boss was a middle-aged Swede given to overeating, overdrinking, and overswearing in a broken English I could laugh at but not imitate. He was tall and fleshy, wide between the eyes, wide between the ears, with the strength of two or three men my size. With a two-wheeler he could heave a packing case or bale out of the elevator, down the aisle, and onto a platform without straining or grunting, and keep going hours at a time without stopping. He expected me to do the same, even for five-hundred-pound bales. When I came to one I could not budge, he laughed a kind of choking gurgle and trucked it into place. Then, with jokes about my weakness, he would put me to unpacking and stacking boxes of glass tree ornaments as light as cotton batting. It was August and breezes never stirred the gloomy aisles of the warehouse. From morning to night the sweat never dried out of our clothes.

Six days a week I worked from eight to five-thirty with half an hour off for lunch. When I got home at night I still had my share of the housework to do. With no other place to go, I asked my cousin Maggie and her husband, Willie Cain, to take me in. They did, though there was not enough room and I would have to sleep on a pallet in the living room. They already had two girl boarders and the house, the one I had lived in when I first went to Dallas, still had only four rooms. All of us had jobs: Cain as a policeman, Maggie in a dress factory, the two girls in a laundry. All of us had to help with cleaning, cooking, dishwashing.

Country people in town, working at the jobs they could get, living from payday to payday with no hope of anything better, they were glad to have another wage earner share the costs and work, though because of my low pay they charged me a dollar a week less. They thought I had wasted too much time in school. I had finished high school and a year of college, but, as they were quick to say, I had no better job, no better prospects than I had when I was fifteen. It was too bad, they said, I had not stayed with a job and prepared myself for advancement by studying typing and shorthand in night school. A man coming up to twenty-one should have a good job and some money in the bank. When he walked with a girl at night he should be able to buy her a treat.

They did not have to tell me that I was not getting ahead. I knew it. I knew also that I had lost some of my hope, some of my confidence in myself. Keeping alive was all I could manage. At times I hoped a way would open up for me to go back to school, but the hope faded fast when I came into the presence of the Swede.

My best refuge—at times my last grasp on hope—was the Dallas Public Library, only a short walk from Butler Brothers. As winter came on I went often at night and read whatever of interest I could find on the shelves. At times I read until the lights began to flicker for closing time. In a back room, surrounded by dark books on dark shelves, I carried on education as well as I could. A part of the education came from rereading W. H. Hudson's *Far Away and Long Ago*, which I took out on my card and read on the streetcar. It was about a land far away and strange to me, but page after page opened to me new ways of thinking about myself and about the land that belonged to my own childhood. I followed it with *The Purple Land*, and the two together separated me even farther from the people I lived with, the people I worked with.

27

Letters filled with distress began coming from my mother almost daily. Dewey, his lungs weakened by pneumonia long before, had come home with tuberculosis, one of the diseases most dreaded in the wet parts of East Texas. Something had to be done at once. Her first step was to give up the place in Paris and move to Brookston, where they crowded in with Monroe and Mae. Dewey was staying in a tent in the yard, away from the children, and my mother was waiting on him as well as she could, cooking his food separately, boiling everything he touched to keep from spreading the germs.

The doctor said that he should be taken to a higher, dryer climate at once, if possible to the tuberculosis sanatorium at San Angelo in West Texas. They tried but the sanatorium was full. The best they could do was to get his name on a waiting list. My mother was afraid to wait. It might turn into galloping consumption and then it would be too late. Much as she hated West Texas, she was selling anything she could to raise money. She had to take him out there and nurse him back to health.

She needed money and all the help she could get. Charles was working in the oil fields around Breckenridge and Graham and would help all he could. She thought I had better stay with my job and send money when I could spare it. I had been trying to pay off the Rotary Club but now the Rotary Club would have to wait. In her mind everything would have to wait till he was well again.

Then her letters began coming from Breckenridge. She was no less worried but she seemed to draw strength from the fact that she was doing all she could. She and Roy were living in a small house in walking distance from town. Dewey had a tent in the yard. It was a healthy place, not far from Mineral Wells, where people went to drink the water, and close enough to San Angelo for her to know it was a good climate for people suffering from tuberculosis. Charles was close enough to be with them at times and to take much of their burden on his shoulders. Roy would go to high school in Breckenridge.

I never saw how they lived there, but I could imagine. They had only the things they could take on the train with them, and very little money. They had to skimp more than ever before. Dewey had to have good food. At times the others got down to cornbread and beans. Life was not easy for any of them. It was harder for Roy. He had been dragged from pillar to post—for us no pillars, only posts—with each step a step down. It would be that way, I began to feel, until he was old enough to quit school and get a job.

There were days when I felt I had to quit Butler Brothers and go to them, but that would not do either, I knew. They would have one more mouth to feed, and no telling when or where I could find a job. As he had done before, Charles was taking up the slack and there was little I could do to help him.

In my discouragement I went to several Baptist churches, including the First Baptist, and finally, to the Salvation Army, looking for a lifting of the spirit and finding little. All the fault could have been mine. I was too ashamed to talk to anybody about what was happening to me and my family.

Not in church but in the Dallas Public Library could I shed for a few hours the things troubling my mind—shed them in reliving through books the lives of other people in other places.

28

Christmas came and I was laid off, without warning, with only a pink slip in my pay envelope. When I protested to the floor manager, he said that I was not needed, that the Swede had reported that he could do without help until spring. Down in the employment office they told me that I had no skills that could be used in another part of the company. I begged to be kept on at any job, sweeping floors or anything, at any wages. It was no use. They would be glad, a woman clerk told me, to have me apply again when work picked up in the spring. She was saying the same thing to the others waiting in line with their pink slips.

At quitting time I went out into the dark and chill of a wintry night and walked along Akard past Commerce and Main to Elm. For the first time that I could recall I felt that life was against me. I walked through the crowds on Elm Street, past Christmas windows and Salvation Army Santa Clauses, asking bitterly why it was. I had been made to believe that education and hard work were the ways to getting ahead. I had worked hard and studied hard. For what? To be out of a job at Christmas?

Bitterness became mingled with anger. Not at Butler Brothers. Butler Brothers did not know how hard I had worked or how much I needed a job. I was angry at the Swede. He was the one who had driven me day after day till at times I was ready to drop. He knew what getting laid off meant to me, and had not tried to help me. I could feel hard toward him as much as I liked, I knew, but there was no way I could get back at him.

Unable to go to my boarding place as if nothing had happened, unwilling to face the others with my news, I kept walking the streets through the Saturday-night crowds. Of one thing I was sure: I would not stay in Dallas for Christmas. I would go to Paris and out to Novice, where I would be not at home but close to home —in the country, safe from the city. My grandmother had a saying: "He goes where the pot boils strongest." For me the pot would boil strongest at Novice. There it would be like Christmas, and I could expect some singing and fiddling.

As I walked I decided to delay telling the others that I had lost my job. For three days I could pretend that I was going to work but hide away in the library. Then on Christmas Eve I could leave a note telling them what had happened, walk out past White Rock Lake, and begin catching rides to Paris.

On a cold afternoon, after a hitched ride for fifty miles in an open car, I went into the Vanlandingham Tailor Shop in Paris, where Mrs. Willie Crockett worked. The shop was warm and smelled of steam from irons and press and of steamed wool. Mrs. Crockett was at a table at one side, sewing by hand on a man's wool suit, with a pile of coats and pants on a chair beside her, waiting to be altered or mended. She saw me come in, called me to come over, and cleared a place on a chair near her table.

"Glad to see you, Billy."

She kept her fingers moving, her eyes on her work.

"You home for Christmas?"

"Yes, ma'am. I'm going out to Novice soon as I get warmed up a little."

While I warmed and she worked we talked about my family, her family, Immanuel Baptist Church, and school. At her age, with two sisters and two children of her own besides herself to support, she had gone back to high school and was studying Latin—not in classes—she could not get off work long enough to go to classes—but by writing exercises at home and sending them to the Latin teacher at the high school. It was a slow way to learn but she had no other.

"When are you going back to school?" she asked.

I had to tell her that I had lost my job and that I could see no chance at all of going back to school. I expected to hang around Novice a few days and then go on the road.

"You'd be better off in school. You asked anybody to help you?"

I hadn't and didn't see how I could, with money still owing to the Rotary Club and my mother needing more help than I could give her. Others working in the shop heard us and began offering help and advice. They would ask the Rotary Club to extend the loan, help me get a job, find a place for me to stay. The winter term had been in session two weeks. They would ask the registrar to let me make up work I had missed. The Lord would provide a way for me to get through. It was Mrs. Crockett who offered the most immediate help.

"You could stay with us. We could let you have the back room for five dollars a month."

I knew how poor she was. She did not need to take on another burden—of somebody not kinfolks.

"It'd help me with the rent," she said quietly, and convincingly. "You'd be paying a third."

Together they made me think that I should go back to school.

When the sun was turning pale in a graying sky I went to the wagon yard on North Main and begged a ride on a wagon going to Spring Hill. Too many people were on it already but they made standing room for me back of the springseat. The mules lagged along on the pavement of Pine Bluff and the gravel out past the golf course. Walking would have been faster but after the golf course there were red clay hills, bogging wet, the clay sticky enough to ball on shoes.

Two country schoolteachers, Mary and Maud Jones, sat on the springseat with the driver, girls close to my age, in new clothes and happy in their teaching. I listened to their talk of Christmas programs and basketball games and spelling matches and was jealous of them.

Past Faught, where a road branched to the right, I climbed down from the wagon, thanked them for the ride, and set out in the dark to walk the three or four miles to Uncle Charlie's house. The road, no more than a lane, wound between fields and through woods, with no more than two houses along the way. I was glad to be walking it alone. I needed time to be alone and to think.

At the road from Novice to Blossom I turned north and then east on the lane to Uncle Charlie's house, where a single lamp shone from the window in the heater room. I knew what it would be like inside and I was glad that I had made the long journey.

After a hello at the gate they met me at the door and took me inside. It was as I had expected. My grandmother sat on one side of the stove with her legs propped up, smoking a pipe, with Ruthie sitting beside her. Uncle Charlie and Aunt Niece were on the other side, with her next to the lamp and the newspaper she had been reading out loud on her lap. Austin was at the front of the stove, where he could keep the fire punched up.

They made me glad to be there, in the way they said "Christmas Eve Gift," in the way they thanked me for the dime-store gifts I had brought. I was their Christmas, they told me, and they were mine.

It was a quiet Christmas, with the pot going strong from morning till night, with Christmas cooking on the table three times a day, with my grandmother telling again the story of the Christmas backstick when she was a girl on the Ouachita. Grandpa Cleaver always let the family celebrate as long as the backstick lasted. Weeks before, the boys cut a sweetgum as big as the fireplace would take and soaked it in mud till the first day of Christmas. They could build up a fire as high as your head but the backstick would still last four or five days or more.

At night we pumped roll after roll through the player piano. Once Uncle Charlie got out his fiddle and played "Over the Waves" and "Red Wing." Once we parched peanuts in the stove and played Hully Gull: "Hully Gull." "Handful. How many?" The one who guessed right got the peanuts.

There was talk of what I would do. My grandmother had only one piece of advice: "You better go he'p yore mammy." When I talked about going back to school the others said, "Ain't you never gonna quit going to school?" They talked about jobs to look for. They said, "Anybody as stout as you air c'n git something." They meant farm work or work in the woods.

Then Christmas was over and I caught a ride to Paris. Mrs. Crockett and the Vanlandinghams had been at work for me. They had a job for me at Joe Gaylor's confectionery on the east side of the square jerking soda. They had taken my case to the Rotary Club. Mr. Carson was willing to extend the note I owed and lend me money to finish out the winter and spring terms. With a feeling that something might still go wrong, I went to the college and to the dean. He was willing to let me enter late and pay when I could get a job teaching.

There was nothing to prevent me from going at once to Miss Hudson's class in English literature.

29

The life I plunged into was full, intense, and opened to the creative in a way I had never known before. Ruth Hudson wanted me to read creatively, write creatively, both with imagination running as free as I could manage. There were class assignments and extra reading for me alone, to be done in the library when I could, or at the confectionery between making sodas and banana splits and washing dishes. She took time—extra time—for anything I wrote and sent me away to write and write again.

For a dollar a week, from the seven I got working in the confectionery, I took piano lessons with Miss Velma Green. I was slow at music, partly because I had to unlearn the system of shaped notes and chording I had learned at Pin Hook, partly because my ear had long been tuned to fiddle music and the minors of English ballads. I had to give up reading *do, re, mi* before I could begin reading lines and spaces. I wanted to learn church music. She made me practice scales, and after a long time, let me try Brahm's "Lullaby" and Beethoven's "Minuet in G." With her the feeling was controlled by the click of a metronome but feeling was there nevertheless.

Mrs. Crockett kept herself and the rest of us running with work and church and school. She worked at the tailor shop from eight to five and often later. After work she cooked and cleaned and did the washing in the bathtub on her knees. As she worked she recited Latin conjugations and declensions. Late at night she studied Latin, read the Bible, and prepared Sunday School lessons. For us, because of her, every day was a becoming, every night a preparation for what the day would bring—for me the excitement of books and music, the drudgery of a methods course in high school teaching.

We lived in East Paris but we still went to church at Immanuel

Baptist in West Paris. Bus fare was a nickel, so we walked. Every Sunday morning with her in the lead we straggled along Clarksville Street to the square, across the square, and out Bonham Street, in time for Sunday School. Attendance was scrupulously taken; absence and tardiness counted against awards of buttons and ribbons. One of the mottoes she recited to us was "Be there and be on time." Every Sunday night we went back to church for Baptist Young People's Union, where records of attendance and tardiness were also kept. After three hours of young people's meeting, of singing and preaching, when the church lights were turned out, we walked back home through quiet streets. If we were not too tired, we recited favorite passages of Scripture to each other and reviewed the truths of the sermon, starting with the belief that if the preacher said it it had to be true, according to his lights. We could apprehend truth through our own lights but the preacher was divinely called to lead us and therefore to be listened to.

Mrs. Crockett's own lights were strong, coming as they did from absolute faith that the Bible is the word of God and that it was best expressed in the Baptist doctrine expounded by the preacher. No complexities, no doubts blurred her light. She was as sure of achieving heaven as she was of escaping hell. She could quote with absolute assurance: "Surely goodness and mercy shall follow me all the days of my life. And I will dwell in the house of the Lord forever." With the stride of a soldier she marched through life with words from a song she had made her own:

> *Richer, fuller, deeper, Jesus' love is sweeter,*
> *Sweeter as the years go by.*

She was not one to complain about hard work or skimpy living. She could work day after day sewing, mending, pressing with a heavy charcoal-heated iron. She did complain bitterly about men like Scopes and Darrow who, to her, were out to destroy literal interpretation of the Bible and raise up the animality in man.

The preacher agreed with her, in the pulpit and out, and added all those who by thought or deed would seek to destroy the church.

He preached against the apostate church, in which he included almost any that were not Baptist. He proselytized openly, with a welcome to all but with a warning that none should come with their feelings out, for plain truths would be discussed—the plain truths of sin and salvation in the light of Baptist doctrine.

In revival meetings at Pin Hook they sang:

> *'Tis a glorious church without a spot or wrinkle,*
> *Washed in the blood of the Lamb.*

The image had stayed with me and now, to me, because of preachers and preaching it was clearly the Baptist church.

30

A week before Mother's Day the preacher announced a ritual he had worked out on his own: a flower-pinning ceremony. As usual, everyone would wear a rose for his mother—red if she was living, white if she was dead. After preaching, everyone whose mother was present would pin a flower on her to show love and appreciation. After the mothers had been honored, anyone who wanted to show appreciation for another person would pin a flower on him. It could turn into a great love feast, he said.

When we got to church, after a hot walk under a bright sun, I saw buckets of roses, red, white, pink, yellow, lined against the base of the pulpit platform. Against the walls on either side there were other buckets of flowers—larkspur, daisies, gladioli, and honeysuckle—enough for the ritual to last half a day or longer.

By a quarter to eleven the church was filled, many of the women —old and young—in white lawn or organdy dresses, the men and boys wearing white shirts and dark ties, the deacons sweating in suit coats. Most of them were wearing roses—white or red—or could get them as they passed the altar.

Before the sermon there were speeches and prayers honoring motherhood. Then a man went to the pulpit and sang a solo:

> *There's a dear and precious Book,*
> *Tho' it's worn and faded now,*
> *Which recalls those happy days of long ago;*
> *When I stood at mother's knee,*
> *With her hand upon my brow,*
> *And I heard her voice in gentle tones and low,*
> *Blessed Book, precious Book,*
> *On thy dear old tear-stained leaves*
> *I love to look;*
> *Thou art sweeter day by day,*
> *As I walk the narrow way*
> *That leads at last to that bright home above.*

When he began there was only the full round tones of his voice, the hushed notes of the piano, and the soft stirring made by a hundred cardboard fans from the funeral parlor. Then there was quiet sobbing from among the women. He came to the end of the song and began the refrain again softly, feelingly.

Blessed Book, precious Book . . .The emotion was too much for a woman near me who cried in a subdued voice, "Oh, mama, mama."

After a final "bright home above" the preacher preached his Mother's Day sermon. He reminded us all of the joys and pains, the blessings and sacrifices of motherhood. He asked us to think of our mothers' toil-worn hands, made old and hard in work for us. I could see my mother's hand, her right hand, shaking at her side, a sign of nervous strain, and feel what the people around me were feeling. He talked of the hard life, the hardships, mothers had to endure on earth, the heartbreaks they suffered over the child who chooses the way of sin and death. Then he talked of their glories in heaven, at the side of the Savior, surrounded by the ones they had loved and served, the suffering of life ended at last in eternal peace and joy. Not ended for the lost, he shouted. Some mothers were looking down at that moment, praying for their sons and daughters in sin, begging them in silent whispers to set their feet on the straight and narrow path. The time is short, the way hard to redemption, the preacher said. For mothers the sadness would never end until all their children had made their election sure.

Time came for him to make the call to the mourners' bench. Instead, he leaned on the pulpit and looked down on the people and there were tears in his eyes.

"Are you wearing a white rose?" he asked, his voice trembling. "Are you wearing a white rose for your mother in heaven? If you are not and she has gone on to glory, I want you to let me pin a white rose on you."

He stepped down from the pulpit and stood beside the buckets of roses. Men and women without roses stood up and began a slow procession down the aisle. As each reached the preacher, he pinned on a white rose and took the person by the right hand.

"God bless you," he said. "God bless your sainted mother in heaven."

Men and women turned from him with tears running down their faces, with their lips shaping unvoiced words. By the time he came to the last one there was a sound of gentle crying throughout the congregation, with here and there a fervent prayer, "Oh, God help me."

The ones who needed red roses marched by and again the preacher was in the pulpit talking. He talked of how remiss we are in expressing our appreciation to friends and loved ones for the many things they do for us. Life is too busy and we let too many things get in the way. He did not complain against flowers for the dead, but he thought it more important to give flowers to the living. On this morning he wanted us to take time out for flowers and words of appreciation.

"Let us all stand," he said. There was a rustling of clothes and a clattering of folding chairs. "The ushers have papers of pins. I want you to look around you, at the faces of mother or father, sister or brother, deacon or friend. I want you to ask yourself if that one has done anything for you during the past year for which you should show your thanks. When you see one, I want you to take a flower and pin it on and say 'Thank you and God bless you.' Go, in the name of Christ, amen!"

At first the people stood still, waiting, staring, or taking a furtive look. Then there was a movement toward mothers and fathers, the shuffle of leather soles on bare pine floors. Mothers and fathers with large families bloomed with flowers across their breasts— roses and honeysuckle pinned on any way, crushed in hugs, wet with falling tears. "God bless you" rose again and again above the sobbing. All at once people began moving toward the buckets and then toward friends, for moments of pinning, embracing, praying, crying. The few who held back had to yield when flowers were pinned on them. Only a few restrained themselves from tears. The preacher stood in front of the pulpit praying and blessing as hands reached out to pin flowers to his lapels, his tie, his sleeves. The air became hot and heavy with the smell of roses and honeysuckle.

I saw Mrs. Crockett near the piano, her face red and moist with perspiration, her breast hidden in roses. Of all the people there, she was the one I needed most to thank. I took a pink rose and waited my turn before her. She was crying, but there was a proud look in her face, a proud lift in her shoulders. I pinned on my rose and thanked her for making possible the way for me.

"God bless you, Billy," she said. "I know you're on the right road and I am praying for you."

There were others for me to pin flowers on: the preacher, the deacons, the teachers I taught with in Sunday School. There was also the girl I had been forced to give up walking with. We met in the aisle, and not knowing what else to do, pinned red roses on each other.

The praying and crying and then the singing rose to the pitch of a revival meeting and began dying away. The preacher went to the pulpit and asked the people to be seated. When they were all quiet again, he looked at me.

"Brother Billy," he said, "will you come to the altar?"

Not knowing what was next, I went up. He met me at the steps and pinned a red rose on my shirt. Then he took my hand and turned me until I was standing beside him in the pulpit. He laid an arm gently across my shoulders.

"Brothers and sisters," he said, "this is a great day in the vine-yard of the Lord. It is a day for tears, a day for rejoicing. I can see the glory in your faces. If I am right, shout amen!"

"Amen!"

"And again, amen!"

"Amen!"

He stood away from me and faced the deacons in the amen corner.

"I think we have another thing to be joyful for today. We all know how faithful our brother Billy has been in the work of the Lord. He does not know what I am going to say, but I pray he will see in it the hand of God moving his wonders to perform. I have talked and prayed with the deacons and now we come before the congregation in conference to ask the favor of a great blessing. We are asking you to license our brother Billy to preach and teach the Gospel throughout the world."

At first I was too stunned to speak. Then I stammered "I—"

I was going to say that I had not felt a call, or the touch of the hand of God, but he stopped me.

"It is the working of God in us and through us. I feel it running through me." He looked at me earnestly. "You have not asked us to show such faith in you, but we know God wills it. We will go with you straight to God. He will open the way to you. Only take this step, and the Kingdom will be yours."

He turned to the congregation.

"I know how our young brother feels. I was once where he is and felt the same way. It is the biggest step a man can make in his whole life, and I am asking you to help him. I want you to search your own hearts before we take this vote. If you feel it is the will of God, I know you will vote for his will to be obeyed. Bow your heads in silent prayer, close your eyes, look not to one or the other —only to God."

I knelt by the lectern and bowed low, putting my face down into the smell of my own sweat and of the roses pinned on me. I could hear the notes of the piano soft on the refrain of "Whispering Hope." I could feel the presence of a church full of people with bowed heads asking God's guidance for me. For the first time I prayed that if it was God's will I would hear a call.

While I was still groping in my own confusion the preacher broke the silence with "Amen!" Heads were lifted; eyes were on the altar, where I was still kneeling, feeling that something was happening inside me but knowing the call had not yet come loud and clear and unmistakable.

"Are we ready to vote?" the preacher asked.

There was a rustling among the people. I could have stopped them at that moment, but I did not. A secure feeling of belonging at last had come over me.

"Only members in good standing will vote," the preacher continued. He looked out over the congregation. "Will all those in favor stand?"

Only the children, the ones who had not reached the age of accountability, remained seated.

"The vote has passed," the preacher said, and helped me to my feet. "Welcome, brother. Welcome to a deeper fellowship in the work of the Lord. Let us all say amen."

"Amen!"

"Now let us join hands and sing 'Blest Be the Tie That Binds.' "

He took my right hand and led me down to the congregation. A deacon took my left and I was soon joined to the whole congregation as the words of the song rose:

> *Blest be the tie that binds*
> *Our hearts in Christian love;*
> *The fellowship of kindred minds*
> *Is like to that above.*

Then it was over and, after a last "God bless you, Billy" from Mrs. Crockett, I was out walking the streets alone, still confused in my own mind, still asking for something—some sign, some sound—that could only be the voice of God speaking to me and to me alone. The guilt of many sins ran through my mind, the sins of the flesh. The more I tried to shut them out, the more they burned till I could feel the blood hot in my face.

31

That night I was back at the church, talking to the preachers, the deacons, trying to find out what was expected of me, how immediate my response had to be. For close to half a year I had been living a life I had planned. Would I have to put that all behind me? There was still time left in the spring term at school. I owed money to the college and the Rotary Club. Would there be time to close out old accounts?

The two preachers were divided, one and one. One, a strict Missionary Baptist, a man who had been a year or two in college, believed that God called a man and then equipped him to preach through the natural processes of human learning. The other, an older man, a farmer preacher, was close to the Primitive Baptist belief that at the call God equipped a man directly and immediately to preach the gospel. The one wanted me to go to school as I could, the other to quit at once and take up the cross. Both advised against going to a seminary. They worried that I might be influenced by the heresies of modernism creeping in. So did the deacons. What I needed most, they assured me, was a willingness to study the Bible and to preach without fear the truths revealed to me.

Preachers and deacons alike, when I asked how I would live, answered, "The Lord will provide." When the time came they would take up a special collection for me. I could expect a dollar here, a dollar there from the good souls who wanted to see the Kingdom advanced. I worried that I might appear to be begging. "Not when you go in the name of the Lord." They quoted "the laborer is worthy his hire" and bade me look forward to the time when some church would call me at a fixed salary.

After meeting, one of the preachers kept me a while to tell me plans he and the deacons had in mind. They wanted me to finish the school term. Then they wanted me to help him with the summer revival. The church had no money to pay me, but a deacon had offered to make a place for me in his home. Some people would give me money and many would take me to their homes at eating time. He expected it to be the greatest revival in the history of Immanuel Baptist. He would do the preaching, and he promised to take the hide off Methodists and other sinners. He needed me to be the reporter, to write daily newspaper stories on the progress of the revival. I said yes at once, happy at the chance to write.

His manner changed, his voice became imperative. He had another task for me, a worthier one by far. A young man in the church, with whom he had seen me from time to time, had not yet been converted, though he was many years past the age of accountability and special prayers had been offered for him many times before. There was serious concern for him. By election, God had chosen him to be a Christian. The danger was that, if he delayed longer, he would be incapable of making his election sure, that he would continue in sin, a dead soul. The revival would be dedicated to his conversion. If he alone was saved, the revival would be a blessing from God. He was asking me to do what I could to help save this friend.

I was free to work with the preacher, and I began to feel, as I talked with him, that the Lord might have cleared the way. Things were better with my family. They had just moved to Dallas, where Charles had a job in an electric shop. Dewey had recovered enough to begin looking for work. After West Texas, my mother wrote, she was satisfied to be in Dallas. She wanted me to come home but now I had other work to do.

The next day, after classes, I told Miss Hudson what had happened to me. She listened quietly and, without saying she was disappointed, let me know how much she was disappointed. As if she was dealing with an assignment she took me back over the work I had done for her, in a way that made me know how hard she had worked to encourage me and teach me. She still wanted to encourage me. She was giving me A in the two courses I was taking with her. She had hoped to follow my development through college. She could have, in literature and writing. In preaching? She did not try to answer the question.

When there was no more to say I went out of her room, sadly, knowing a change had come between us.

That night I found David Phillips and, as we had so many times before, we walked the streets and talked. He was glad to have me join him in the work and was puzzled at my worries and fears. God had taken care of him. He would take care of me, and I should never feel that I was begging. He quoted, "And whosoever shall compel thee to go a mile with him, go with him twain." That was the challenge of the call.

He was now a senior in Paris High School. He might go on to junior college, he might not. The learning he needed most was the learning he got at the feet of the Master. He had survived as a licensed preacher; he was about to be ordained. God had provided: he was supply pastor of the First Congregational Church and had more calls from country churches than he could accept. The sooner I got to work in the vineyard, he told me, the sooner I would be relieved of doubt and fear.

32

Through the end of May and the first days of June preachers and deacons prepared themselves for the drama, the ritual of the revival. Every sermon had in it some part that showed the despair of sin, the hope of salvation; every Sunday prayer brought to our minds the impending fire for the lost; every song reminded us of our duty to rescue the perishing. Women and girls prayed fervently in morning prayer meetings; men and boys prayed as fervently at night. Men and women made prayer lists for private devotionals morning and night and any pause through the day. In a sermon the preacher set the theme: "Behold how great a matter a little fire kindleth." The fire of sin, he said, could be quenched only by the blood of Christ. The sinner had to be brought to the blood. That was the work of the revival.

I spent my days and nights working for the revival and studying the Bible and Baptist doctrine as passed on to me by the preachers. I memorized passage after passage from the Psalms and Proverbs and in the early-morning hours said them aloud in the empty church, inspired with the sounds of poetry echoed from bare walls. Doctrine was not so easy, but I took it on faith so much that I could argue in favor of total immersion and closed communion and the historical belief that the Baptist church was there before Roman Catholicism came into being. Conversion of the sinner was the first work of the revival; bringing him into the Baptist church the second.

The revival tent was set on a vacant lot not far from the Methodist Church, close enough, some of the Baptists hoped, for singing and preaching to carry. It would be a good thing, they thought, for backsliding Methodists to hear some good old-time hell-fire preaching and get a whiff of burning brimstone.

Opening night, I sat near the front with a tablet in my hand, ready to take notes for a report to the newspaper. We had done our work well; the crowds were there. Every chair was taken and people stood around the edge of the tent, rows of faces barely visible in the light that glowed under the tent through fringed valances. Heat of a summer night stifled us. With our fans we stirred air that smelled of talcum powder and dew-damp dust. Everything was right for a revival.

The preacher came in from the back of the tent, followed by the gospel musician, a young man hired to play and sing and lead the singing. The musician sat at the piano and looked out over the congregation, waiting for the whispering to cease, the moment of silence to come. When it came, he let his fingers race up and down the keyboard faster than the eye could follow, making such music as I had never heard before—an emotional music that reached inside me and made me know we were going to have a great revival. I looked at the people around me, sitting motionless, their eyes fixed on him as if a spell had come on them. The music, unfamiliar at first, shifted to old tunes, revival songs that raised memories of brush arbors and sawdust and people on the glory road.

When the spell could hold no longer, the musician stopped, gave his place to another pianist, and stood before the congregation.

"My ministry is music," he said. Then he talked of how every night before preaching we would lift the spirit with music and singing, every night we would have a sermon in song. He asked prayers for his ministry, that the depth of his feeling could be felt by all.

The pianist played an opening and, at a signal from the leader, the people rose and sang in a kind of determined rapture:

> *I shall not be, I shall not be moved,*
> *I shall not be, I shall not be moved,*
> *Just like a tree that's planted by the water*
> *I shall not be moved.*

After the refrain had been repeated, the leader divided the congregation by the aisle in the middle of the tent and set the two sides to competing with each other for number of people singing and volume:

> Jesus is the Captain,
> *I shall not be moved;*
> Jesus is the Captain,
> *I shall not be moved . . .*

He brought us together again for the chorus, urging us all to sing, urging us all to open up our voices and let all of West Paris know how to praise the Lord in song:

> *I shall not be, I shall not be moved . . .*

He marked time with his right hand half-extended, with a turn of his wrist right, left, right, left, in the motion of turning a gimlet:

He is mine forever,
I shall not be moved,
He will leave me never,
I shall not be moved . . .

Before the spirit could flag he brought us down to a last chorus, sung low, hardly above a whisper, clear enough for the ear to pick out the parts in the harmony. Then he cut us off with a hack of his hand and the quick drop of his head.

An old woman near me said in an intense voice, "That song sure gits to the gizzard."

More songs, more prayers, and the way had been prepared for the preacher, who went to the pulpit when he felt the people were ready to hear him. He stood like a prophet in shirtsleeves and looked out over the congregation. He had two weeks of revival before him, two weeks in which to convince the doubting of the horrors of hell, the glories of heaven. He began his sermon, "Paris at the Judgment Bar of God," with a description of hell as a great wide field of glowing coals and rising flames through which souls crawled like worms, weeping and wailing and begging mercy of a God who had been denied and who now refused to hear their cries. He talked to the young people about their sins. Each sin, no matter how great or small, was recorded and would have to be faced at the Day of Judgment. He pleaded with parents to save their children from eternal damnation wrought by a jealous God.

The mother of my unconverted friend sat near the front, a small woman with gray hair partly covered by a black straw hat, a woman with a life-weary face and eyes red from weeping. As the preacher talked I could see her shoulders shake with sobs and hear her choked cries. She was begging for help and I wanted to help her. Somehow or other he had to be brought to preaching. The revival could not end till he had confessed his sins and prepared himself for the judgment bar of God.

When the preacher had brought the people as far as he could that night he leaned on the lectern and in a sad, hollow voice began the call: "Who will be the first to come?" The song leader began "Softly and Tenderly Jesus Is Calling" and the people took up the song with him. No one came to the mourners' bench but many went up to shake the preacher's hand and reaffirm their faith. After the last amen people lingered in the tent to pray that the Holy Spirit like a dove would come down.

My story written, I took it to the newspaper office, to Miss Maude Neville, an exacting editor who kept the essential details but cut out what was in reality my own importunings for people to come, to hear, to be saved. Quietly she showed me that as reporter and participant I had to be two people. No matter how much I was involved in the revival, as a reporter I had to stand at the side, an observer, a recorder, detached emotionally, setting down the who, what, and where, and no more.

As meetings followed each other, day and night, day and night, people close to the preacher knew that the spirit was hovering over us and that great things would be done in the name of the Lord. The young man came some nights and sat at the back of the tent, his face grim, his soul unyielding. He had come, friends told the preacher, to quiet his mother and keep her from grieving. The preacher took it as a sign that God was working with us and in us that he had come.

Near the end of the week, after the sermon, when the preacher gave the call, a family of Methodists came forward to confess the error of their way and beg to be taken in as Baptists through the true baptism. They knelt at the mourners' bench and men and women began crowding around them crying and praying. Others came up, old men who had never taken the step, whose eyes showed they had seen death just ahead; young women who, no more than a week before, had been dancing and playing with no thought of the wages of sin, bent their silk-stockinged knees into the dust.

A young girl went into a faint and fell on her back on the ground. Older women crowded around her, pulled her dress down over her knees, and fanned her wet face.

"Don't touch her," one of the women said. "Don't raise her up. She's in a trance. It looks like the Spirit's working in her."

"Thank God," another woman said. "Just let her lay. I've

knowed 'em to lay twenty-four hours not knowing nothing, just wrastling with the spirit of God. They come to a-shouting and you know they've been saved."

One girl in a faint changed the temper of the meeting. The mourners' bench filled up and people began kneeling wherever they were, praying out loud, the sinners in the agony of the knowledge of sin, the saved asking God's mercy on the poor sinners.

After a time the girl opened her eyes and women helped her to a seat. It was not a trance and there was yet no wonder-working of God. She kept crying that she was a sinner and begging for mercy.

When the people were beyond cries and tears the preacher stood in the pulpit for a final exhortation. They had seen the glory, he told them. For one brief time they had been allowed to see it. A greater glory awaited if only they would seek it.

The fervor increased. Young men and young women prayed openly and secretly for the lost; some pledged themselves to the Lord's work for life if there could be a sign of grace—a soul converted.

The next night the people came expecting the glory. The young man was there, after a long day of revival visits, sitting near the edge of the tent, not far behind his mother. He was quiet and alone and there was a sadness in his face. The preacher nodded to me and then to him on the way to the pulpit.

"It'll be a good sermon tonight," the people said. "It'll have to be a good'un to beat last night's."

There were songs and prayers, all directed toward the young man, as if tonight had to be the night when he would cross over. Then the song leader leaned on the lectern, and pleading, close to weeping, looked down on the congregation. His eyes found the young man and remained on him while he sang:

> *There were ninety and nine that safely lay*
> *In the shelter of the fold;*
> *But one was out on the hills away,*
> *Far off from the gates of gold;*

Away on the mountains wild and bare,
Away from the tender Shepherd's care,
Away from the tender Shepherd's care.

The song ended and we were implored to pray and pray for the one that was lost, we who were safe in the Shepherd's fold. We knew there were rewards in heaven if only we would pray without ceasing. There was rejoicing among the angels when a soul was saved and Satan confounded. Anyone who would bring a soul to God would have a star in his crown on that great day.

As the preacher preached I knew he was talking to me. I was one of the ninety and nine who had been blessed. He was laying on me the need to go out and bring in the lost sheep—the young man—by convincing him of the danger of delay. I looked at his face and thought there was a trembling in his lips, and I prayed, "Lord, if there ever was a time, let this be it."

The preacher finished his sermon and called for the invitation song: "Almost Persuaded."

"Before we sing, I want you to do one thing. Look around you. If you see anyone who is not saved, go to him and put your arm around him. Ask him in God's name to come with you to the altar." He drew himself up to tiptoe and shouted, "Now."

I put my hand out and leaned toward the young man. A deacon came and stood on the other side of him. Boys from a prayer group gathered around. Then the people were singing:

"Almost persuaded" now to believe;
"Almost persuaded" Christ to receive;

The preacher paced back and forth before the mourners' bench calling, "Why not? Why not be persuaded before it is too late? Why not prepare to meet thy God?"

Seems now some soul to say, "Go, spirit, go thy way,
Some more convenient day on Thee I'll call."

The preacher was now going up and down the aisles crying, "Talk to them. Labor with them. Bring them to the altar before it is too late. Let them not harden their hearts forever against God."

There was a sound of talking and praying and crying and through it the pleading of the singers:

> *"Almost" cannot avail; "almost" is but to fail;*
> *Sad, sad, that bitter wail—"Almost—but lost!"*

I spoke to the young man. So did others: men old and young, boys half his age, a few women who shook his hand and gave him a word of encouragement. The mourners' bench was filling up and the laborers gathered there, kneeling, praying. The song leader took up a different song:

> *What have I to dread? What have I to fear?*
> *Leaning on the everlasting arm?*
> *I have blessed peace with my Lord so near*
> *Leaning on the everlasting arm.*

During the refrain the prayers became a layer of chant under and around the song:

Leaning *(come to Jesus)*, leaning *(he is waiting)*,
Safe and secure *(Oh, safe and secure)* from all alarms *(Glory, glory)*;
Leaning *(Help me, brother, help me)*, leaning *(Oh, help me, Jesus)*,
Leaning on the everlasting arms.

Something moved the young man. He leaned away from the people talking to him and took a step toward the altar. Once started, he went fast, working his way among people reaching out to touch him and at last reaching his hand up to the preacher.

Then a cry rose, a sharp shriek of pain and joy, like the cry that ends a birth, and his mother leaped from near the mourners' bench and landed flat-footed with knees bent. "Glory," she shouted, and leaped out into the aisle, and "Glory, glory, glory, glory," with every word a leap. At the edge of the tent she turned and I could see her face, dead white, and her eyes, open and fixed, as if she were staring at a light brighter than we could see. Her black straw hat went to one side. Without breaking her step she pushed it back down on her head and shouted, "Saved at last, hallelujah, amen. Oh, that I should have lived to see this day."

The singing stopped. People at the mourners' bench ceased their pleading. The time was given over to one devout woman who had toiled and prayed and lived to see her son saved. There was weeping, but it was happy weeping in joy with the woman dancing because the Lord had been kind. She danced near her son but did not touch him or speak to him. Her words, in rapture, were only for the Lord. After a time her steps slowed, her voice became a whisper. She went around one more time and then stood with head bowed, waiting for the benediction.

The young man spoke after the meeting.

"I knew she would do it."

Back at the home of a deacon, after a late prayer session, I worked on my account for the newspaper. It was easy to report text, main points of the sermon, and the number converted. I could stand aside, uninvolved for that. I was not able to write about the depth of emotion that had infused the meeting, partly because I did not understand it, no matter how glad I was to see anyone join the church, partly because I could not find in myself the need to dance and shout to express my feelings.

To the last day of the revival I kept writing accounts for the newspaper. When it ended, people said it had been the biggest in the history of Immanuel Baptist, or of West Paris. There had been enough conversions to require two baptisms, one in the middle, one after it had closed, to bring in any who waited till the last night to confess.

The last night came and the sermon was on the crucifixion. The people, worn from days and nights of meetings, gathered to listen, to sing "Count Your Blessings," and to thank God for His special presence during the revival. They hated to see it over but they knew it had to end. Held too long, people lose interest and begin to drift away.

At the last the song leader, already packed to go on to another revival, asked the people to join hands and sing the parting song:

> *God be with you till we meet again!*
> *By His counsels guide, uphold you.*

With His sheep securely fold you;
God be with you till we meet again.
Till we meet, till we meet,
Till we meet at Jesus' feet;
Till we meet, till we meet,
God be with you till we meet again.

The last amen said, the people gone, the tent dark, a few of us lingered to clasp hands once again, knowing we would never meet again in just this way but certain that in some distant day we would join the throng of the elect.

33

The preachers and deacons, ever in search for stars for their own crowns, urged ordination on me at an early date. David Phillips was to be ordained at the end of August. They wanted me to follow soon after, though I told them I felt a long way from being ready. I did not want to be, in the words of one of the deacons, "a narrow-gauge train on a wide-gauge track." David Phillips was not. He was already a preacher with a following—people who went to hear him wherever he preached. They said he was going to be one of the great Baptist preachers. I did not have his easy flow of speech, his knowledge of the Scripture, his understanding of Baptist doctrine, and proved my inadequacy the one time I entered the pulpit, when I elected to talk about one word that kept coming back to me: *work*. Work had a meaning to me in everyday life. My search for moral and spiritual meaning in the word brought me to the Epistle of Saint James—his letter to the world, his sermon about having a care, one for the other. What he was saying I accepted intuitively and from living experience: "Even so, faith, if it hath not works, is dead, being alone." I could see Mrs. Van Dyke warming and feeding the poor who came to the Salvation Army —the body cared for first and then the soul. This was the sermon I preached and the people were not with me. At the end I knew why. A grim-faced deacon and his grim-faced wife waited for me just down from the altar. "Too Presbyterian," the deacon said. Justification can only be by faith.

I went away from the church and walked the streets alone, feeling regret for my failure, doubting the fervor of my call, perplexed about directions to take. I could read the Gospels on my own, but this was not enough and I knew it was not enough. Christ crucified was at the center, but that was not enough. There was a doctrine to which the Baptist had to conform, in many ways intuitively. My intuition seemed to be leading me away from that doctrine.

The preacher, when I went to him with my perplexities, immediately suggested an alternative: working with young people, while I grew in faith, while I read the Bible and searched for the Baptist meaning. The Baptists in Fort Worth were sending a young woman field worker to Direct for a week of missionary work with the women. She had asked for a young man to go with her and work with the young people. This was an opportunity for me and he wanted me to go. There would be no pay, unless the people at Direct wanted to make a contribution, but it would cost me nothing and I would get some good experience. I would stay in homes and go to dinner and supper wherever people invited me. One of the deacons would take us out Monday morning and bring us back the next Sunday night. He was persuasive, and willing to try, and I agreed to go.

Monday morning I met the young woman and the deacon at the church. She had recently been graduated as a home missionary from the seminary in Fort Worth and was on her first assignment. She might have been pretty except for the plainness of her dress and the severity of her face. She smiled rarely, and when she talked at all, echoes of missionary Scripture and songs pervaded both words and tones.

We went in a model-A, with the deacon keeping his eyes on a road that was gravel for a few miles and then rutted sand, out past Sumner and Tigertown and on toward the Red River. The missionary sat beside the deacon, saying little, holding herself rigid even when the axles scraped the earth. I sat on the back seat watching houses and barns as we passed and worrying about how I would get along in this kind of work.

Direct in the dog days was a place of stagnant, punishing heat. It was a cluster of two-story houses around a store, a church, a school on the high ground above the Red River bottoms. All the roofs and walls, painted or not, had a reddish tinge from Red River dust. We arrived in the heat of the day, at a time when anyone who could rested in the shade of a porch or a chanyberry tree.

A place to stay had been arranged for the missionary, but not for me. She would be in a house in walking distance of the church. At the store the deacon asked directions for her and about a place for me. About the time that I was beginning to feel unwelcome they found a deacon who said I could share a back room with his son if that would be all right. It had to be. No one else offered anything.

The room was as comfortable as I could have expected. The main problem was that the son, two or three years younger than I, was not very glad to see me, or to share his room with a stranger. He showed his feelings by going ahead with what he was doing and saying no more than he had to when I asked him questions. He certainly had no interest in coming to a church meeting that night; he had heard enough preaching.

It was clear before the Monday-night meeting was over that most of the people in Direct had had more than enough religion for one summer. Between the Methodists and the Baptists, there had been preaching nearly every Saturday night or Sunday. The Baptists had just closed a protracted meeting that had lasted for two weeks. Now the Baptists had sent a missionary they had not asked for. Not many came to the meeting.

After songs and prayers the missionary gave the plans for the week. During the day she would meet in homes with the women, while I visited the young people or held conferences at the church. Nights, we would meet at the church for classes. She would teach a class in missions, I a class in Bible study. Each night we would end with singing and a prayer meeting. She gave the theme for the week in the words of the song:

Into my heart, into my heart,
Come into my heart, Lord Jesus;
Come in today, come in to stay;
Come into my heart, Lord Jesus.

Then she gave a talk on the work of the Southern Baptist Convention in foreign missions. As a student she had studied with men and women who had gone out to rescue the perishing in China, Africa, and South America. They had told her of heathen souls won, sometimes only with the kindness of a crust of bread.

She ended her talk with a prayer that someone there that night would feel a call to carry Christ to some dark, unfriendly shore. It was an earnest talk, a sincere talk, with none of the fire and brimstone of a revivalist. But the people were not moved, even with the singing of the closing song:

Throw out the lifeline! throw out the lifeline!
Someone is drifting away;
Throw out the lifeline! throw out the lifeline!
Someone is sinking today.

She had work on Tuesday. I had none. I waited in the church, sitting on a bench at the front, waiting for someone to come. No one came. I read song books and the Bible and prepared a New Testament lesson for that night.

Wednesday was the same until the missionary came, and somewhat embarrassed, told me of a young man in the community in need of help and advice. She gave me his name but was so indirect in what she said that I did not know at all what she meant. She did make me understand that it was my Christian and missionary duty to help this young man if I could.

That night, in the black heat of the room, I gave my roommate the boy's name and told him what the missionary had said.

"What's his trouble?" I asked.

"They say he knocked a girl up."

He said it in a matter-of-fact voice and would say nothing more except "It's his business, not mine."

The next morning I got more of the story from a deacon. The boy was a baptized believer, and so was the girl. They went to church together and everything was fine until this happened. Then he turned hard-hearted and would not darken the door of the church, even during the revival meeting. He had refused to marry the girl and if he did not do so soon there would be a wood's colt in the community.

"He don't seem to have no feeling about nothing," the deacon said. "Most daddies would a taken a shotgun to him before now."

Later in the morning the deacon came to see me at the church to say, what it seemed to me, the church people of Direct wanted said to the young man. They wanted him to come back to church. Chances were that if he would come back to church he would see how he had ruined the girl and would marry her. It was my Christian duty, the deacon felt, to persuade him to come back to church.

He felt it so strongly that he had his son waiting in a pick-up at the store to take me to the young man. I walked with the deacon across to the store and got into the pick-up for a ride that took us away from the river on a narrow road that wound in and out through scrub timber. Deep in the woods we came to an unpainted boxed house without a porch front or back.

"He lives here by hisself," the driver said. "I reckon he's around. He wouldn't a gone off and left the door open."

We got out and met him coming around the side of the house. He was a big man, my age or a little older. He had been working in the woods: his jumper was sweaty, and there was sawdust on his shoes. In the way of country people we howdyed and then stood around, all waiting for somebody else to talk. My name was not said, and I did not say it. The meeting was going to be tougher than I had expected.

"You heered about the classes at the church," the driver said.

"Somebody was telling me about them."

The driver looked at me in an offhanded way.

"He's one of them, doing the teaching."

The opening made, I had to do what I had been sent to do. I looked him straight in the face and held out my hand.

"Brother," I said, "we want you to come with us tonight. We need you, you need us."

He started to take my hand but stepped back. From the sudden anger in his eyes I knew I had started out wrong, but I did not know how to make an abrupt change of subject, or to keep quiet.

"Somebody must a been meddling," he said.

"It's not meddling. Lots of people have got you on their hearts and consciences. They're praying for you. They'd kneel down with you if you'd come to the church tonight. They'd pray it all through with you—"

"You mean my trouble?"

"That's what they say."

His voice became hard.

"It ain't my trouble. It's hers. She's old enough and she let me. I don't care what anybody says, she was willing." He gave a harsh laugh. "I may be going to hell but I sho God ain't going to church. They can pray for me till they're blue in the face, or till they find out it ain't none o' their business. I ain't a-caring which."

He looked angry enough to hit me in the face.

"You can go back and tell 'em what I said. Now I've got some woodcutting to do."

He turned and went toward the woods. When he was out of sight we got into the pick-up and went back to Direct, neither with anything to say.

I found the deacon and told him what had happened.

"Sounds like he's the one," the deacon said. "We was right, thinking it was his'n, but that ain't gonna be no help to the gal or her mammy and pappy."

He let me know what would be said to the community: The boy did not scare easy.

That night I slept, the little I slept, in the church house, sitting or lying on a wooden bench. I felt that I had worn my welcome out in the deacon's house and no one else had offered me a place to stay. Worse, I felt that the men at the store as well as the boy I shared the room with were laughing at me. By the night meeting most of the people in Direct knew of my visit to the young man and how he had put me in my place. So I stayed in the church and the night was mine, a time for thinking over again the direction I had taken.

It was too dark within the walls to read, but not too dark to remember, and I had enough passages of Scripture to think on the night through. Red letters of my red-letter edition of the New Testament glowed in my mind. These were the words of Jesus—not the words of Paul or James or any of the others. There were the words I had accepted as the truth of life, the words I had set myself to live by, and the heart of them I began to feel: *If ye believe in God, believe also in Me.* These first, and after them others, the command: *Feed my sheep.* How one without the other? And how to feed the feeder? In the hours when he feels cut off, reviled?

Late in the night when lamps in all the houses had been turned out, I began the soft singing of hymns, trying to draw from hymn makers lights that had guided them. One was an old song that took me back to brush arbor nights at Pin Hook:

> *Amazing grace! how sweet the sound,*
> *That saved a wretch like me!*
> *I once was lost, but now am found,*
> *Was blind, but now I see.*

The blindness I knew, and human sight. What I needed was an inner sight that would make clear the way.

Later I went to a song new at the time, a favorite of men who sang solos in churches:

> *I come to the garden alone,*
> *While the dew is still on the roses,*
> *And the voice I hear, Falling on my ear,*
> *The Son of God discloses.*

I liked the scene and the sound of the long o's in the rhyme. The voice eluded me, try as I might to hear it, as everything else did when I tried to come close to the Son of God. The refrain was closer, more personal, placing Him and me as it did side by side, or face to face:

And He walks with me, and He talks with me,
And He tells me I am His own;
And the joy we share as we tarry there,
None other has ever known.

Some voice spoke to me that night, when or in what words I do not know. What I do know is that from some time in that night I knew that believing was right, doubting was wrong—not through a voice of thunder or a flash of lightning—not through any special baptism or communion I came close, first to the historical Jesus, the teacher, and then the divine Jesus, whose essence touched an essence in me, whose red-lettered sayings forever grieved my mind. To believe in Him was to accept the word of God.

Again I came to the question of how I was to serve. I rebelled at what I considered the tyranny of the collection plate, of having to do the kind of preaching that would keep the money coming in. How could one have the call to preach and not the gift of words that touched the hearts of people? A gift I never had. If I was to serve, I was beginning to see, it would have to be in a way not depending on money, and not with young people, because of a worry in my mind. Once in the revival a young girl had put her arms around me as sister to brother in Christ. In my feelings I was as sinful as the woodcutter.

Having come that far, having found peace for the moment, I slept till I was awakened at daylight by my roommate.

"You slept here all night?" he asked, conviction growing in his voice. "How come you slept here all night?"

I could not tell him I felt unwelcome in Direct, or that I had needed time to be alone.

"I don't know."

He turned and went toward the door.

"Well, you better come git your breakfast.".

His words said clearly what I had thought the night through. I would eat a breakfast I had neither worked for nor bought, and that would make me a servant not of God but of man, a deacon but still a man. I felt trapped. I had to be beholden for my breakfast or go without. Too late to eat with the others, I took my breakfast

153

from the back of the stove, and suddenly hungry, cleaned the plate.

Most of those who came to the morning meeting knew I had slept in the church the night before. I could have explained myself by saying that I had gone there to pray and had prayed most of the night through. Then they would have marveled at such devotion in one so young. I said nothing and they guessed I had gone there because I felt unwelcome. Some said it was a crying shame they had not asked me home with them the night before. Others said it was a slap at the good people of Direct. One thing became clear: the meeting was not going well and they knew it. The missionary knew it better than anyone else. She looked sad and hurt and eager for it to end. A deacon assured her that I would be made welcome and invitations came from two homes, in one of which I was already staying.

The deacon had a talk with some of the boys. Then one of the boys came up to me.

"Some of us boys is going to walk out to the river Saturday morning. We want you to go with us. You reckon you can?"

All week I had waited for such a chance to get acquainted with the boys. I was not sure how much they wanted me but I decided to go. Anything would be better than waiting around the church for people who never came.

The sun was no more than a hand high when eight of us trailed out the red dusty road past fields of corn and cotton toward the line of trees that marked the bluffs of the Red River banks. As we walked heat rose in waves ahead of us and the trees shimmered a silver green. Sweat dripped from our faces and our mouths grew cottony from thirst. We could go on and drink red water from the river, or we could turn back. I wanted to turn back but one of the boys thought of another way to wet our whistles.

"It ain't no piece to that watermelon patch. We could git us some watermelons. The juice is as good as water when you're dry." He looked me straight in the eyes. "He ain't gonna mind none."

Suddenly the boys were more friendly than they had been all week, and I was glad they had taken me with them. Talking and laughing, we went along a turnrow and came to a patch where watermelons lay ripening in the sun.

"Get you a good'un," they said to me. "See if the curl's dead and then thump it. If it sounds hollow, it's ripe."

They did not have to tell me. I knew a ripe watermelon when I saw one. We separated and went up and down the rows till each one had a melon in his arms. Then we went back to the turnrow and busted them in the shade of tall bloodweeds. They were ripe red inside and juicy. We ate the hearts with our fingers and then drank the juice and no longer felt dry.

We went back to the church and arrived just in time for meeting. There were songs and prayers and a talk by the missionary. The boys sat with me and the missionary was greatly encouraged.

The next afternoon, while I was on the store porch with the men and boys, waiting for time for the last meeting, a man drove up in a wagon. He got out, hitched his team, and came up to the porch.

"Somebody's been stealing my watermelons," he said. "They busted 'em and et 'em right in the field, and trompled the vines."

"Any idee who?" a man asked.

"No, and I better not find out. I got my shotgun loaded with a meatskin. I'll burn his hide."

Suddenly I knew that I was a watermelon thief. I looked around for the boys. They had quietly disappeared behind the store and I could feel them laughing at the watermelon-stealing preacher. They had set a trap and I had fallen into it. I knew that I should confess to the man, but I could not. Better to be laughed at silently than laughed out of town.

Though it was too early to go to the church I went, embarrassed, angry at what had been done to me. Too ashamed to show my face, I stayed in the church, staring across at silent, unfriendly houses, until the people began arriving for the meeting. The missionary came first and then the deacon from Immanuel Baptist, there to take us back to Paris. They talked about the week's work and reconciled themselves with the belief that it was too early to judge how successful we had been. People from Direct came at dusk and waited in groups outside, waiting for the lamps to be lit. Most of the faces looked as they had looked at meeting every night before. Some did not, and I knew the boys had tattled. Before the meeting was over everybody in Direct would know the young preacher had been stealing watermelons. Talking, whispering, the people moved inside and I shrank against the wall behind the pulpit.

I sweated through prayers and songs and a final talk by the missionary, who said she could see the hand of God working through the meeting and prayed that He would always be close to the good people of Direct. She thanked me for my fine leadership of the young people. I watched the faces and felt relieved. Whatever they knew about me they would not tell her.

She came to the most important moment of the week: the call for men and women, boys and girls to dedicate themselves to missionary work at home or in foreign lands. She asked us to sing and dedicate ourselves as we sang:

> *Ready to go, ready to stay,*
> *Ready my place to fill;*
> *Ready for service, lowly or great,*
> *Ready to do His will.*

She looked at me steadily and I knew she was willing me to come forward and take her hand. I could not, no matter how strong the appeal in her words and in the words of the song. No one else moved. No one went forward, even when the song was sung through a second time.

The meeting over, I went outside without speaking to anyone and climbed into the back seat of the model-A. I knew at last what I was going to do. The next morning I would be on my way, hitchhiking to Dallas to find a job. Liscensed or not, I had no call and I was through with preaching. Whatever else I might be, I would not risk being a jackleg preacher. The decision left a sadness, for the friends I was leaving. David most of all; for the kind of communion of good people I had found and loved; for the weakness that left me cringing in body, naked in soul.

34

Again we were all under one roof, this time in the four-rooms-with-bath bungalow at 4916 Santa Fe Avenue, next door to the house that had been my first home in Dallas. There we were faced with the problems of making a living, a home, and, most important, a life. My mother would keep house in a house with bare floors, furnished with only enough beds for sleeping, a few chairs, and a table in the kitchen. Roy would go to Bryan High School. Making a living depended on the three older brothers. Dewey had been injured while working for the power company and was waiting for compensation through his insurance. Charles had a steady job. I had to go to work as soon as possible.

This time I tried to get a job that would go on after Christmas, but ended up at Butler Brothers again as a stock clerk, with only a halfway promise that I would be shifted to a regular job when one opened up in the fall. Though all of us knew the job might end at Christmas, it was the best I could do. All of my work experience had been in retail or wholesale or mail-order houses. Now, though I was twenty-two and had worked at jobs off and on since I was fifteen, no one else would hire me. It was clear that I should have learned shorthand and typing, or operating a comptometer, but I had not, having been convinced that if I would go to college I would not need such skills. So I was back at Butler Brothers again, pushing a two-wheel cart and stacking boxes of merchandise in bins, all for eighteen dollars a week.

This time my boss was a young man, under thirty, who expected me to do my work but did not drive me from morning till night. He was a kind of clairvoyant who claimed to have second sight and to be able to read minds. In the few slack minutes we had he stopped me to tell me about meetings in boarding houses on South Akard in which people achieved direct communication with God and with the dead. He thought that I was religious and that I would get great benefit from attending these meetings. The more I listened, the more I knew that such meetings were not for me. I was still too much a Baptist.

Making a living was hard enough. Making a life was harder, for us and for all the people on our block. The men were barbers, policemen, and streetcar conductors. Most of the women worked six days a week operating sewing machines in garment factories. They caught streetcars about sunup and came home about sundown. Saturday nights they bought groceries, and if they were through in time and had the money, they went to a picture show on Beacon Street. Charles and I fell into the pattern. Saturday nights at supper we studied the newspaper for the specials at the supermarkets. Then we walked to the stores on East Grand and went from one store to another to save what money we could on the advertized loss leaders. Then, with bags as heavy as we could carry, we walked home again. Sunday was our day for living and the two of us spent from nine to one and six to nine at the First Baptist Church.

My mother, it was soon clear, was not learning to live in Dallas. She was glad to have us together and to do for us, but she kept longing to go back to Pin Hook. She scoured the floors and cooked, read the Bible and the *Daily Times-Herald*, but she rarely left the house, either to talk with neighbor women or to go to the corner grocery. It was owned by *Eye*talians, whom the people on Santa Fe Avenue called "Jew babies" because they were foreigners. She felt repelled by the number of their children, their noise, their broken English and thought it was better for us to stay away from them.

She did not want to go to as fine a church as the First Baptist but she missed preaching. Once she asked me to take her to a revival meeting in a tent off Fitzhugh Avenue. The evangelist, nicknamed Pitchfork, was a man with a reputation as a hellfire preacher and a political troublemaker. There had been threats against him, both for his preaching and his statements about politicians. My mother was not interested in the political. She was sure we would get some good old-fashioned preaching.

The night was hot and still, and the people were crowded into an open-sided tent with a dirt floor covered with sawdust. We got folding chairs near the back of the tent, not far from a purplish-faced man I had seen at Fair Park rallies for Jim Ferguson. His color, I had heard, came from a heart leak. Whatever it came from, it gave him a strange, almost frightening look.

A tall thin man in a light-colored suit came in and took a seat back of the pulpit.

"Brother Pitchfork," someone called him.

He was followed by two men, one of whom went to the piano, the other to the pulpit to lead the prayers and songs. During one of the songs he yelled, "Put down your fans and clap your hands." The tune was like a jump-up. People clapped their hands and stomped their feet, working up the revival spirit. One song ended, they began another and sang and sweated together. At times there was the yip yip of a woman shouting; at times loud amens from the men on the front rows. My mother did not clap her hands but I could hear her murmuring songs she did not know.

At a nod from the song leader the evangelist came forward and stood leaning his elbows on the lectern. When the people were quiet he stretched his hands out, palms down, and asked for silent prayer for the Holy Spirit to come down as it came down with a rustle of wind at Pentecost long ago. There was a silence and a stirring of air with fans and a moving of lips in prayer.

Before the sermon, the evangelist announced that he had something to say about corruption in Texas politics. Before I could get the meaning of his next words the purplish-faced man stood up and shouted, "Liar!"

It was the beginning of a free-for-all. Men started swinging fists at the purplish-faced man and at each other. Men ran in from the edge of darkness and joined the fight. Young men came sliding down tent poles, from the canvas top where they had been waiting for trouble to start. They were there to break the meeting up. Afraid of what might happen to her, I got my mother by the arm and began forcing our way out of the crowd.

By the time we were safe on the sidewalk the fighting was over. The song leader said the meeting would go on and started them singing. We did not go back.

At home, my mother said quietly, "I do wish they'd a let him preach."

She never went to preaching again in Dallas, and I was sorry. Little by little she had withdrawn into her own house, her own life. She said that her boys were enough to keep her busy. What she did not say was that she was increasingly afraid of the city, the people—even the people who lived next door.

35

The First Baptist Church did more than keep me off the streets Sundays. It opened to me the teaching and preaching of Dr. George W. Truett, the leader of Baptists in Texas, the South, the world, a man who, while he held strictly to Baptist doctrine and Baptist tradition, brought us back week after week to the teachings of Jesus, the need of us all to use what talents we had for the uplifting of poor, sinful mankind. With the look of a close-shaven, well-groomed prophet, with a deep, full voice tempered to the prophecy of doom or the gladness of salvation, he held his people —as many as five thousand at a time—more than an hour in the morning, an hour at night, in sermons that touched on all varieties of human and religious experience. His was a religion of simplicity. He had no kind of symbol—neither collar nor cross—nor did he permit vestments for the choir. He made the ordinances of baptism and the Lord's Supper as simple as possible. To him, preaching was what mattered, oratorical preaching, and in his sermons he drew on the richness of the Bible, the daily language of Southern people, and at least some of the English Victorian poets. When he needed to be he was emotional in his preaching, and unperturbed when, though rarely, a woman burst into a shout during a sermon. He was missionary in spirit, and when he called on people to become missionaries at home or abroad, but especially at home, it was a call I felt.

Partly in response to his call, partly in gratitude to Mrs. Van

Dyke, I offered to work for the Salvation Army and was assigned to a hall in South Dallas in one of the poorest sections in the city. Our neighborhood on Santa Fe Avenue was poor and people had to scramble to make ends meet, but they were able to live in bungalows or weather-boarded shotgun houses, with flowers in the front yards, peach trees in the back. In South Dallas, the people were crowded into run-down houses, sometimes living one family to a room, their facilities a water hydrant and an outhouse in the back yard. I walked past these houses on the way to the Salvation Army and thought that we were well off.

From these houses came the boys and girls I taught in a mission Sunday School, pale, hookwormy, hungry kids drawn to the hall by hopes of something to eat, something to wear. Their clothes came from barrels of cast-offs brought on trucks and handed out Saturdays and Sundays, at times ill-fitting, at times party clothes grotesquely out of place. They sat quiet and afraid while I told them Bible stores and what would happen to them if they were not good girls and boys. Then, in general assembly, they watched such object lessons as the turning of water to wine, which the lieutenant in charge performed with trick glasses. After a song and a prayer they got what most had come for: a paper cup of fruit juice and a handful of cookies.

Once the lieutenant asked me to see him after Sunday School.

"I heard about a family that needs help bad," he said. "Can you go to see them for me, and find out what we can do?"

"I reckon."

"When can you go?"

"After work tomorrow night."

"Good." He gave me the name and directions to the address. I had to take the Lamar streetcar and get off in front of Sears Roebuck. Then I would have to walk several blocks, asking as I went because some of the streets were unmarked.

It was after six when I found the house, an unpainted shotgun in a row of unpainted shotguns on an unpaved block, with the space between houses too narrow for anything to grow. The yards were black mud and black mud had been tracked on doorsteps and porches. From the looks of the houses everybody on the block needed help.

I knocked on a porch post and a young woman came to the door, holding a little girl by the hand.

"I'm from the Salvation Army," I said. "Is your husband at home?"

"He ain't now but he will be any minute. He works at the iron works. You want to set and wait?"

She brought a chair to the front porch and I sat where I could look inside at a table set for supper between a bed and a cot. The woman took the little girl to the table and brought out her supper. It was white lightbread, purplish baloney, and milk the color of blue john—three things and no more.

Her husband came, a husky man, no more than twenty-five, with a boyish sweep of hair brushed back but no boyishness in his face—with a weary sag of shoulders under the blue chambray shirt and blue ducking galluses. I told him who I was and mentioned the Salvation Army but he did not shake hands. He told me with a shortness in his voice that he had not gone to the Salvation Army.

His wife came to the door.

"You want to eat now?"

"If it's ready." He looked at me and his face softened. "You want to come in?"

They gave me a chair at the table but I lied to keep from taking from them even a slice of baloney and bread. They told me they were from the country in Navarro County and had been in town over a year. They had come hoping to better themselves but things were no better. If they got worse, they would starve to death. Living in town was sure not what it was cracked up to be. A man had to have a trade to make a living in town. The man was more than discouraged, he was sullen.

When I asked if there was anything the Salvation Army could do, his sullenness changed to anger. He had not asked for help. He did not want charity, or even advice. All he wanted was to get back home to the country.

"Dang it," he said, "I cain't make a living in town. It's hand to mouth all the time, and they ain't nobody around here any better off, after no telling how many years of trying it. If I'd a knowed what it is like before I come, they couldn't a drug me here. They can say what they like against the country, but it's good enough for me."

In his anger he opened a bitter way of looking at the city—at the squeeze a working man was in if he had only his hands to work with, caught between high prices and low wages, with having to buy everything and pay rent, fifteen dollars a month for a place not fit for hogs.

He was not about to take help from the Salvation Army, and I understood why. The saying was general: You have to be bad off to take help from the Salvation Army. It was like admitting you were a bum.

I reported back to the lieutenant, who did not seem to understand why, when so many came to the Salvation Army for help, a man who needed it so much would be stand-offish. Perhaps because he did not understand, he asked me to go again to see the man.

The next day he was not there, and the house was empty. A neighbor woman told me he had skipped with his family in the night, leaving his junk behind and owing more rent than the junk was worth.

I went to the lieutenant with what I had learned and at the same time told him I would not be back again to teach my Sunday School class. It was not the Salvation Army, nor the pride that could have been false that kept me away. It was new knowledge of how the city can squeeze lives, a new determination not to be squeezed.

The result was a turning inward. I started piano lessons at a dollar an hour with Marie Jensen Skavenna, a tall, hard-driving woman who had seen most of Europe and was having a hard time making ends meet in Dallas, so hard that she had to take any pupil who came. I tried out with church songs and was told firmly they were not to be played for entertainment, that there were other kinds of music to be played outside the church. She lectured me on my ignorance and set me to work on two pieces that she said would open the way for me to study two kinds: the classical and the popular. They were "Le Papillon" and "Kitten on the Keys," neither of which was in my technical range. She was scornful of my work-thick fingers and tried to limber them up with these pieces and five-finger exercises.

At times during a lesson she became so exasperated with me that she took over the keyboard herself, and almost as if I had not been there, played the pieces she had prepared for a concert tour that never came. When she had played herself out, she would turn back to me and beg, cajole, threaten me into playing better for the moment. She must have known it was no use. She could make the fire come leaping into my brain. She could make me see and hear the music, but she could not force my fingers to keep up with my reading. No matter how frustrated she was she kept on week after week, the dollar an hour her slender reward, unless she could count moving me a little away from the church, a little toward a broader way of looking at music and literature.

She was Scandinavian, and though I recall no direction on her part, I went on a binge reading Scandinavian writers. Johann Bojer was first. I found a wild and wonderful book by him called *The Prisoner Who Sang*, a story of the cupidity of mankind and the perverseness of human nature. It put me to reading everything of his in the library. Among them was *The Emigrants*, which showed me a way of life in America—an accumulation of hardships—I had never known before, and *The Great Hunger*. From him I went to Sigrid Undset and in *Kristin Lavransdatter* immersed myself in another time, another place, another people. Then I went to Knut Hansen and *The Growth of the Soil*. He knew country people and how they felt about the land. He knew their beliefs about harelips. I recalled a harelip boy I had seen down on Red River and the creepy feeling people got when he was around. Knut Hamsen showed that with an operation a doctor could have made him like anybody else. People down on the river did not know that. All they knew was that his mother had looked on a rabbit when she was carrying him. For that, people would draw away from him and he would have to go through life with an ugly gap in his upper lip.

The wonder for me was that a Scandinavian could tell me what I needed to know about people around Pin Hook.

36

Then I had more reason than ever to be bitter about the city. I managed to stay on at Butler Brothers through the Christmas layoffs and annual inventory. Then, just as I was beginning to feel less worry, the pink slip came in my pay envelope. I pleaded with the floor manager, but it did no good. Business was slack. Christmas merchandise had been packed away for the next season. Spring orders had not started coming in. The branch manager had been ordered to let people go on a store-wide plan: last hired, first fired. My date had come up. He was not dissatisfied with my work. In fact, he asked me to come see him personally in late spring, when he might be able to hire me again. When there was nothing more to say I walked the streets as I had walked them before, crying inward tears of frustration, bitterness, anger.

For a little while I was able to live a lie. Thinking it better not to tell my family, I went through days of worry and job hunting. I left home at the regular time in the morning and returned at the regular time in the evening. Once out of sight of the house I walked back streets where I could not be seen from the streetcar. It was bad enough to be out of work; it was worse for the neighbors to know about it. Money was scarce and I saved every carfare I could. As soon as my money ran out we would all be living on what Charles brought home, and that was no more than seventy-five dollars a month.

On a Monday morning in late January I was so desperate that I went to the employment agency on Lamar Street that had sent me to the University of Dallas four years before. Standing with a group of jobless men, I studied the postings on a sidewalk blackboard: farm hands, a dishwasher in a restaurant, a stock clerk in a chain grocery. Slim pickings, but I went on up stairs to a room crowded with men in work clothes. I stepped inside, and then wished I had not. Dewey was sitting near the counter. He saw me and came toward me.

"You lost your job?" he asked.

His voice was not accusing, but it was full of worry. Of all of us, he was the one who worried first and most. Now his deep-set brown eyes seemed deeper set with this added worry.

"When did you lose it?"

"Not long after inventory."

"What you been doing in between?"

"Looking, tearing the place upside down looking."

With no luck. I did not have to tell him that. He knew when he saw that I was willing to pay an employment agency to get me a job. We stood together against the wall and he told me how many times he had come to the agency and now he came almost without hope. He had been out of work so long that he was ready to take any job they offered.

"If anything comes up you'd better take it," he told me.

I knew he was right. He knew I had lost my job. The others at home would know before the day was over. Facing them with any job would be better than with no job at all—the sadness and fear that would come in their eyes.

Toward midmorning they called his name and I went with him to the counter. They were ready to send him out on a job—the dishwashing job in a restaurant. It was off Elm Street and paid two dollars a day and meals. He took it, and signed for the restaurant owner to deduct the agency fee from his pay. They gave him a card and he left.

I filled out an application and, when the room was almost empty, was called for an interview. The man reviewed my work experience and told me he would have a hard time placing me. I had none of the skills employers wanted. He did have some farm jobs at a dollar a day and board, and one working in the barns at a Dallas dairy. Men were waiting for a chance at these. If I wanted to go out, I would have to sign up at once. If I wanted to wait, something might turn up the next day, or the next. I decided to wait.

With nothing to do, no place to go, I went to the Union Station. It was warm in the waiting room and pleasant with the sound of the Negro caller calling trains to San Antonio and St. Louis and all the way to New York. There were travelers waiting for trains, and bums waiting for life to pass, or for a handout from a traveler, and station police to protect the travelers from the bums. Every half-hour or so a policeman made the rounds, tapping sleeping bums with a nightstick to wake them, keeping them moving so there was no real rest for them. Begging went on, inside the waiting room and on the broad steps leading up to it. The shrewd beggars worked the crowd fast, asking only for a nickel for a cup of coffee, and made more money than they could have at a full day of work. When they were caught they were threatened with a trip to jail in the Black Maria, but I never saw one go.

After an hour or so of watching and dodging the police I began to feel like a bum myself. I had been around too long to be waiting for a train, as policemen and bums knew. Bums sidled up to me, just for company or to find out my racket. A boy my age told me how he had come in to Dallas riding the rods and was waiting for a chance to go out riding the blinds. He would take me with him if I wanted to go. I wanted to go—to see some of the places he talked about, to smell strange flowers and feel salt water, and most of all, to be free of the things that bound me—but I also wanted to stay. Because I was afraid? Yes. Because I needed to stay? Also yes.

He went his way and I went to the public library. Bums were there, too, sleeping in the big reading room with their heads resting on tables. Here there were no policemen to stop them from sleeping, or begging, or stealing a hat or a coat when a reader was not looking. With so many men out of work, I could see little hope for me.

I was too restless to enjoy reading or to profit from it. The day was passing, and by dark I would have to go home and tell the truth: I was no longer an earner; in a few days I would begin to be a burden. I had already stopped piano lessons. The piano itself might have to go back for the few dollars I still owed on it. All of us would have to go on slenderer rations.

As I walked home I was glad to be going—to a country kitchen, a country supper. I was a long way from my breakfast of cold cereal with milk. My mother was cooking over an old black-and-white gas range. Her kind of cooking took three hours or more, to boil pinto beans and vegetables and bake cornbread, to season with side meat or a shoulder bone.

"How come you're home so early?" she asked when I went in.

Quietly I told her that I had lost my job. Quietly she cried. She rarely raised her voice and she did not now. She did not blame me. She blamed living in town. It was the trouble with trying to live in town. You always had to depend on somebody else. She was right.

My brothers came home and after supper we tried to figure how to get along. Though there was never a word of blame for me, I knew I would have to take any kind of job I could get, and that two years of college would be no help.

37

Grocery clerk, the employment agency had posted. The job was not to my liking but I had to take it, at a chain grocery on Elm Street, twelve hours a day, six days a week for fifteen dollars. First in the mornings I had to meet delivery trucks at the sidewalk, and with a two-wheeler, truck cartons and bags to the storeroom at the back. The deliveries all in, I had to fill shelves and bins and straighten display stacks on the floor. Vegetables had to be trimmed, apples shined, potatoes scrubbed in a big sink in the storeroom. In between, I had to tote and carry for customers or for the men at the checkout counters. Just before closing time I had to stack garbage by the back door and sweep down the floors. No one could think of going home until the manager said the store was ready to open the next morning.

From the first day I hated the work. It was heavy. By the end of a day of running and lifting I was too tired to read or even to think. By the end of the week I could think of Sunday only as a time for rest. The manager was a hard driver, the work dull. No education was needed for the job I had. Something had to be wrong, I thought, if this was the best I could do after two years in college.

Within a few days I knew the store was crooked, though the only complicity required of me was to keep my mouth shut. The system was simple. Daily specials were advertised to bring customers to the store. These were the loss leaders. Checkout men were told to make up the loss. This could be done by underweights or by overcharging a penny or two here, a penny or two there. Checkout men skillful enough could make the loss leaders turn a fair profit. These were the men the manager favored most in raises and time off. When they were caught or questioned, they could apologize so abjectly that less suspicious customers accepted the overcharge as an honest mistake. It was easy in a rush, they agreed, to strike the wrong key. The most skillful of the checkout men claimed to be able to spot the penny-pinchers before they got to the counter, in time to charge them correct amounts and avoid arguments. Thievery became a kind of game, and the men sometimes boasted about how much extra money they had taken in a penny or two at a time.

What I hated most was that I was expected to wear a long white apron, the badge of a groceryman. It was bad enough having people see me working at a grocery store; it was worse to have them see me wearing a grocer's apron. The manager called me stubborn and then stupid for not wearing an apron when it was paid for by the store and I was getting myself muddy washing potatoes. I kept quiet and did my work, but did not put on the apron.

Then in three days in late March I was fired from one job and hired on another. The new one came from a newspaper ad for college boys to work in promotion, with salary and commissions guaranteed, plus bonuses for those who earned them. I applied at a room in the Southland Hotel and was hired without references. I looked the right age and that was enough. It was a magazine-subscription scheme. As boys working our way through college we would go from town to town and door to door taking subscriptions for home magazines. We would get three dollars a day, to cover our traveling expenses. Our commissions would come from the sales we made. Those who sold a certain number of subscriptions would qualify for a college scholarship. I had to have a job, and anything sounded better than working in a grocery store. I agreed to go and was assigned to a team of six working south from Dallas, with the first stop Ennis.

Our team captain was a man in his thirties whose sales pitch came not from college but from years of selling from door to door. He never seemed to get away from his sales pitch whether in conversation or in the lessons he gave us on the tricks of the canvasser's trade. Before we left Dallas and on the train to Ennis he lectured us.

"Get your foot in the door. That's the first and most important thing. Get your foot in the door and then get their sympathy. Sell them yourselves. Make them believe how much you want to go back to college. Only a little help from them and you can go. Convince them they're helping you get an education and you can sell them anything."

Of the five salesmen on our team, I was the only one who had been to college at all and the others had no intention of going. That did not stop them from working up hard luck stories of why they had been forced to drop out of college. The captain helped each one work out his story and made us practice them on each other. He knew the arguments we would get and told us how to get around them. We should always be obliging but vague: Spin the story out as much as they wanted but never let ourselves get caught. My story was factual enough, but no more convincing in sound than the others.

If we failed to get their sympathy, he told us, we were to rely on the magazines themselves. He showed us how to open a magazine at an eye-catching page, hold an illustration close enough for a prospective subscriber to glimpse but not really see, and read aloud passages that would whet curiosity but not give away the story. He had us go through our samples, mark pages, and work up short spiels.

In Ennis, the captain spread us out, two to a boarding house, to cover as much of the town as possible. The boy with whom I shared room and bed but fortunately not the clap he was doctoring had grown up on South Browder in Dallas. He had not finished high school but had acquired a special kind of education from living in cheap boarding houses and working street jobs. To him, Ennis was the jumping off place. Anyone living there had to be a hick—as much a hick as the men and women working in fields along the interurban tracks—and vulnerable to his salesman's tricks. He demanded and got the paved streets in the middle of town to work. My streets, mostly unpaved, ended at the edge of cotton fields or became country roads.

My first call proved that I needed more brass if I expected to make any money as a magazine salesman. I never got my foot in the front door. In fact, the door was slammed in my face before I could get into my first spiel. I wanted to quit then but could not. Before I could draw the three dollars allowed me for the day, I had to report by name and house number the blocks I had covered and the people I had called on. All morning long I went from house to house, telling anyone I could get to listen how I was working for a college scholarship. By afternoon it was clear that the people I was talking to had no interest in whether I went to college or not. As a matter of fact, few seemed to know what college was.

The next morning, following the advice of my roommate, who had done well the first day, I changed my pitch to telling the women about the love-story serials they could follow month after month if they were subscribers. When I found women working in their yards or gardens I praised what they had growing and then opened up a magazine. Radios had not reached the back streets of Ennis. Reading love stories was a chief form of entertainment. If I could tell a little of a plot, I was almost sure to have a sale. Late in the afternoon, on a street where a single row of houses faced plowed fields, I sold a magazine subscription at almost every house. The women knew the names of the magazines but not how to subscribe for them and were glad I had come along. Some took three-year subscriptions; some asked their neighbors to subscribe, not for me but for themselves. They wanted to trade with each other. One woman told me, "I sure hate to miss a month once I git started on a story."

We canvassed every house in Ennis and moved on to Corsicana, a larger town still feeling the effects of an oil boom. We had to take what places we could find in boarding houses and share tables with roughnecks and women who followed oil booms. Money was plentiful and we expected our sales to go up.

Again the captain sent me to streets near the edge of town, in a neighborhood of fine houses next to rows of poor houses. He told me to turn back when I came to a colored section—no sales there. At the fine houses I went back to my story of working my way through college, and the people knew what I was talking about. Some gave me subscriptions; some gave me sympathy. Wherever I got a foot in the door the people listened. One woman especially wanted to be helpful.

"You ought to go see Mrs. McKie," she said. "She helps lots of boys through college. They made money in the oil boom and she's a good woman. Just talking to her would do you a heap o' good."

She wrote out the address and I promised to go when I got through work.

Late in the afternoon I found the house and went as far as the front porch. I could not go any farther because I did not know how to say what I needed to say without sounding like begging. I walked around the block and came back, planning to start by trying to sell her a magazine subscription. Then I talked to myself: People living in a house that large would not need a magazine subscription, or want it. When I could not get up enough nerve I went back to the boardinghouse, promising myself I would go back first thing in the morning.

When morning came I had a cold and was running a fever. The captain was angry. He had neither time nor money for a sick salesman. He promised to pay what I owed the landlady and put me on the interurban back to Dallas. He also promised to mail me the eighteen dollars in commissions he owed me, but I had seen him break too many promises to feel that he would ever pay. I was bringing nothing home, but I could not help getting sick.

Glad to see me, my mother met me with good news from down home. The Pin Hook school had not hired teachers for the next year. There was a good chance for me if I wanted to apply.

As much as I had ever wanted anything I wanted to apply. Fever or not, I would go. At last I might be doing what I had set out to do.

38

The next morning, after five years of trying to make a go of it in the city, I was on my way home to Pin Hook, hitchhiking from Dallas to Paris, glad to be going, glad of a chance to escape the kinds of jobs I had been forced into. It was a warm clear day, good for crops, and all along the way men and women were working in the fields. Between rides, when I was walking, I spoke to people beside the road because I wanted to, not because I wanted to sell them something. I felt like saying "I'm coming back to the country" but did not.

In Paris, late in the day, I went through the Kress store, but not to see Mr. Watkins. He was already making good in New York. It was a sort of wanting to go back to old times, old places. Then on to the junior-college registrar to see if my certificate was still good. There I learned that Mignonne Chennault, also a college student, had applied to teach the lower grades at Pin Hook. When I called, she gave me names of the school board members and her father offered to drive us out the next day to see them. Of the three trustees I knew two, U. S. Swindle and Preston Goolsby, and they would be easy to talk to. Mr. Swindle and I had long since got over the differences we had when I was his hired hand. I was again like a member of the family. Preston, not much older than I, had married Amy Haley, who had been only a year or two ahead of me in school. The third trustee, a man named Webster, was new to Pin Hook. Mignonne had not found him on her first trip but she had heard that he was tough on teachers.

My trip back to Pin Hook, this time in an Overland car, was a retracing of old roads—out past the golf club, up and down red clay hills, through stretches of scrub-oak timber and open pasture land. The Novice church was sagging to one side; the old Addison house, once home to us, was filled with hay. Then we came to the Swindle place, to a house unchanged, set in fields where as a hired hand I had chased blackbirds from young corn.

Mr. Swindle was on the porch when we turned off the road and stopped in front of the gate. Mrs. Swindle came through the door of the fireplace room. He was in striped overalls, fresh shaved, his hair and mustache turned whiter. She wore a gingham apron over a gingham dress that came almost to her ankles. White showed in streaks in her black hair; there was more white than black in the high wave pushed back above her forehead. She had brushed white face powder over her nose and high cheekbones, so lightly that the darkness of her complexion showed through.

"Come on in, Bill."

Mr. Swindle spoke to me as he had when, a ten-year-old boy, I had brought buckets to his well for water. As a little boy, as his hired hand, I had feared him. Now I did not, though I was again coming to him for a job, a job I wanted more than anything else in the world. He spoke to "Miss Mignonne" and her father and said he was glad he was not in the field this time. All of us went in and I helped bring chairs to the porch while they told me that Pat was working in West Texas, Lois and Dahlia were not at home just then.

"It's like having you home again," Mrs. Swindle said. Then she told us of the old woman, a neighbor, who went to a restaurant in Paris and ordered eggs. "How do you like them?" the waitress asked. "God, I like 'em," the old woman replied. We laughed and then talked about the weather and crops and the places I had been. We talked about the school, but not much. Both teachers had left; they had to hire new ones.

"You can have the school as far as I am concerned," Mr. Swindle said to me. "If the others are willing to sign your contract, I will."

He was less certain about Mignonne. I thought I knew why he was holding back. The Pin Hook school had always been taught by teachers raised in the country. A teacher from town would have town ways. A teacher from town might not know how to get along with country boys and girls, or she might feel herself above them.

Mr. Swindle talked to her and said they were considering her application but made her no promises.

Back in the car, we followed ruts, rattled on the Little Pine Creek bridge, and came to the crossroads that was Pin Hook. It had not changed. Tom Baxter was in his store on one corner, Billy Redding in his blacksmith shop across the road. We found Preston Goolsby at the store and talked to him about the school. He was willing to hire me—it was like hiring a boyhood friend— but wanted to know more about Mignonne. He wanted us to see Mr. Webster. Nobody could be hired until we had seen Mr. Webster.

Mr. Webster was at his house on the road north from the store, a stern man with one eye out, the other sharpened by double duty. Because he felt they should hire the principal first, he said little to Mignonne. I had to tell him that I had been raised at Pin Hook partly, and that I had gone to the Pin Hook school close to four years, from the sixth through a part of the eight grade. He wanted to know if I had ever had trouble with my teachers. I suspected then that he knew quite a bit about me. When he asked whether I had ever been whipped in school, I told him yes.

"You believe in whipping?" he asked.

"If I have to. If the boys behave too bad—"

He made it clear that he was talking about girls as well as boys. He wanted to know if I would whip "gal young'uns" if they needed it, and was not satisfied until I had assured him that I would—that I would not let girl troublemakers off easy. He expected the teachers to ride herd on the pupils; he expected to ride herd on the teachers. The school would run right or the trustees would know why. He would have a daughter, Chloe, and a son, Felix, in my room, and wanted them treated just like anyone else.

Convinced that I could keep discipline, apparently unconcerned about my other qualifications, he said he was ready to sign when the others had their names on the line.

Back in Dallas with my good news I found more good news. Sears Roebuck had called me to come to work in the stockroom, the next Monday if possible. They had decided on me from an application I had filled out when I lost my job at Butler Brothers.

They had checked my record and found that twice before my work for them had been satisfactory.

The next Monday I was back at work at Sears Roebuck, moving boxes and bales in the warehouse for eighteen dollars a week. It was heavy work and I went home sweaty and tired every day, but it was a job and it gave me time to think. Loads had to be wheeled from the elevators to a stockroom on the west side of the building. On the way to the stockroom I had to keep looking straight ahead to guide the load. On the way back I could pause at the west windows and look across the open space of the Trinity River bottoms and count the days left of this kind of work. I did not tell the floor manager that I planned to leave him at the busiest time, and felt no guilt. I had been left jobless too many times when the busy season was over.

My rejection of the city was by then almost complete. I could pass by the Salvation Army hall and fell no urge to go inside, or to join in their mission work. At the First Baptist Church I could sit through singing and preaching and not respond at all to the calls for young Christians to go out to the poor and bring help to the needy. There was not enough help from all the churches to overcome the evil of the city. Faithfully I went to church; as faithfully I went to the library. It was like living the known, exploring the unknown.

Paradoxically, life was better for us as a family than it had been for months. Charles and I had regular jobs, Dewey a few hours of work each week here and there, plus several hundred dollars from his insurance settlement. We moved away from Santa Fe Avenue all the way across town and to the edge of Oak Cliff, to a small white California bungalow at the dead end of a new street. It was not country but close to it, close enough for my mother to feel less closed in. We bought furniture and made the house comfortable for her, with the hope that at last she would be satisfied. She seemed to be, and before long Catherine Street began to feel like home to us all.

It was best for Roy, to be taken away from living beside the railroad tracks, from a downtown high school to Sunset High, where he could have new friends and spend the time in sports he had spent riding a streetcar. It was his fifth school in as many years. School was not yet a problem for him but it could be, even before he finished high school. Two more years and we would have to find a way to send him to college.

39

Instructions came to me and Mignonne from the county superintendent's office. In a move to achieve uniformity, country schools in Lamar County would, for the first time, have the same opening date, October 15. The date had been announced. We were expected to be on the job.

On the Friday before, I quit my job at Sears Roebuck. The floor manager became angry at me for quitting during the rush, and for the first time I talked back to a boss. I could leave them, I told him, as easily as they had left me. He told me he would mark my record "Fired," but I did not care. All I wanted to do was pack my duds and get out of town.

The next day I took the train to Paris. Carrying my suitcase, I walked from the station, around the square, and through the Kress store, glad to be at home among country people in town for Saturday e'ening. In the store girls worked behind the same counters they had been assigned to when I left Kress more than two years earlier. They told me it looked natural to have me walking down the aisles. Some hoped I was coming back, but I shook my head.

"What you going to do?" the girl in charge of notions asked.

"I start teaching Monday."

"Where?"

"Faulkner."

She looked at me, puzzled.

"Where's that?"

"Pin Hook."

"Oh, Pin Hook."

She made it sound like the last jumping-off place. Then she

added, "It's good you got a job." A customer interrupted and she said to me, "Well, come to see us when you're in town."

I looked for people from Pin Hook on the square and out North Main past where the old wagon yard had been. No one from Pin Hook that I knew. It was a long trip and people did not make it often. Anybody in a wagon would already be on the road.

At a store on Bonham Street I bought two essentials for a country schoolteacher: a watch for keeping time and a bell to call the pupils to books. Then, as she had been hired to teach the lower grades, I called Mignonne Chennault and asked for a ride to Pin Hook.

Sunday afternoon I rode with the Chennaults out the gravel and the dirt road past Faught and Novice. Summer still hung on, hot and dry, and we left behind us pools of dust like sand-red cloud banks in low places. Mignonne sat primly in a corner of the back seat, a little afraid, I thought. I tried to tell her what Pin Hook was like, what the people were like, and ended up saying, "You have to live there to know it. It's not like any other place I know of."

She had arranged to board at the home of Mr. C. P. Phillips. I had not made my own arrangements, but Mr. Phillips had the most to offer. His house was the biggest in Pin Hook, he set a good table, and he had a piano in the front room. Hard-working, hard-driving, he was looked on as the richest man for miles around and as the natural leader in Pin Hook. He rarely sat around the store on Saturday afternoons as the other men did, but when he came he could expect a nail keg for a seat and the other men gathered around to listen to him. He ran the voting box and his word usually carried the box for a candidate. A man with very little education, he was a natural speaker, always to be depended on to say the right things at church or school meetings or graveyard workings.

We came to the four corners at the Pin Hook crossroads. The store and blacksmith shop were closed, and there was no one in sight. A half mile farther, down the Woodland road, we came to the Phillips place: on the left a large barn, on the right a white house, L-shaped, with a porch across two front rooms and a hall between. The hall became a gallery with doors opening into another room and then the dining room and kitchen. We stopped in grinding sand.

Mrs. Phillips came to the porch, a white-haired woman in a Sunday dress. She was expecting Mignonne, but did not appear surprised to see me.

"You all get out and come in," she said.

We went through a gate and across a bare strip of broom-swept yard to the steps.

"I see you made it all right," she said. She shook hands with us and turned to Mignonne. "I'll give you Dollie's room. Dollie's married to C. H. and lives at Woodland."

They followed her inside. I stood in the hall, looking in, seeing the room as I had seen it many times before, a tall-ceilinged room with enlarged pictures of Phillips relatives in a solid row around all four walls, hung so high that the scrolled and flowered frames almost touched the ceiling. There was a fireplace at the east end and for furniture a piano, dresser, bed with a white counterpane, and chairs. The floor was covered with a many-flowered rug. People often said it was the prettiest room in Pin Hook. They left Mignonne's things and came back to the hall.

Mr. Phillips crossed the road from the barn and came to the porch. He shook hands with us and, when he spoke, his voice had the after-resonance that made it different from any other voice in Pin Hook. I had heard it in deep fervor, deep sorrow, but never in anger.

Mrs. Phillips turned to me.

"You want to stay with us, too?" They did not have a hired hand at the time and there was plenty of room. "Oren's room has two beds in it. You can have one to yourself. You used to set together at school. He always did say you were the best speller in Pin Hook."

I did not consider long. When I left Pin Hook I was living in a house so ramshackle that it was torn down as soon as the last member of my family left it. Now I would be living in the best and putting my feet under a good table. They would welcome me, they said. I would be a heap of company to them. Mignonne and I could play the piano all we wanted to. I had thought of going back to Mr.

Swindle's, to the shedroom I had shared with Pat when I was a hired hand, but it was across the creek and I would not be able to get to school in times of high water.

"I reckon I'll stay," I said quietly, keeping from my voice the pride I felt at coming back as a teacher and being taken in by the ones some called the best.

Mr. Phillips took me and my valise to a door that opened on the gallery. It was a dark room with a fireplace on the south wall, windows on the west, a door on the north to the room where Mr. and Mrs. Phillips slept. There were two beds with headboards against the north wall, the door between, and a cane-bottomed chair at the foot of one. Mr. Phillips put his hand on the bed by the window.

"Oren sleeps here," he said. "I reckon he's out with the dry cattle, but he'll be home before it's very late. Workday tomorrow." He stopped and then began again, answering a question I had not asked. "Oren is used to having somebody in the room with him."

When we came out again Mignonne was at the car with her parents. She kissed them goodbye and came back through the yard gate, looking as people in Pin Hook said of her "not bigger'n a minute." Mr. and Mrs. Phillips went to the kitchen to warm up supper, leaving us facing each other awkwardly in the hall. We knew we had to get along together all day at school. We also had to come to the table together at breakfast and supper, day in and day out. It was our first job. We had to get along, and with no sparking. At the moment we could only talk around the problem. Then we were at the table with Mr. and Mrs. Phillips, passing the biscuits, the cornbread, the meat and vegetables, and talking about the first day of school.

"You're in good per now," Mrs. Phillips said to me. I knew what she meant and told her I was much obliged. In my schooldays at Pin Hook, when we played rolyholy, we tried to maneuver our marbles into good "per"—"persition" as we pronounced "position"—to shoot. She was saying that, after my years of work and study, I was in good "per" to be a teacher.

After supper Mignonne went to her room and I went out to walk the road and recapture the feeling of home.

The night was warm and soft under a star-filled sky. The dirt under foot was also warm and soft and damp enough for the smell of dew-wet dust to rise with every step. I walked west toward the store, past the one house between, where Mrs. Baxter lived with her bachelor son, Tom. The light was out; it was already late enough for them to be in bed. When I came to the crossroads the smell of dew on dead and drying oak leaves brought back many times when I had been here before, going to mill, playing roly holy, carrying a girl home after snap or preaching. Standing in the middle of the road, I could see the light of stars pale on the plank walls of the store, walls rebuilt from the walls of the house in which I was born. I could also see the blacksmith shop, a black mass in the shadow of oak trees. There were houses on the roads north, west, south that I could not see, dark houses, the lamps blown out. People, I knew, went to bed early Sunday night unless there was a singing at somebody's house.

Four roads met at the Pin Hook store. Sooner or later, closer or farther away, three of them crossed Litttle Pine Creek. In three directions the creek cut Pin Hook off from the outside world. A few houses across the creek were in the Pin Hook district, and boys and girls living in them came to the Pin Hook School, but they did not really belong to Pin Hook—they were not called Pin Hookers. Pin Hookers were the people living in the half-dozen houses on the road east to the beginning of Woodland, three houses north to the creek, one house west to the creek, half a dozen or so on the road south to the creek, and a few houses in the fields and woods. The schoolhouse and graveyard were on the road south.

I walked the road south past the blacksmith's house but not as far as the schoolhouse. I knew that, once there, I would want to go on, past the graveyard, to the lane and down the lane to where our house had stood. It was not the walk of a mile or so there and back that stopped me. It was that I was faced with too much all at once of looking at myself through all the stages of growing up in Pin Hook. It was enough for the moment to sit on a road bank and look at myself as principal of the Pin Hook school.

This was my work, I knew. At last I had found my work and my place in the country. I wanted to make the country my home.

I had seen the lights of the city and felt its excitement. I had also seen men and women picking through garbage cans on South Akard looking for something to eat.

When the milky way had whitened across the sky I walked slowly back to the house and through the gate. A lamp had been left burning for me. I blew it out and lay down with a greater sense of peace than I had felt since I first went away from Pin Hook when I was fifteen.

40

Breakfast was by lamplight, cooked by an old Negro man for men who had already fed the teams and milked the cows, a breakfast solid enough to last them till they come back in the middle of the day for dinner: big soda biscuits, salty side meat, and fried eggs. There was a molasses pitcher for a sweet to end with—butter stirred in molasses and sopped with a biscuit—and a pile of sweet potatoes baked without peeling, to be stuffed in pockets for midmorning hunger. While I ate, the cook made my dinner: one biscuit cut open with a piece of meat between, one with butter and molasses, a baked potato, and a piece of cake, all piled in a half-gallon molasses bucket with nail holes in the lid to keep the grub from sweating.

Before sunup the men, wearing duckings and jumpers, brogans and wide hats, went off in a wagon to the field. Soon after, in my coat and tie, I started my walk to the schoolhouse. The morning was clear and crisp, and people were out early, the men in the fields, the women getting out their Monday wash, the smoke rising from washpot fires. The blacksmith was hammering steel on his anvil with a sharp ringing sound. The store door was open. A man on the porch spoke to me and said he hoped the scholars would do good in their studies.

A half-mile south and I turned into the schoolground. It was brown in the front with dying grass and weeds left to stand since the end of school, red-brown at the back with falling leaves. The schoolhouse looked dusty and deserted. Clean up days would have to be set. I opened the unlocked door to the big room and went in. Nothing had changed in the years I had been away; five rows of single desks faced the blackboard at the other end of the room, a few double desks faced the black-jacketed stove. I went to a double desk and found the initials WAO I had carved years before. Then I tried the pump organ. It was wheezy from dirt daubers and dust but there was enough voice for an opening song. The floors had been cleaned and oiled with an oil that smelled of cedar shavings. There was nothing for me to do but open windows and put out chalk and erasers. The little room at the back, for pupils from the primer through the fourth grade, smelled of cedar and buzzed with wasps from a nest under the eaves. I knocked the nest down with a broom and left the door and windows open wide for the wasps to fly out. The water fountain, a varnished oak keg with a shiny nickel bubbler, stood on a rack near the cistern. Under the new school laws the zinc water bucket and tin dipper could no longer be used. I drew water and filled the keg. Then I searched the walls of the two outhouses at the edge of the woods for smut.

Still alone, I sat on the front steps in a warming sun. At that moment boys and girls were walking toward school, on paths through fields and woods, joining in groups on the roads, some traveling as much as three miles an hour or more at a child's pace. Children had been walking these same paths and roads since the school was set up and named Pin Hook soon after the Civil War. The principle then, a principle beginning to change, was that every child should be within walking distance of a free public school—a principle that resulted in many small districts and one-room schools through the century it was in force.

The state, I had learned in education classes, was trying to raise standards, to improve both town and country schools. It had passed compulsory attendance laws, which I was charged to help enforce but knew I could not. How could they be when parents needed the children to work in the fields, or moved to a new district every year? The state furnished free textbooks, partly for the sake of uniformity, partly to make certain that the poorest child had books to study. For the first time Lamar County was going to require county-wide testing and a county-wide graduation for the seventh grade, the last year of grammar school. A part of my work was to prepare my seventh-grade pupils to compete in that test: Pin Hook against places almost big enough to be called towns.

The state, through visits by county supervisors, was attempting to reach into the communities and improve schooling generally. Regulations were sent out, but there was no way to force the schools to comply. For sixty years, isolation being an advantage, Pin Hook had been able to operate under laws of its own, with a few exceptions, one being redistricting thirty years earlier and changing the name from Pin Hook to Faulkner. I had little expectation of change. Parents remembered the school as it was when they were children. What was good enough for them was good enough still.

Mignonne came, and close behind her the pupils, the boys in khaki or in blue denim duckings and blue chambray shirts, the girls in homemade cotton dresses. Among them were younger brothers and sisters of boys and girls I had gone to school with. There were also children of renters who might move on by Christmas or soon after. In book satchels made from cotton sacking they carried nickel tablets and nickel pencils. They carried their dinners in sacks and buckets and Sears Roebuck lunch boxes. Some were from families starving poor; some from families who lived by strange beliefs. Some, if they started the day with a garment wrong side out, had to wear it wrong side out all day. Turning it right side out was certain to bring bad luck. Some smelled of assafoetida, some of Watkins liniment.

The boys put their things in the boys' coat room, sidled past me, and gathered at their outhouse. The girls leaned on the curbing of the cistern. All of them were sizing me up. At eight o'clock I spoke to Mignonne. She was ready to take up books. I stood on the front steps and rang the bell. Boys and girls for the big room lined up in front of me; the ones for the little room lined up at the side door. I counted quickly: seventeen for me, about the same for Mignonne. There would be more when cotton picking was over.

"March in."

I stood aside for them to pass. The girls marched in primly and stood beside the desks they had chosen. The boys clumped in after them. When they were quiet I went to the front of the room and led them in The Lord's Prayer and the pledge of allegiance to the flag, though we had no flag in either room. Then I began reading the Twenty-third Psalm: "The Lord is my shepherd, I shall not want . . ."

It was the ritual I had followed when I was a boy, a ritual being repeated with variations that morning in country schools all over Texas. Some would end it with singing "My Country, 'Tis of Thee," but on this first morning I skipped the song.

From the report cards they brought I worked out the roll: Alton, Felix, Dahlia, M. E., Chloe, Pleasant, Myrtle Lou, Kirby, Jimmie. Then I put names I did not know with faces I did not know, and tried to see them as a school. Some were healthy, some yellow from malaria, some pale from hookworm. A saying came to my mind: "Nobody harder to teach than a hookworm kid." Their report cards were marked "promoted" or "retained." One by one I separated them into grades, fifth, sixth, seventh, eighth. Those without report cards had to be guessed at or placed by what they remembered. They gave me names of others still to come, the ones still working in the fields at home, the ones whose families had not come back from picking cotton out at Altus, Oklahoma. Then I gave out books as prescribed by a list from the county superintendent's office.

After morning recess, a fifteen-minute period with a bell to march out by, a bell to march in by, I began working on the daily schedule, following the way it had always been done. The day was divided into four periods; each pupil had to recite in five subjects. A period each had to be assigned to reading, writing, and arithmetic. The subjects left over—geography, history, civics, and spelling—had to be crowded into the last period. The fifth grade had always recited first, and then on up, with each recitation a review for anyone who wanted to listen. I followed the same plan, and assigned arithmetic and algebra to the first period.

I ate dinner at my desk, surrounded by books, some of which I had never seen before but would have to start teaching the next morning, wishing there had been some chance to see them ahead of time. Outside there was quiet and then the sound of shouts and laughter of boys and girls in a game of "Wolf over the River." Quickly I looked at books and made assignments by numbers of pages or first chapters. Adjustments would have to be made when I knew more about the material and how much the pupils knew. All the lessons I had been compelled to take in education courses now seemed far away and impractical. They were taught by teachers who had never heard of Pin Hook. They were all town teachers, college teachers, who overlooked the fact that country teachers would have to teach four grades or more and make up lessons for any older boys and girls who might want to come back to school. I had watched other teachers work at this same desk. I saw no way but to make their methods my methods.

But I knew this was not right either. More had to be done but in a different way. The same books were furnished in Pin Hook, Paris, Dallas, but the children here were different, because they lived a long way from town, some a long way from each other— too far for participating in much besides school. They lived on the farm and most would live out their lives on the farm. I had to find a way, if I could, to make them know more than was held in these narrow boundaries.

After dinner I gave out the lessons, going from grade to grade, book to book, watching the pupils to see that they wrote their assignments in their tablets and did not mark their books. Borrowed books had to be returned not later than the end of the year. Borrowers had to pay for torn or dirty pages, and I would have to collect from parents too poor to pay. I could be charged personally when I did not collect. The system was supposed to teach them good citizenship. It taught me to keep careful records.

Roll book, textbooks, assignments kept me busy through the last recess. Then there was time for spelling and nothing else. I started with the word columns in the spelling book for the fifth and sixth grades, alternating from one class to another, asking them to write as I pronounced each word twice. Then I had them exchange papers and mark errors as I spelled the words aloud. For the first time that day I was discouraged. The fifth graders were very poor spellers, the eighth graders not much better. I went from desk to desk examining the papers. The problem was greater than that of spelling; it was handwriting and also reading.

After the pupils had been dismissed for the day I sat alone in the quiet room studying their papers. It was not all their fault, I knew. They had been out of school since April. Since April, most of them had not seen a book. Most of the homes had only the Bible. Older girls in the room were passing around a sentimental novel called *The Blonde Creole.* This was no surprise to me, but for the first time I was seeing the problem as a teacher. Suddenly it seemed almost too much for me to cope with.

Before I could go home, blackboards had to be cleaned, floors swept. I could clean up all right, but I worried about my teaching. I did not know enough and I had not been trained well enough. Seven months of contract stretched out ahead of me, and, though I knew the diameter of a basketball hoop to be ordered, I did not know enough arithmetic to figure the length of iron required to make it. Worse, there was no one to ask.

Before sundown I closed the doors and started back to the house, but the work day had not ended for other Pin Hook people. Men were still working in the fields. Boys and girls were bringing in wood and water before they could get down to their books. Billy Redding was hammering away in his blacksmith shop. I went to the door and watched him shaping a piece of red hot steel on the anvil. He finished the shaping and dropped the piece into a tub of water. Steam rose around his face. He turned to me and smiled.

"How's school?"

"Pretty good."

He put the metal back into the coals and began cranking the bellows. A man I had never seen before stopped across the road.

"Whupped any yet?" he asked me.

"Not yet."

I laughed with him and then went toward the house. When I was in hearing distance I heard the piano. Mignonne was playing "Silvery Waves." Suddenly I felt better. The first day was over. Looking back on it, I began to see boys and girls, not the words they had misspelled.

I went in and Mignonne let me have a turn at the piano. I had been trying to memorize a part of "The Storm," the part that builds up to the rush of wind, the roll of thunder. I played it over and over and by time for the lamp to be lit I was again glad to be back at Pin Hook.

41

My first full day of teaching lay before me, from eight to four, with an hour and a half for recesses and, at the end of the day, half an hour of "keeping in" for helping the lagging or for punishing the whisperers, note writers, noise makers. For worse offenders—boys caught smoking or swearing or writing dirty words—I had birch switches, cut that morning in a grove down toward Little Pine Creek, standing tall as the blackboard in a corner. I was there early. Trouble would start if pupils were there ahead of the teacher.

Arithmetic came first—fifth grade, sixth, seventh—and then algebra for the eighth. The sixth and seventh grades had to be set to work reviewing fundamental operations—addition, subtraction, multiplication, division, both short and long—the eighth to reading the introduction to the first course in algebra. That done, I began reviewing the fifth. After five months out of school, five months of swinging hoes or dragging cotton sacks, with no need to count in anything more than pennies, they shook their heads on words like *minuend, subtrahend, dividend, quotient.* I had to take the review back farther and farther to know where to begin. They knew their numbers and could count to a hundred by ones and fives and tens; they could add two-digit numbers and say the multiplication tables through the fives.

The sixth and seventh grades were a little better, but not much. A girl in the sixth grade stood timidly by her desk and recited "one times seven is seven" and on through the sevens and eights. She started on the nines but got stuck on nine times seven, unable at first to see that nine times seven is the same as seven times nine. In the seventh, boys and girls labored over stated problems, translating words into numbers, writing numbers on rough tablet sheets with short pencil points wet with spit. I thought of putting all three grades together and going back with them almost to the beginning of arithmetic, but that would have been against regulations.

Time for algebra came, and with it the question: "How come we got to study algebra? I cain't see no need for algebra in Pin Hook."

As Pin Hook saw it, they were right. Several teachers before me had tried to teach algebra and nobody could se any good that had come from it. All I could answer was that it was required by the state. I had to teach it and they had to study it. At the same time, I knew that most of these boys and girls would live in Pin Hook or places like Pin Hook. Better to spend the time preparing them to live there and make a living on the farm. There was no way in the school to give them any kind of vocational training. They could learn algebra but they would go on as their fathers had done wearing out the land with corn and cotton.

The best I could do for the first lesson was to read the first chapter aloud with them and try to show them how letters could be used to represent numbers. Even this they resisted. I was not well enough trained to counter their resistance.

Reading was easier for me to teach than either arithmetic or algebra. One by one, grade by grade, boys and girls stood and read passages from the assignments in their whangy East Texas voices. Between readings, they talked the grammar of barn and field. Their way of talking was as local as their way of thinking. The readings took us through the far reaches of the world in time and place, from King Arthur's Roundtable to Robert E. Lee's horse, in the realm of fantasy from the Arabian Nights to German fairy tales. For some, the reading was leaden, a slow plodding no matter where the mind was invited to wander. Some heard of far-off places with imaginations too unaroused to be able to leave Pin Hook. A few, for whom I was grateful, were eager to leap on and on, wherever some voice from the past called them.

This was especially true in poetry. When I was a pupil in this room I had memorized "Abou Ben Adhem" and responded to such lines as "I pray you then, write me as one who loves his fellow men." Now boys and girls were reading it for me, silently at first and then aloud couplet at a time, and I was trying to get them to listen and imagine.

"I cain't stand poetry," some of them said. "You all the time got to memorize something."

No need to argue, I knew. I thought quickly. Teachers had been there before me. There must be residues from their teaching.

"Would anybody like to recite something he learned last year?" I asked.

A thin-faced boy named Kirby put up his hand. When I called on him he stood with shuffling feet and eyes staring out the window. The sounds were East Texas, the words and rhythm Walt Whitman:

> O Captain! my Captain! our fearful trip is done,
> The ship has weather'd every rack, the prize we sought is won,
> The port is near, the bells I hear, the people all exulting,
> While follow eyes the steady keel, the vessel grim and daring,
> But O heart! heart! heart!
> O the bleeding drops of red,
> Where on the deck my Captain lies,
> Fallen cold and dead.

He stopped and smiled gently.

"That's all I know of it," he said. "It's about Abraham Lincoln."

I looked around the room. All work had stopped. All the boys and girls were listening to Kirby, whether they liked poetry or not.

No one else wanted to recite. For a time I spoke to them about reading I liked and heard in my own voice and words that I had dropped back into the speech of Pin Hook.

"It's dinnertime," I heard myself say. "We'll get to the word study this e'ening."

While I ate my biscuit and fried meat at a desk in the schoolroom I worried about what I could do with these boys and girls to make them see more of the world outside and, having seen it, use it to make their lives in Pin Hook better. I had to try to put myself in their place and them in mine. Five years before, frustrated by my own sense of isolation, I had left this room. Now my own view of the world was wider but Pin Hook remained as isolated as ever. One family, at times two, subscribed to the Paris *News*. There was not a radio in Pin Hook; most of the boys and girls in school had never heard a radio. Except for what they read in schoolbooks, the world outside was what they saw on a Saturday in Paris, and there they saw mostly people who had moved to town from places like Pin Hook. The state required that I teach reading, writing, spelling, arithmetic. I knew that I had to teach a great deal more. The tools were there, good books. My task was to help them see beyond the printed page.

After dinner the fifth grade had geography; the sixth, Texas history; the seventh, civics; the eighth, United States history. All this period we were reaching back in time, out in space. Geography was the introduction; the way of teaching, the way I had learned it, made it less so. Memorize the names of the states by section: New England, Middle Atlantic, Southern, and on west to the Pacific. Next, memorize the names of the capitals. Make it into a game: see who will be first to say the names of the states and capitals without missing. There was a colored map with the capitals starred. There were also a few pictures of far-off places, too far off for the boys and girls to imagine visiting them. Some of them had been to West Texas with their families to pick cotton. Some had been across the Red River to Hugo. Most of them had no more sense of Boston than they had of Tibet, of which they had never heard.

Texas history was more interesting, once I decided to pass over the periods of French and Spanish conquest and relate the story to American settlements. Then the past seemed a little nearer. The Pin Hook school was on a land grant made to Wiley Witherspoon. I could tell them that Wiley Witherspoon was my great-great grandfather and that he had settled in the fields south of the school house while the country still belonged to Mexico. The houses and barns he built with his slaves were no longer standing, but the fields he cleared were still being worked. That much of Pin Hook history I knew, but not much more. There was a story that Davy

Crockett had come up the road from the Red River on the way to Honey Grove, but no one was certain of that.

Civics was harder to teach than, or as hard to teach as, algebra, and Pin Hookers had as little use for it. For them, government hardly existed, though people came to the store to vote and knew the names of the sheriff, the constable, and the road commissioner. Words of government hardly existed for the boys and girls of Pin Hook, or for their parents. Their law was, for the most part, "Mr. Phillips says." They paid their taxes when they could, county and school, and the men worked the required number of days a year on the roads. The boys and girls knew this, and that the constable or sheriff would be sent for if there was trouble, but to most of them the county courthouse in Paris was a place where they could go to the outhouse when they were in town, or where older boys and girls had to go to get marriage licenses. Authority at home rested in the flat of the hand, at school in the birch switches in the corner.

There were those in Pin Hook who did not want their boys and girls to know more about the outside. They might do what some had done: go off from home and never come back. The state was encouraging consolidation, the combining of several small school districts into one. The advantages were obvious. There would be more pupils, more teachers, a wider range of studies, especially the vocational. Pin Hook was not ready to join with anyone. The roads were all dirt, impassable in wet weather for a wagon, let alone a school bus. Little Pine Creek on a rise could put off consolidation a long time.

42

On a Sunday morning, before people were stirring, I walked past the store and schoolhouse and stopped at the graveyard long enough to read inscriptions on the few gravestones, among them

Remember, friend, as you pass by
As you are now so once was I;
As I am now so you shall be;
Prepare for death and eternity.

Then I went to where our house had stood, now a place of emptiness. The barn was still there, but it was beginning to lean as logs rotted away. It was a homestead abandoned, the yard and garden now grazed by cattle. Thirty years or so before, my father had built there in the shade of oaks. The oaks spread their branches farther and farther out. The well he had dug with pick and shovel still yielded good water, but had started caving in. A few more years and all the signs of his work would be gone, as was the work of others before him.

I crossed the road and walked the fields that Wiley Witherspoon had cleard and worked while Texas was still a part of Mexico. Toward Little Pine Creek he had built his houses and barns and quarters for the slaves he had brought with him. All but one building had rotted back into the earth. It was a square cabin, built of logs on which I could still see the marks of ax and broadax, the spaces between the logs chinked with postoak clay held together with grass from the fields. It now had a rough board floor, added later perhaps when the cabin was moved farther up the creek. In this house my father's mother was born.

It was easy in these silent fields to wonder what compulsion, what hope of reward made Wiley Witherspoon and his wife load their four daughters and belongings on a wagon, and with others in a train, make the long journey, beginning in Virginia or Kentucky or Tennessee, across Arkansas, and a hundred miles into Texas, to this spot. What had made them choose this when there were so many acres open for choosing. The land had belonged to the Indians and they had used it. In gullies close to the creek I could still find arrowheads and pieces of clay pots. For the Indians it was good land. Away from the creek it was wooded, with an upper canopy of oaks mixed with hickory and here and there a black walnut, with a lower canopy of huckleberry and other bushes. Along the creek there were dense cane brakes, where deer and buffalo came to graze.

Wiley Witherspoon came quietly in 1834. He labored and accumulated for fifteen years, and with his wife left as quietly in 1849. He cleared the land. Any other marks he had left had now disappeared, and his name with them except where it appeared on land grants and a will—documents that proved he had lived there and prospered under Mexico, Texas, the United States, no doubt left alone by all three.

A little farther on I came to the Witherspoon graveyard on a knoll back from the creek. Here, among some smaller ones, was a granite marker, bearing the name of Catherine Duval, my great grandmother, the marker put there by her daughter Harriet Wiley Hall. The graveyard yields its own story. Here were buried the four daughters of Wiley Witherspoon, three of them dead while Pin Hook was still wilderness. Here also lay John M. Hall, who by some circumstance drifted down from New York City, where he was born, met and married Catherine Witherspoon, fathered children, and died, still probably in his thirties. Near him lay his only son, James, who did not live beyond childhood. Near him also lay William Duval, Catherine's second husband, and their daughter Melinda, my grandmother, who was married at fifteen, a mother at sixteen, and dead at seventeen. The graveyard was far off the road and the graves had settled down to brush-covered earth under black locust trees.

The black locusts had their own story, handed down from generation to generation. The child of one of the Witherspoon slaves died and there was no separate place to bury it. The mother was allowed to bury her child in a corner of the family graveyard. She marked the grave with a small black locust. After the graveyard was abandoned the locust spread and became a grove; in winter, black, gnarled trees against the sky, in spring, a cloud of snowy blossoms sweet on the air, drawing wild bees from tree hollows all up and down Little Pine Creek.

I wondered how master and slave lived and shared in what had to be cramped quarters of the wilderness, what tensions they developed, what tenderness. Another story told me a little. A preacher passing through on horseback agreed to hold a meeting in the master's house. There was no church and preaching was seldom heard. A slave, old Aunt Minerva, was as hungry as anyone else to hear the Gospel, but it was not fitting for her to be in the house with the preacher and the white folks. It was finally decided that she could sit on a chair behind the door where she would not be seen. The preacher began preaching with all the oratory of a frontier evangelist. Aunt Minerva got happier and happier. When she could hold in no longer she burst from behind the door and shouted and danced until she was worn out. Then, like a member of the family, she listened to the preacher till the last amen.

In 1865, June 'Teenth the exact date in Texas, the separation between masters and slaves came, and the slaves moved to their own settlement to the north and west of Pin Hook. There, in a school that was part of the Pin Hook district, I might find boys and girls whose ancestors made the journey into the wilderness as slaves of Wiley Witherspoon. I had no desire to go. I had been there before and seen how they lived, in boxing plank cabins, poor, illiterate, slaves in another sense, needing the care of whites who took little heed of them. They had owned no land, left no record.

I found myself looking back over four generations of life in Pin Hook. I was the fifth. No one remembered how it came to be called Pin Hook, but the name had been known a long time, perhaps for nearly a century—or why. Perhaps as a joke on a place at the back end of nowhere. In a hundred years life had changed little—for many not at all. The life cycle might still be as short as forty years: birth, marriage, death, the years between filled with a little schooling, much hard work on worn-out land, begetting of children who would begin the cycle all over again.

The day was, I realized, another journey in search of myself, of trying to find out what spark from what generation had sent me away from Pin Hook, what spark had brought me back, what spark made me content to be back. If not a spark, then a chemistry of the soil? I could see the boys and girls in my grades following the life cycles of their parents, too many hookworm kids begetting too many hookworm kids. In me the cycle had been broken, by what I did not know.

Of one thing I was sure: what had happened to me might happen to someone else. My job was to discover and to prompt. Back at school I went through lessons and recesses and talks after school asking boys and girls where their families had come from, where they themselves thought they were going. On the way back to the house I asked the same questions of men hanging around the store and blacksmith shop, and of Mr. Phillips at the table after supper. The answer to where they were going, when there was an answer, was, "I got this old piece o' wore-out land I got to hang onto"; the women, quicker to answer, said, "I got people buried here. It wouldn't be right, going off and leaving them." A thing just as sure: Pin Hook was full of porch sitters and store sitters. "If you got a living," they said, "you don't dast leave it." They said it with a fear of the unknown, a fear I had seen in the eyes of their children, and in the eyes of people on starvation in Dallas.

43

Staying all night was a part of Pin Hook life, an event important enough to appear in the "Pin Hook Notes" in the Paris *News*, especially when news was scarce: "The Misses Blank spent Saturday night at the home of Miss Blank." A reader away from Pin Hook might not know that one lived half a mile down the road from the other. I found staying all night a way to know pupils better. Parents would send word by the children that they wanted me to come and stay all night so we could visit. I decided that no matter how poor or crowded the home I would go. Something they said might make me know Pin Hook better; I might work better with a boy or girl knowing what the life was like in the home.

In a few homes I had pie or cake for supper and a bed to myself to sleep in. More often I had cornbread and side meat and beans or greens and slept in a double bed with one of the boys. I learned to know them as teeth gritters, teeth chompers, snorers, and bed wetters, but once I had gone to one place I had to go to others. I could not afford to make anyone feel slighted.

Talk around the fire at night was usually worth the discomfort. There was always talk of school and pupils, the ones that were smart in their books, the ones who had to stay in after school because they were behind. There was usually talk of gathering and plowing and hog killing. Sometimes when the wick had burned low in the lamp we turned to fortune-telling and stories of haints. Some nights we popped corn or parched peanuts in the fireplace. Some nights a young wife or an older daughter would bring out a "ballet book" and we would sing through a dozen or more ballads and songs, with many repetitions of "Little Mohea":

As I walked out for my pleasure one evening in May,
For a sweet recreation, I scarcely can say;
As I fell to amusing myself in the shade,
Oh, who should come near me but a young Indian maid.

She sat down beside me, and taking my hand,
Says she, "You are a stranger, not one of our band,
But if you will follow you're welcome to come
And share in my cottage, the humblest of homes."

The sun was fast sinking far o'er the blue sea,
When I was a-rambling with my pretty Mohea;
Together we wandered, together we roamed,
Till we came to a log hut in a coconut grove.

With kindly expressions, she said unto me,
"If you will consent, sir, and live here with me,
And go no more rambling all o'er the South Sea;
I'll teach you the language of the little Mohea."

"Oh, no, pretty maiden, this never can be;
I have a true lover all o'er the South Sea;
I could not forsake her and live here with thee.
For her heart beats as true as the little Mohea."

This fair young lady, she's handsome and kind
She acted her part as though heaven designed,
For I was a stranger and she took me to her home,
And I think of Little Mohea as I wander alone.

The last time I saw her she stood on the sand,
As our ship passed by her she waved me her hand,
Saying, "When you get back to the girl that you love,
Just think of little Mohea in the coconut grove."

Now I am safe landed on Hudson's green shore,
Where my friends and companions can view me once more;
The girls all crowd around me, but none do I see
That can compare with my little Mohea.

There was no attempt to find out more about the song than could be found in the words and melancholy tune. It was a sad story of love, no matter who the singer or how far from Pin Hook the experience that mingled an Indian maid, the South seas, and a coconut grove.

In one way or another, the people were superstitious, enough to avoid giving a knife for a present because it would cut the love in two, or carrying an ax into the house unless it could be carried out over the same shoulder and with the same number of steps taken backward. They were also religious according to their lights, which were mostly fundamentalist. The Bible said the world was square—that there were four corners to the earth—and they wanted this taught in school. For some it was against the Bible to teach that the world is round. Better not to teach at all than to teach against the Bible.

Once I went to the home of a widower who, his wife dead, kept house with his two daughters. One was in school; the other had to quit because she thought she was too old. I was invited that night because the man had shot a squirrel and the older girl had made squirrel stew.

After a walk of a mile or so through fields and woods we came to a boxed and stripped house facing a road that seemed to go nowhere. We were late getting there and the lamp was already lit on the kitchen table. I talked a little to the man and then we went to the kitchen before supper could get cold.

In the middle of the table there was a bowl of squirrel and flour dumplings, with the squirrel head in the middle, the eyes glazed and staring. We took our chairs and the man returned thanks. When I looked up again I was looking straight at the squirrel eyes. The older girl must have seen the look on my face. Before the bowl was passed to me, she turned the head over. I dipped once and the head turned back. The bowl went around and the others dipped, but the head stayed in the middle, the eyes up. The older girl grew red from embarrassment, the younger from trying to keep from giggling. Without saying we should, we hurried through supper and went to the fireplace room.

The man asked his daughters to sing "Too Late" and the squirrel eyes were forgotton for the moment in the sad words:

> *So you've come back to me once more*
> *The old, old love is growing yet*
> *You've tried through all these many years*
> *You've tried though vainly to forget.*
>
> *So you've come back to me once more*
> *Since time at last has made you free.*
> *To ask again of me the heart*
> *Whose early ties are bound in thee.*
>
> *Come near and let me see your face,*
> *Your chestnut hair is tinged with snow,*
> *Yet still it is the same old face*
> *I loved so many years ago;*
>
> *The same that on that summer's eve*
> *Bent over me and kissed my brow—*
> *Those happy, happy hours of love,*
> *Ah, well, they are all over now.*
>
> *Oh, no, you cannot take my hand,*
> *God ne'er gives us back our youth;*
> *The gulf between can ne'er be spanned,*
> *Our paths must lie apart in sooth.*
>
> *Forgive—you do not speak the word;*
> *You never meant to do me wrong.*
> *God sent this anguish to my heart*
> *To teach me to be brave and strong.*

A woman's soul, a woman's tongue
Must know and speak the truth;
You left me when my heart was sore—
No voice can e'er restore our youth.

Farewell, I think I love you yet
As friend loves friend—God bless you, dear,
And guide you through life's darkest ways
To where the skies are always clear.

We lingered over the words, which were already stretched from stanza to stanza to fit the slow, mournful tune.

The next morning the younger girl and I walked back to school together. There was no mention of the night before until we were around the porch with the other pupils and I was about to take up books. Suddenly she looked at me and giggled.

"Old Squirrel Eyes," she said, and set the others to laughing. In line and marching in she told the story to the ones in front and behind her and with merry impudence said again, "Old Squirrel Eyes."

The nickname stuck far longer than I wanted it to.

I went oftenest to the Swindle home, where I felt as much at home as if it had been my own. Dahlia, a laughing, curly-haired seventh grader, would wait for me to sweep the floors and close up. Sometimes she led her white pony and walked beside me; sometimes she rode and I walked a fast pace to keep up. Either way, we went north to the store and then west across Little Pine Creek, squinting into the setting sun.

The winter rhythm was in force. When we came in sight of the house we could see smoke rising from the chimney and the kitchen flue. By the time we turned in by the well we could see Mr. and Mrs. Swindle on the path from the barn, coming in from milking, their shoulders lopsided from buckets of milk. By the time we put the pony in the barn and came through the hall, Mrs. Swindle was in the kitchen cooking, Mr. Swindle laying more wood on the fire. I was family but also company. Something extra would be done because I was there. Lois, pale and pretty, would come out of the east room, listen up the road, and if she heard nothing, go to the kitchen or fireplace room.

She was listening for Roy Bell's truck. Sometimes, if his trip to Paris had gone well, he would come before sundown, pull off the road, and stop for a little while, a young woodsman with clear blue eyes and ruddy skin, with breeches that fitted close around his knees and ended in high boots with bands of red socks at the tops. His first year out of school, he was logging up and down the creeks and selling the logs in Paris. Lois would stand at the truck or gate with him and I did not have to be told a love story was unfolding.

Lamps lighted, supper called, we went to the table in the kitchen where, as if I had earned it as my own, they gave me the place that had been mine three times a day when I was their hired hand. For me, there was hot bread, sometimes ham fried in amber gravy, sometimes blackberry cobbler, the berries showing purple through cream fresh dipped from a crock or pan. At supper Mr. Swindle talked, of weather, farm work, events he had read in the newspaper. We listened. Our turn would come later.

By the time the dishes were washed and put away, he was in bed, a roundish lump under the covers, with only a point of a moustache or a tuft of white hair showing. Then the rest of us pulled our chairs close to the fire to talk and tell stories and laugh about goings on at school. If we got too loud, if he stirred under the covers, someone would say anxiously, "Did we wake him up?" He would raise his head long enough to say "I ain't dead" and then drop back down on his pillow.

Warned, we talked in whispers till it was time for me to cross the hall and go back to the shed room, glad that I had come.

44

A problem in Faulkner #2, the Negro school in our district, was solved by the trustees before I heard about it. The problem was overcrowding: too many pupils for one teacher in one room. The trustees solved it by dividing the room with wagon sheets strung on a wire and hiring one of the older girls to teach the primer. This done, they asked me to visit the school and report on the teaching.

On a damp gray day in November I left one of the older girls in charge of my room and went on foot across Little Pine Creek and through the woods to the Negro school, an unpainted boxed plank building on a clayey, little-traveled road. First I looked through half-raised windows. The school was full all right, on either side of the dirty gray sheets.

The door half open, I sidled my way in and found myself in the primer room, a gloomy, dank-smelling rectangle no more than ten by twenty. The girl teacher had moved her class close to the window to get what light they could. It was arithmetic time and she was teaching them addition by rote. She glanced at me and went on with her lesson: "One and six is seven." They chanted after her: "One and six is seven."

When I did not move she pointed past the wagon-sheet barrier.
"She in there."

I found an opening and went through. A middle-aged woman sat at a desk hearing some of the younger boys and girls counting to a hundred by fives. They saw me and all work stopped, their eyes on the stranger.

I went close to the desk and gave my name but did not offer to shake hands.

"The trustees wanted me to observe," I told her.
"Yes, suh."

She said it, not hostilely, only matter-of-factly, but she did not make me feel welcome. I looked at the boys and girls waiting for something to happen.

"Will you please continue?" I asked.

She nodded and set another pupil to counting out loud.

I stood by one of the two windows, where the air was fresher, and watched and listened. Boys and girls sat two to a single desk, or in rows on old-fashioned school benches, the kind that had been abandoned in white schools at least ten years earlier. They had books, furnished by the state, the same we were using at the white school, but as I soon saw, the pupils were not graded by achievement or by age, at least not by age. Even the oldest seemed to be in the third or fourth reader.

"Let the man see you at work," the teacher said when there was a rustle of restlessness in the room. To me she said, "You can pass up and down."

Feeling the warmth of so many bodies around me, I went down a row of benches, looking at the books the boys and girls had on their laps. Most of them had not progressed beyond big type and colored pictures, even the ones beginning the gawky age.

I stayed for all of arithmetic and a part of reading. The older boys, I thought, might know enough arithmetic to count the money they would make, or to read the scales in a cotton patch. In reading, they stumbled on the simplest words and, when the teacher told them to spell the words out, they halted at letters in the alphabet. Some had memorized so that they read as well without the book as with it.

Dinner recess came and I was able to talk to the older woman while the girl monitored the playground. The woman did not seem resentful but her voice was sad and troubled.

"I got so many," she said, "I jes' cain't see after 'em all."

I asked about the girl teacher.

"She do her best, but she ain't got no experience. Hers gets noisy, I have to drop what I'm doing and go shet them up. They ain't paying her but ten dollars a month, and that's out a what I'm getting."

The woman had never been off to school. She would never go. She would teach out her years here, secure in the belief that she was doing the best she could. Texas, I knew from classes at Commerce, had many Negro teachers, Negro schools no better than this. Many Texas Negroes could neither read nor write. Many would never have a chance to learn.

I walked away from the racket of the schoolground and through the woods toward Little Pine Creek, my mind full of questions. I did not question the fact that there was a separate school for Negroes. That's how it had always been. I did question the kind of schooling. They needed two rooms, but would not get them, nor a better qualified teacher. Negroes did not pay enough taxes to amount to anything, the whites said. How could they expect anything better?

I went to a trustee to talk about what I had seen, knowing that nothing I could say would change the Pin Hook belief: "You might as well try to educate a mule as a nigger."

Besides, I was reminded, the big room in Faulkner #1 had been divided with wagon sheets before the little room was added.

45

I knew that sooner or later the older boys in my room would try me out in some way of their own. The trying out came just after Thanksgiving and I did not recognize it for what it was, a kind of snipe hunt, without a bag to catch the snipe in. I had spent part of the time before morning recess telling the boys and girls about our Christmas program. Everyone would have to take part, at least in singing the carols. I set three girls to copying three carols on the blackboard: "Silent Night," "O, Little Town of Bethlehem," and "It Came Upon the Midnight Clear." The others copied the words in their tablets, and began memorizing them. There were poems to give out and Santa Clauses to stencil on the blackboard and color. All of them seemed willing to do anything I asked.

At recess some of the bigger boys came out to the steps where I was sitting in the sun.

"Let's go 'possum hunting," Pleas Smith said.

The hunting and trapping season was in. Each morning the air in the schoolroom was tainted with the smell of 'possum and polecat, brought in by boys who had run their traps before school. It was a good way to get Christmas money.

"I wouldn't mind. When do you want to go?"

"How about tomorrow night? It's a good moon and cold enough for 'possums to be after the persimmons. You ever been in the woods over by the old Ward place?"

"Many a time. We used to catch 'possums over there."

Fall, winter, spring I had roamed these woods for hickory nuts, 'possums, sheep sorrel, or just for the pleasure of being in woods that had been only lightly touched by ax or crosscut saw. With the Farmer boys I had followed hounds on the trail through them and slept in their great silences.

"We can eat supper at our house," Pleas said. "We killed hogs. If you was a mind to you could stay all night. It'd be a heap easier'n walking all the way back to Mr. Phillips' house. You and me can sleep in the front room."

He lived at the old Farmer place and I had slept there many times with the Farmer boys. My mother had lived in the house the year I was a hired hand. It would be like going home. I was glad to stay all night.

The next afternoon Pleas helped me sweep and clean up and then, when it was almost sundown, we cut across broom-sage pastures and through woods till we came to a low, unpainted house a mile or so from any other house. Though five years had passed since I had seen it, I could see no change, except that it sagged a little more. The porch was across the front, sheltering the two front rooms and the hall. Smoke was coming from the chimney in the west front room and from a stovepipe in the shed room behind it. My mother had always called it a lonesome place. It looked so to me as we approached it in the dusk.

Mr. and Mrs. Smith, who looked as if they had always worked too hard in the field, met us in the fireplace room and shook hands. She said she was proud to have the teacher. He was glad I did not feel myself too good to come around and see how po' folks live.

"I cleaned the lantern and fed the dogs," he said. He looked at me and laughed. "If they hunt for snipes, don't you hold the bag."

I laughed with him.

"I learned better'n that a long time ago."

Pleas did not laugh with us. For the first time I thought he might have some other kind of snipe hunt in mind.

Mrs. Smith said, "You all can come on in and eat."

She took the lamp from a stand table and we followed her to the kitchen. The table was set, the plates upside down on the oilcloth, the wood-handled knives and forks laid beside the plates, the peppersauce jar and syrup pitcher in the middle. We sat down and she put supper on the table: a big bowl of boiled backbones, a bowl of turnips and greens with pieces of turnips showing white on top, and crackling bread in the pan it was baked in. She sat down and I bowed my head for the blessing. There was none. He said to me, "Go ahead and dig in if you feel like eating it up from my old woman and children."

It was an old joke and he smiled as he said it.

Mrs. Smith told me to not pay attention to him and said, "Help yourself to what you want and then pass your plate for cornbread. I reckon you like crackling bread. Most folks raised in Pin Hook does."

The bread, mixed with pieces of fat meat from which the lard had been rendered, was thick and heavy but rich and chewy with dried cracklings.

"The greens needs peppersauce," she said.

I poured peppersauce from the Mason jar and forked out a couple of pods of long green pepper. Peppery vinegar flavored the greens. To cool my tongue I took alternate bits of meat, greens, and crackling bread.

We ate without much talking and finished with molasses poured on crackling bread for a sweet. Just as we leaned back at the table we heard the faraway sounds of blowing on fists.

"Time to go," Pleas said. "They'll get there agin we do."

We were meeting two other boys at the persimmon trees on the other side of the first patch of woods. Pleas took the lantern and a flashlight and called the dogs from under the house. In moonlight almost as bright as day we crossed a stretch of pasture and took a trail through the woods, walking under oaks with half-bare branches, wading ankle deep in drying leaves.

"Good night for hunting," Pleas said. "Dew's wet enough for the dogs to trail good."

He blew on his fist and there was a quick answer.

"They beat us there."

We came to the persimmon trees and saw the two boys like shadows in the moonlight.

"Any 'possums?" Pleas asked.

"I shined my light but I ain't seen no eyes," one of the boys said. "They ought to be here. I never tasted better persimmons."

Pleas traced the trunks and branches with his light.

"They ain't out yet. We'll come back this way. I'll bound you they's a possum here then."

We gathered persimmons for ourselves and followed the dogs into the woods, chewing the sugary sweet fruit, forcing out the flat, oval-shaped seeds between tight lips. We let the dogs lead and kept up as well as we could. They roamed ahead, around, at times behind us, all the time getting deeper and deeper into the woods. When they were close we could hear them running in the leaves; when they were farther away, we had to listen for the bark that would tell us they had hit a trail. Pleas held us together with the light of the lantern.

"Don't get lost, " he said to us. "If you get separated, stay where you are and holler. Sound carries on a night like this."

When we were deep in the woods we heard the dogs, far ahead of us, barking on a trail. Pleas stopped and the lantern made a circle of light at his feet. We came up to him and stood listening to the dogs as they circled and circled and then seemed to be barking together in one place.

"Treed," Pleas said.

He started running and soon the lantern was a point of light flickering in and out among the trees. We ran after him but I was soon falling behind, stumbling over leaf-covered limbs, barking my shins on logs and tree trunks. For a time I lost sight of the lantern but I could hear the dogs.

When I came up to them the dogs were rearing against the trunk of a big red oak and barking frantically. Pleas and the other boys were flashing their lights up among the branches. Suddenly Pleas spied him, and yelled.

"I see him, way up there. Must be a coon."

He gave me the light and I moved it till I found a pair of eyes, shining like blue-green jewels fifty feet up.

How to get him down? The tree had a wide spread of branches, the lowest at least twenty feet from the ground. It had shaded out other growth and stood alone. The trunk was too large for anyone to get a leg around and there were no toeholds. Pleas flashed his light up among the branches and circled the tree. The coon followed the light but did not come down.

"We've got to try to chunk him out," Pleas said.

They broke dead branches into clubs and threw them as high as they could. Sticks rattled against branches but missed the coon by twenty feet. He did not move.

"Consarnit," one of the boys said.

When the moon was riding high enough for midnight the dogs settled down from their barking and the boys gave up. They stood around the lantern talking, trying to decide whether chances were better on the upland or along the creek. Pleas decided on the creek and led the dogs whimpering away from the tree.

After a time we were walking among sweet gums and through patches of cane green and shoulder high. Leaves under foot were wet and the woods smelled of dampness.

"Good for mink," Pleas said.

We came to Little Pine Creek and followed up it till we came to a place narrow enough for leaping. As we went, the dogs picked up trails, barked excitedly for a few minutes, and then lost them in water as a mink or a coon took to the creek to shake the dogs.

Tired and chilled, we went back away from the creek and found a knoll where huckleberries grew. We built a fire, and while we warmed ourselves, bent huckleberry bushes down and quenched our thirst with frost-sweetened berries. We huddled close to each other and laughed at the kind of hunters we had turned out to be. I did not really mind that we had caught nothing. It was a fine night to be in the woods and all of us would be better for it.

"Can you spell huckleberry?" I asked them.

They laughed at me, the teacher. This was a 'possum hunt, not a spelling match.

"I'll tell you a new way."

Standing close to the fire, I spelled it a way I had learned it long ago at Pin Hook:

H U buckle, B U buckle,
H U buckle Y;

H U buckle, B U buckle,
Huckleberry pie.

They laughed and then had me say it over till they knew it.
Then they said rhymes they remembered:

Up the hill and over the level,
Grandma's hounddog chased the devil

and

Did you eaver ever over in your leef life lofe
See the divel devil dovel beat his weef wife wofe?

Then they wanted to teach me their way of spelling Constantinople. Laughing self-consciously a boy said:

Gitchigee, gitchiguy,
Gitchi Constanti,
Gitchi nople, gitchi pople
Gitchi Constantinople.

We ran out of rhymes and were three miles or more into the
woods. I wanted to turn back. They were not ready to go.
From the looks they exchanged I began to feel they were not
ready for me to go. They wanted to cross the creek again and
go on toward the Ward pasture. We could count on a 'possum
in some persimmon trees and polecats sometimes holed up in
the banks of gullies up out of the woods. I reminded them with
some firmness that we had school the next day, but they were
determined to go on.

"We ain't wanting to go back without'n some 'possums," they
said.

We talked until I began to feel that they were after the teacher
more than the 'possums. It was not a snipe hunt but they wanted
me to have a turn at holding the bag. Knowing I could not make
them turn back, I agreed to go on. I had hunted the Ward pastures
at night before and could hunt them again.

Pleas called the dogs and struck out with the lantern. We crossed
the creek and a long stretch of bottom woods. At the edge of a
pasture we came to a clump of persimmon trees. The dogs began

barking and Pleas focused his flashlight on a pair of eyes high up in the branches.

"'Possum," he said. "You hold the dogs and I'll shake him down."

I took the lantern, the boys held the dogs. Pleas climbed partway up the tree and began shaking it with a rhythmic swaying back and forth. The 'possum crawled to the end of a branch and swung farther and farther out. Then his hold gave way and he fell, a furry lump.

"Sull him," Pleas yelled and swung to the ground.

One of the boys put a foot on him and he sank into the grass and leaves, looking dead, "playing 'possum." Pleas jerked him up by the tail and held a flashlight on him.

"Good'un," he said. He handed him to one of the other boys. "You tote him."

The 'possum stayed sulled. The only sign of life was in the curl of the tail wrapped around the boy's hand.

Pleas swept the trees again with his flashlight and then started at a fast pace up into the pastures, following gullies cut deep in the earth. A scent of polecat hung in the air but the dogs were not able to roust one. The moon was bright enough in the open for us to walk without a lantern. Indian file, we followed Pleas along a gully, going farther and farther away.

Suddenly Pleas stopped.

"Ready to call it quits?"

All of us were ready, and I felt relieved. If they had planned a trick on me, the chance had passed. I wanted to take what I remembered as the shortest cut along old trails. They wanted to go another way, a little longer but through woods rarely hunted. We might find another 'possum. Pleas took the lantern but did not light it.

"It's light enough for us to spread out with the dogs and cover a lot of woods going through," he said.

We kept together to the edge of the woods. Then, with the dogs ranging ahead of us, we spread a hundred yards apart, with me at about the center.

"They's an old road on the other side," Pleas said. "I'll light the lantern when I get there and you come to it."

They were soon out of hearing and I began my walk through the woods, in leaves ankle deep, pushing aside limbs and bushes, stopping to listen for rustling, or to look for rounded shapes among the branches. After a time I began to smell something dead—a cow or something. I hoped the dogs would smell it. You could nearly always find a 'possum around something dead. I stopped to listen but there was no sound of dogs or boys. The farther I went, the stronger the smell. Leaves high on the branches shut out the moon and I was walking in a strange glow of light and darkness, and breathing the smell of death.

Trying to go faster, trying to escape from whatever surrounded me, I bumped into a sapling hard enough to make the upper limbs crack against a tree. There was a noise, a flapping of wings and I looked up to see a shape, a big bird struggling to fly and thrashing against branches. Then there were more noises, more flapping and crashing into branches. Buzzards. A buzzard's roost. They had walked me into the stench and filth of a buzzard's roost. Buzzards woke buzzards. All overhead buzzards were flying and trying to fly, strange shapes in the strange light, and the air was filled with the sound of flapping and crashing and the sickening smell of carrion.

I tried to turn back but could not find my way. There was nothing to do but push on ahead. I tried running but my crashing only stirred the buzzards to wilder flapping. Then I tried crouching, stooping under branches, feeling my way past tree trunks. After a time I noticed that the buzzards had quieted down. The stench was less and I was outside their roost.

I came to the old road and saw the lantern light half a mile on toward home. When I came up to it the boys were waiting quietly. I expected them to say something about buzzards but they did not. Neither did I. If it was a trick they had played on me, everyone at school would know the next day. So would I.

After a long silent walk the two boys went their way and Pleas and I went to his house. He put the 'possum under an iron washpot in the yard. In the front room he blew out the lamp and we lay side by side in a double bed. Long after he was in a deep sleep I could hear buzzards flapping and even my underclothes smelled of rotting flesh.

46

Preparation for the Christmas program took more and more of our time. The days were full and happy and peaceful. If the older boys had been trying me out on the hunt, I had apparently met their test. They never mentioned the buzzard roost; they did everything they could to help get ready for Christmas. I had decided against a Christmas tree. Too many boys and girls would have no presents at all, either on the tree or at home. It was not fair to make them watch while some man in a Santa Claus mask handed out presents to other children and the teachers. In the program, any child who wanted to say a piece could. They were all expected to come on the stage and sing carols.

The week before Christmas we put up a platform at the end of the big room for the stage. Two of the girls brought sheets for curtains and with safety-pin holders hooked them to a wire clothesline strung from wall to wall. Then we began decorating. People in Pin Hook rarely had Christmas trees or decorations in their homes. Everything we used had to come from the woods. With some of the older boys I roamed up and down Little Pine Creek cutting branches of red haw and pieces of stretchberry vine. The red berries and green leaves could be arranged to look like holly. We added some pieces of pine brought from down toward Red River. We had no ribbons, no ornaments, but we did have a look of Christmas.

Friday morning we brought the children from both rooms together and went through the final practice. Friday afternoon we dusted erasers, washed blackboards, and cleared off desks. Then we let the children go early to get dressed and return with their families. I swept the floor and built up the fire in the black-jacketed stove. Last, when dark was coming on, I lit lanterns and hung them as well as I could to light the stage. Then, for a little while, I could warm myself at the stove and enjoy the Christmas scene we had built.

Soon after dark families began arriving on foot and in wagons. Women sent their children to the little room and squeezed themselves into seats made for fifth and sixth graders. Men stood around the outside, talking. They would come in at the beginning of the program. The room was warm and a smell of coal oil hung in the air. The excitement of Christmas was with the children in the little room. I could detect none among the parents.

When the time came I gave my final shush to the children and stood in the center of the stage, waiting for the two boys to slide the curtains back to the walls. There was a sound of safety pins sliding on wire and I was face to face with the audience, husbands and wives scrooched together on narrow seats, some men and older boys standing with their backs against the coat room walls, their eyes invisible in the shadows, the reddish lantern light turning to a glow on their cheeks. Most of Pin Hook was there, the Methodists, Baptists, Holinesses, the believers and unbelievers, silently awaiting the opening prayer.

I bowed my head and began "Our Father, Who art in heaven . . ." They bowed their heads in silence, most of them too shy to pray in public except in revival meetings. One of the Holinesses, an older woman, large enough to take up a seat by herself, began a kind of descant, beginning after me and finishing before me, in a voiced whisper that reached me as *glory, glory, glory* and *praise His holy name.* I finished the prayer, stepped out of the way of the curtain pullers, and motioned Mignonne to send the big boys and girls in for the first carol.

They shuffled in, shy and frightened, and took their places, girls in front rows, boys in back. There was a reedy sound from the organ and then they began "O, little town of Behtlehem, how still we see thee lie . . .," too softly and then stronger as they found their voices. I stood with a curtain puller where I could see without being seen. At that moment I understood best what it meant to be

213

a country schoolteacher, seeing every head turned toward the stage, seeing tired country faces brought to life with music, with pride in the singers, with memories of a procession of Christmases back to the times when they were the singers.

Again I was at the center of the stage, welcoming the people, telling them how proud we were of their boys and girls. There was not even a handclap when I finished—Pin Hookers almost never applauded—but their faces glowed feelings as warm as mine.

Mignonne brought the boys and girls from her room in for their first song and then gave her own welcome to the parents. She did not sound like a town girl; she sounded like a country school-teacher.

Piece after piece, song after song, we went through the program. I knew it was going well. Boys and girls, as they finished their parts, went around outside to the front door and crowded along the walls. They had seen it, no telling how many times before, and were still eager to watch another time. I knew also by the way people said to boys and girls, "You sure done good."

When only "Silent Night" was left, I called on Mr. Phillips to say a few words. He came and stood in front of the platform, his shoulders a little bent from years of hard farm work, the strength of his face half-hidden in the shadows. In a voice that commanded attention, he began with praise for "these young people who are doing so much for our children." Then he talked to the children, urging on them the need to study hard, to get an education. It was the kind of talk I had heard from him when I was a boy. I could almost hear the words I had heard so many times: "If you don't get your schooling, you'll spend your life following old Beck down a cotton row." I looked at the boys and girls crowded at the back of the room. They were listening, but I could not tell by the looks on their faces whether they would be better pupils because of his talk. He ended with words to old and young alike, words in which his voice trembled with seriousness. He had come to the plea with which he ended most of his talks, a plea for religious humility and moral righteousness. He brought us close to the Judgment gates and then eased us back to the close of our Christmas program.

He went back to his seat and I called all the boys and girls to the platform. After some pushing and giggling they found their places, the little ones in front, the tall ones at the back. A chord on the organ and they began "Silent night, holy night." They no longer needed me, or Mignonne. They were singing together, and better than anyone had thought they could. I went to the porch and then out in the yard to hear the sounds floating into the night.

The song ended. The boys pulled the curtains to. People began crowding toward the door. Some who had known me a long time said to me, "I knowed you'd be a good teacher."

When the people had gone, I went first through the little room, putting it in shape to leave it for Christmas. Then I went to the big room. The sheets had been taken down but I had to knock the boards of the platform loose and stack them outside. Then I straightened the desks and swept the floor. When there was nothing else to be done, I blew out the lanterns and shut the front door.

Pin Hook was dark and I could see only the shapes of houses as I passed.

47

For the week of Christmas I was in Dallas in the midst of family and family problems. My mother still had not got used to living in town, and told us again that she never would. She talked of how much good a visit to Pin Hook, even for a few days, would do her. She talked once, quietly, tremulously, of going back to keep house for me, if I could find a house, but then she had the other boys to think about. Charles was working and she had to help stretch his money as far as it would go. Roy had played a season on the football team and was passing in school. Better for him to stay where he was. Dewey did not have a job, and she worried about him most. He was now twenty-nine, still a bachelor, shy when strangers came around, increasingly secretive about himself. He would read long stretches at a time and then pace the floor with feverish eyes and restless turns of his body. At times he became angry because he could not find work, and bitter because he was not carrying his part of the family load.

He needed a job. Even more, I thought, he needed friends. On a Sunday night we took him to a young people's meeting at the First Baptist Church. My friends welcomed me and tried to bring him into the group, but he remained at the side, standing awkwardly, sitting awkwardly, speaking when he was spoken to and no more. Only once did he relax, and that was during a period of entertainment, when a young man with a deep bass voice sang "Asleep in the Deep."

His expression remained almost unchanged through the song to the last line: "Many brave hearts are asleep in the deep, so beware, beware." Then there was almost laughter on his lips, in his eyes as the singer took the last *beware* down an octave a note at a time. Not the words but the performance had touched him, I could see.

When we were on the streetcar going home Dewey said to me what he had said before, "You've got the gift of gab. I don't."

Before we got home I knew he had to leave the city. He would be better off at Pin Hook or anywhere else in the country than he was in Dallas. That night I worked out a plan. I would take him and my mother back to Pin Hook through New Years. They would have a good time visiting. Dewey might find a place somewhere working on a farm.

We went, but Dewey did not go with us. He backed out the morning we were ready to start, on the excuse that he might miss a job. I thought there must be something else. So did my mother. No matter what we said, he would not go.

48

January brought a little snow, a little ice, and weather cold enough to keep us indoors most of the time, with the boys and girls taking turns warming themselves at the stove. Unable to wear themselves out with sheep-board's down or wolf over the river, they fidgeted around the stove or made too many trips to the water fountain or privy. When I was writing on the board I could hear whispering and at times a book pushed from a desk to the floor. I reprimanded them gently and then severly. Misbehavior increased. I tried keeping the worst noise makers in after school. They looked on this as a favor. If they were kept in long enough they got out of carrying wood and water at home.

Every day they were bolder and all I had left for control was the switch. I cut new birch limbs and stood them in the corner. For a few days the room was quiet. Then, on a gray afternoon, when the pupils were more restless than usual. I caught one of the boys hitting another in the back. I knew that if I lost control of him I would lose control of the school. I moved him up near my desk, close enough to be able to watch him till school was out and the others had gone home. With sullen looks and shrugs of his shoulders he let the others know he was not, as they said, "a-scai'd o' the teacher." Boys in trouble backed each other up with, "He c'n kill me but he sho God cain't eat me."

When we were alone in the room I was not certain what to do. My instructions from the trustees were clear enough: Don't be easy on them. Better to whup early than late. I had caught this boy making trouble and they would expect me to whip him. I was not certain that I wanted to whip him, or whether I could force myself to. I laid two switches across my desk and faced him with his crime. He did not deny it. If I did not whip him now he would tell the others and I would have more trouble. I took up a switch and took him by the left arm where I could whack him on the backs of his legs. I raised the switch and was glad he could not see how much I was wavering.

Suddenly he began crying.

"I won't be mean any more," he said.

I knew then that I had an excuse not to whip him and was relieved.

"How do I know?" I asked him.

He wiped a sleeve across his face.

"If you give me a whupping, I'll get another'n when I get home. I won't do it again."

217

I knew his family well enough to know the kind of whipping he would get at home. Licks from me would mean welts at home. I had to let him go and take my chances with the others.

"I'll let you go this time," I told him, "but don't you let me catch you again. I'll skin you alive."

He let the tears roll down his cheeks and drop on his shirt.

"No, sir. C'n I go home, sir?"

I watched him out the door. Then I put back my switches and took up the broom.

Before the next day was over a woman said to me, "I heered you didn't switch him. I heered you let him go. What's your reasons?"

As my real reasons would never have been understood by her I gave her another, not true.

"I gave him a good tongue lashing. Next time he does it I'll skin him alive."

She was not willing to let me off.

"They say he just had to cry a little and you give in." Her laugh had little knives in it. "You mark my words, they done lernt that crying's easier'n taking a licking any day."

Whatever he told the other boys and girls, they were quieter and as tractable as they had been the first day of school.

Then there was another kind of trouble. For the first time, seventh-grade pupils would be required to take county-wide examinations. They were afraid. So was I, and eager for them to perform well. I began drilling them daily. At first they were all below average on the sample tests I gave them. Then one girl was far ahead of the others, especially in civics and composition. At first I praised her and then knew she was copying from books. I found some of the passages, copied almost word for word, and showed them to one of the trustees.

"You'll have to whup her," he said.

When I showed them to her, she began to cry.

"I didn't mean to do anything wrong. I wanted to do good on the test and I didn't know enough. If you won't whup me, I won't do it again." I did not whip her and she did not copy again. In fact, she hardly studied again. She made up her mind not to take the test, and I could not persuade her.

218

49

Then a never-lifting shadow was cast over my family. Dewey had disappeared. Without a word to my mother he had gone off—in search of work, of a new life? We did not know. I first learned of it from my mother, in an anxiety-filled letter written in pencil on a scrap of tablet paper. Two questions were uppermost in her mind: Where he had gone? Why he had gone? I had no answer for the first. The second I thought I knew. It lay not in anything we had done but in the harshness of the city and in his own nature, his inability to cope with the city. I could see now that he was by temperament a recluse and a romantic, a recluse too conscientious to exist on the work of others, a romantic imbued with a dream of finding a better life on some other road.

I worried over the ways I had failed him as a brother, the times when I went with friends when I could have gone with him, the impatience I had expressed that in business school he had learned to write a better hand but not enough of office skills to hold a job in an office. My conscience hurt most over the book he had been writing on so many years. It had seemed absurd to me that, with no schooling beyond the fifth grade, he should be trying to write a book. I discouraged him, not knowing then that it is better to write than not to write once the urge becomes compelling.

More of his story came from my mother. She had heard from him in Houston, where he was staying in a cheap hotel. He had been living among Bohemians in South Texas, perhaps doing farm work though he did not say so. He was waiting, for what he did not say. We thought later that he might have been waiting for a ship to South America. He had once confided a dream of going to South America and starting all over again.

There was never another word. we had neither the money nor the knowledge to make a search for him. We delayed in hope that we would hear again, as we had before when he had dropped out of sight for a time. Then my mother began listing his name in the missing-persons columns of farm magazines.

At first there was hope and then despair, and for me, anger, especially at one faker who claimed to be Dewey. From many there was also sympathy and understanding. We were still close to the frontier, and the frontier was full of stories of men and boys who had simply disappeared, never to be heard from again. There were also the stories of Confederate soldiers who marched away and never returned, stories repeated in my family one generation after another. Despair over lost sons had been distilled into the song "Where Is My Wandering Boy Tonight." In my early days in Dallas Aunt Vick, whose own son had spent his youth wandering, where she never knew, sat in front of a phonograph, her eyes sometimes alight with understanding, sometimes dulled when her mind was clouded with forgetfulness, irrationality, listened over and over again to a haunting voice singing the haunting words:

> *Where is my wand'ring boy tonight,*
> *The boy of my tend'rest care.*
> *The boy that was all my joy and light,*
> *The child of my love and prayer?*
> *O where is my boy tonight?*
> *O where is my boy tonight?*
> *My heart o'er-flows, for I love him he knows;*
> *O where is my boy tonight?*

Even with the many disappointments, the continuing silence, my mother never gave up hope.

50

Corn planting began in late February. School would be over before corn-thinning time. Some of the boys had to stay out for flat-breaking and bedding land. In spite of compulsory school laws some never came back to school at all. They sent back their books.

I would have to send them report cards marked "Retained." Almost before I knew it we were working toward the end of the school year and the closing exhibition.

Pin Hookers looked forward to a play at the end of school, with skits and jokes and songs between acts. Except for it they had no drama, unless they managed to go to a picture show in Paris on a Saturday afternoon. I could look back on *The Winning of Latane* and other plays put on by the school in the past. The people wanted enough comedy for some good laughs, and a love story that ended happily.

Finding a play was fairly easy. In the T. S. Denison catalogue I could get the names, plots, and number of characters of two dozen or more recommended plays for small schools or country schools, including three popular in Lamar County: *A Poor Married Man, A Winning Widow,* and *That's One on Bill.* With my own limited knowledge of plays and how to put them on I decided to use one of these rather than try something new. Getting a boy and girl to play the leads was not so easy. In all Pin Hook there were no more than a dozen girls of acceptable age, and some of them were too shy to stand up before a crowd and say a piece or act out a piece. The most likely one was Lois Swindle, who came to school irregularly and studied whatever pleased her. She was fair-haired, pretty, of a romantic turn of mind, and willing to take a part if Roy Bell could. I offered him a part and he took it.

Practice started and in no time at all I was involved in parallel love stories: theirs and the one in the play. The one in the play was fixed, theirs constantly changing. From the first read-through all of us had trouble distinguishing between real life and play life, between real names and play names.

The play cast, I worked at other parts of the program. M. E. Bruce, a very pretty girl, wanted to do blackface with jokes and jigs and a fiddler to play breakdown tunes. There also had to be a tableau, with tableau powder burning to light up a scene. People always expected a tableau.

Play rehearsals had to be at night, in the big room, under the light of a coal-oil torch. We could build an outdoor stage but we could not have scenery. I had only words and voices and country boys and girls with which to create a life never seen in Pin Hook.

5 1

One night I came home from play practice to find another man in my bed, asleep and snoring. I lit the lamp and saw that it was a wandering farmhand who stayed around the countryside, working for room and board, when there was work to be done, moving on when the work ran out. At once I knew what this meant. Spring work was piling up and he had been hired. The only place for him to sleep was with me. It was too late for me to say anything that night, so I crawled in beside him. But there was little sleep for me. I was awakened time and again by his snoring and the grinding sound of his teeth.

The next morning when I was on my way out to school Mrs. Phillips came down the gallery toward the kitchen.

"I cain't sleep with him," I said.

"Why?"

"He grits his teeth and no telling when he's had a bath."

There was a flush in her face and an edge in her voice.

"It's as good as you was ever used to."

For the first time since I had come back to Pin Hook I was being reminded of the kind of life I had had as a child. To her, it was as if I had never been away from Pin Hook or got used to other things, like having a bed to myself. She was firm.

"He's working for us and he's got to have a place to sleep."

Mr. Phillips was already in the field. I would have to wait till night to tell him I was paying board and should not have to share my bed with anybody else.

All day I worried over what had happened. I had come back, partly with the aim of proving that I could be somebody in Pin Hook, and now I felt that I had failed.

That night I walked home with Dahlia Swindle and slept in the shed room where I had slept when I was their hired hand. I made a joke about sleeping with the hired hand but they knew I was not joking.

"You can stay with us," they said.

"I'll have to talk to Mr. Phillips," I said.

The next night I had my bed to myself. The man had gone on to some other place. Mr. Phillips did not bring the question up. Neither did I. I knew without their saying it that when another hired hand came along I would have to sleep with him, and like many other people in Pin Hook, they would not think it unreasonable.

The next afternoon I took my stuff in my suitcase and moved to the Swindles', to the shed room. It was like going home. The roof leaked and the dog was raising a batch of whimpering puppies under the floor. I had to walk a mile farther to school and would not make it when the creek was up. Still I felt more myself with a room of my own and sure that I could bring school to the end with a good program.

52

One warm afternoon, after slogging in deep mud through fields and up the road, I came home to find Mrs. Swindle waiting for me on the porch.

"Lois wants to see you," she said. "She's waiting in her room. Just go on in."

I pushed the hall door open and put a foot across the door sill. The dark green shades were half drawn and there was a dim green-gold light in the room. Lois was sitting on the side of the bed, her pink-white skin and pale hair a glow in the shadows.

"Roy's quit me."

Her voice was sad, close to tears.

I began to worry. He had missed the last play practice without saying a word to me. If he and Lois were at outs, there would be no play. Something had to be done, for her sake, for their sake, for the sake of the play. Reluctantly, she answered my questions. She had not seen him or heard from him since the last play practice. She was afraid she would never see him again.

"If I could only see him and talk to him."

"You will—tomorrow night at play practice," I told her, but she would not believe me. There was a party that night at Woodland and he had not asked her. She was sure he would go. He might be taking another girl.

"You want me to go find out?"

She wanted me to go and she wanted to go with me, but not to go in. She would feel too plagued to go in, but she would wait in the car. He could come out and talk to her if he wanted to.

At dark we took Mr. Swindle's model-T coupe and went down the road toward Little Pine Creek. Lois was silent and I had all I could do to keep the wheels in the ruts and the motor from stalling. We got to the creek bridge, past the deepest mud of the bottom road, but we still had a red clay hill to climb before we came to sand again. By double-clutching and racing the motor I got up the hill. We let the motor cool a bit and then the going was fairly easy till we got to the crossroads at Pin Hook. There were lights in houses but no one out to see us or to wonder where we could be going.

Three miles to Woodland. A half-mile up the Detroit road. I got out and in the car lights examined the road. A car had gone through and opened ruts.

"We've got somebody ploughing out ruts," I told Lois. "If they make it, we can."

The party might be over when we got there. Roy might not be there at all. Still we had to go on. In low gear we crawled past houses with lamps burning, a lamp to a house, in kitchen or front room.

We came to Woodland and turned right and slowly climbed a hill. The party was going on. There were lights in every room and we could see people on the porch and standing in doorways. I stopped the car in the road and we sat watching the people as they came and went. After a time Lois leaned across me.

"There's Roy," she said in a low, intense voice. "See him?"

I saw him, standing just inside the front door, the light from a lamp reddish on his face and hair.

"I'll go get him," I said.

"Wait," Lois cried. She was no longer looking at him. "I don't know what to say to him when I see him. He was the one that broke us up."

I got back in the car and waited and talked to her. If she did not want to talk to him in front of me, she did not have to. I could get him and go down the road out of earshot. She did not want that either. She had been slighted and did not know what she wanted. Then she could not bear to have him see her there.

"Let's go home," she said.

Feeling that we had been on a wild-goose chase, I got out and cranked the car, turned it around in the road, and we began the trip back, with nothing to say to each other. On the clay hill above Little Pine Creek I got a wheel into a deep rut and could not get it out. I tried pulling backward and forward till I could hear the water in the radiator boiling. There was nothing to do but leave the car and walk home.

We took off our shoes and I rolled up my pants legs to my knees. The earth was cold to our bare feet. At times we walked in almost liquid mud, at times on sharp sand. The sky was luminous with stars and the milky way, but the ground was shadowed and we could not see where to step.

I was both sympathetic and baffled. Nothing had been settled and I would have to call off the next play practice. I might have to call off the play. My courses in education had not prepared me for anything like this. Worse, I had no one to talk to or turn to for help.

53

On the road through Pin Hook the next morning people stopped me with the question: "You gonna have a play?" When I said yes they said, "I heered Roy and Lois was broke up." At school, boys and girls asked me the same question. It was time to begin building the stage outside. At the first recess I started the boys laying logs for the foundation.

The mail carrier brought a letter from the dean's office at Paris Junior College. The principal's job at Forest Hill was open and I would be recommended if I wanted to apply. It was a three-teacher, seven-month school and the salary was one hundred and fifty dollars a month. I would teach the seventh, eighth, and ninth grades, and the tenth if there were any pupils. Forest Hill was north of Petty, in a part of Lamar County I had never seen before. The job was better than anything I could ever hope for at Pin Hook—a real step up for a country schoolteacher.

On Saturday morning, with the problem of the play still unresolved, I borrowed a car in Paris and drove west through Brookston and High and on to Petty. Then I turned off north on a dirt road that was wet but not too sticky for a car. On either side there was good farmland, more gray than black, much better than the sandy land at Pin Hook. People had better houses, some of them painted white, and some of them had cars.

The first glimpse I had of the school was across a stretch of prairie. It was a white building, bigger than the Pin Hook school, on a treeless ground, the girls' privy on one side to the back, the boys' on the other. I drove up to it and sat in front staring at the closed doors and windows. Everything looked fresh and clean. It would be a good place to work.

I spent most of my time with one trustee, Mr. White. He was friendly and as we talked I learned he and the other trustees had already asked about me at Pin Hook and that my recommendations were good. They had asked before the play became a problem and I did not mention it. Then he told me why they were not rehiring the principal. He was not a good disciplinarian. The big boys ran over him. They preferred basketball to books and he let them have nearly every Friday evening off for basketball. The trustees did not object to basketball; they did object to running all over that part of the county to play games. The trustees felt they had to make a change, though school was not yet out and they had not told the principal. What they wanted was a man who could control the pupils. If a boy was caught smoking or swearing, they wanted a man who would set him straight with a good whipping.

Before the day was over I had seen enough of Forest Hill to be willing to adjust to almost anything the trustees might ask. I liked the looks of the community. I liked the people I had met. It would be a good place to settle down in, and much as I liked being in Pin Hook, I had decided against settling down there.

I left wihout a promise of a job but with the feeling that the job could be mine, if nothing went wrong at Pin Hook before a contract could be signed.

Eager to get back—to talk to Lois and Roy about the play—I walked out from Paris toward sundown and caught a ride to Pin Hook on a logging truck.

Pat met me at the gate, home unexpectedly for a visit. He had already talked to Lois. The next day he would talk to Roy.

For me, everything looked better. He had traveled the country many times and crisscross in every direction during the five years since we had gone our own ways from Dallas. He had worked at many jobs, and lived through many times when he had no job at all. I was older in years; he now seemed older in experience, but not hardened by all he had gone through, or less ready to laugh at the garbled line of a neighbor who had asked, "Did your tomatoes get killed by the frost and potatoes?" I knew more about books; he knew more about life. I began counting on his knowledge of life.

54

I never knew what Pat said to Lois or to Roy. One afternoon when I came home from school he took me outside for a talk.

"Everything's all right with Lois and Roy," he told me. "He's coming over to see her tonight."

Roy was there that night. The next night we were back at play practice after missing about a week. Again people stopped me on the road. "I heered you was putting on the play all right." "Yes." "Lois and Roy still in it?" "Yes." "It ought to be a good'un." There had never been anything like it before in Pin Hook: a play with the same couple acting out a love story at the same time they were living their own love story.

One night when I came home from play practice I paused at the yard gate and looked through the window. Mrs. Swindle was sitting by a lamp with sewing on her lap and a magazine in her hand. The light shone on her face and her hair, turning it white where it was pushed back from her forehead. There was a look of peace, of serenity. Suddenly I could see a tableau: Mrs. Swindle sitting just so on stage with Mignonne singing "You Are a Wonderful Mother." It would do us all good.

When I went in, she showed me the pink crepe de chine on her lap. She was making a wedding dress for Lois. On the Saturday a week before the play Lois and Roy were going to Paris to get married. Mrs. Swindle was willing to be in a tableau.

The boys and I worked after school finishing the stage and setting planks on blocks of woods for seats. I took the two girls who had completed the seventh grade to Paris to the countywide graduation, and while in town, signed a contract to teach at the Forest Hill school.

The last week of school we practiced every night till near midnight. The play was going well and Lois and Roy as husband and wife were better in it than they had ever been as sweethearts. After practice, in the warm night air, I walked through woods and fields to the creek and on the road to the house. They were happy walks. I felt sure that I was what I wanted to be: a good country school-teacher.

55

By sundown the night of the play I knew we had not built enough benches for the people to sit on. All day long boys and girls had been telling me who was coming. One of the boys said, "It looks like everybody and his dogs and cousins is coming." They had heard of people coming from Woodland, Novice, Walnut Ridge, Post Oak. The ones coming so far in wagons had to be on their way.

By dusk people began arriving on foot, the pupils in school among them. By good dark, headlights of a few cars shone on the road. Men drove their wagons close enough to sit on their own chairs and springseats and watch the play.

We had curtained the stage with wagon sheets. Two coal-oil torches lighted either end, and we had hung coal-oil lanterns for lights at the back. We could have only one stage entrance and that was from the little room, where the boys and girls in the play had to dress and make up and where the others had to wait for their turn on the program.

When we were later than we should have been, the boys pulled the curtains for me and I stepped forward to make my welcoming speech. Never had I seen so many people at a Pin Hook gathering —school or revival or graveyard working. The benches were filled and people sat wherever they could on quilts on the ground. Behind them, people stood, so far back that the lights barely showed pale outlines of faces. Farther out, where they could see but not be seen, more people waited in their wagons for the play to begin. They listened to me politely, but they had come to see Lois and Roy in the play.

The curtains closed and opened again, this time on the first act of the play. When Lois came on wearing her pink wedding dress, her face flushed a livelier pink, I could hear women whispering, "My, ain't she purty." "She's as purty as a doll."

We got through the first act with a minimum of prompting and it was time for M. E. and me to do our blackface. While a fiddler and guitar sawed and picked into "Eighth of January" we pulled black stockings over our faces. Her costume was an old dress that came to her ankles; mine, overalls big enough for me to put on over my clothes. The crowd was silent when we came on, but they began laughing when M. E. pretended to be rubbing clothes on a washboard. I jigged past her and said, "You knowed my name?" She shook her head. "Ain't never knowed yo' name." "You knowed my face?" "Never knowed yo' face." People began to laugh again at the joke we were acting out. "When does you wash?" "I washes Tuesdays and Thursdays in the same old place." Then, with arms waving and feet flying, we danced an exaggerated dance, making most of it up as we went. As we danced off the stage together we knew it had not been much of a dance but it had been funny to Pin Hookers.

The tableau came after the second act. The lights had to be turned low or blown out and the curtains left open. Then Mrs. Swindle came and sat in a rocking chair, a dark shadow, holding a magazine and with sewing at her side, waiting for the tableau powders to burst into flame. I put the powders in a bucket lid on the edge of the stage and stood at one side with match in hand. Mignonne, out of sight, her voice soft and sentimental, sang words that reached out to the people in wagons and beyond:

> *You are a wonderful mother, dear old mother of mine,*
> *You hold a spot down deep in my heart where the stars will*
> *always shine . . .*

By now the audience had heard enough words to know what to expect. I struck a match to the tableau powders and stepped back to watch a scene that was both dramatic and beautiful. The words might have been written for Mrs. Swindle. Her face, naturally dark, some said from Indian blood, was composed and serene. She had combed her hair and piled it in such a way that the white on top took on a pinkish glow in the red light. She sat motionless, appearing unaware of the part she was playing, as the words rolled hauntingly over the crowd:

> *The moon never beams without bringing me dreams of that*
>   *wonderful mother of mine,*
> *The stars never rise but I see the bright eyes of that*
>   *wonderful mother of mine . . .*

The flames rose till the whole scene was suffused with red from a light that framed her and reflected on the faces in the crowd. People looked wonderingly at the changes made in each other's faces. Then the flames died down and darkness slowly returned as Mignonne came to the final words:

> *There never will be another to me like that wonderful mother*
>   *of mine.*

After a short silence a murmuring ran through the crowd. They had never seen a prettier tableau.

The third act went quickly and happily. Then the play was over and my year at Pin Hook had come to an end. The girl in the play may have been called Zoie. The name sounds like the one I heard floating on the air as I walked home.

56

At last I was on the ladder—some called it the treadmill—of teaching in the winter, studying in the summer, my goals a permanent teaching certificate, a job teaching in a school where I would be happy to stay year after year, and a farm that I could cultivate Saturdays and after school. I was halfway through to a college degree. For the first time I had enough money saved to go to school without working, if I would go to Paris Junior College.

In the weeks I had to wait for summer classes to open I chopped cotton at Pin Hook, and liked it. Like everyone else I went to the fields before sunup and worked till after sundown. All the people who could work were in the fields, and I felt part of them, eating my dinner from a molasses bucket, drinking water from a glass jug, going to the bushes "to see a man about a dog" as everyone else did when the urge came. Each night I went home bone tired; each morning I took pride looking at the strip we had chopped the day before. I looked forward to the time—maybe a year, maybe two—when the cotton I chopped would be my own.

Then I was in summer classes—Spanish and chemistry—and happier than I had ever been in school. I loved Spanish and hated chemistry, but each opened new worlds to me. So did my leisure time. I learned to play tennis and croquet and how to make friends with new kinds of people, among them the Sayers Boyd family. Mr. Boyd was editor of the Paris *News*; Mrs. Boyd owned rent houses. Their son Jimmie, who was in my Spanish class, took me home to dinner with them one night, into a home that seemed to me enormously wealthy, but at the same time a home remarkably friendly. They talked of books and music and the importance of learning to work with the hands. They did not think it strange that I had been out chopping cotton. Jimmie, under Mr. Boyd's direction, had been tarring a roof. Mrs. Boyd did ask if I had set my sights too low in my ambition to be a country schoolteacher. Even that ambition she understood when I told them about the boys and girls I had taught at Pin Hook.

My classes had a number of country schoolteachers studying to get ahead, among them George and Mary Belle Haley. She was the "Miss Molly" who had taught me in the first days of school at Pin Hook and later in the second grade at Linden. Year after year they had taught in winter and gone to school in summer. They had earned their first certificates by examination on perhaps a seventh-grade education, had progressed through high school equivalency, and were now in college. Some time in the future, if they kept on working, they could hope to get baccalaureate degrees at Commerce. Whether they got degrees or not, they knew they had to keep on. Year after year standards for certification were raised.

They had to keep up or give up teaching. Every year new requirements for degrees were added, among them a foreign language.
Good-humoredly they struggled over beginning Spanish when
they were old enough to be the parents of anyone else in class. I
was already a long jump ahead of them, but they did not seem to
mind.

In them I could see myself, but with the advantage of having
been born later in time.

57

When the end of summer school was still a week away a frightened
letter came from my mother. Charles was out of work and had left
Dallas to find a job wherever he could. She was out of money and
had to have help at once. I sent her what I had and went back to
studying early and late. There was no way of knowing when I
would have a chance to go back to school again.

Examinations over, I hitchhiked to Dallas and found my mother
worried over Dewey, from whom she had not heard, worried over
Charles, who was roaming from place to place, worried over
money, and sick of living in town where there was nothing she
could do to help. Things were not much better for Roy. He could
carry a paper route but he was still too young to get a job.

After breakfast the next morning, after I had bought milk and
bread, I lacked a penny of having enough for streetcar fare to town,
to look for work, and my watch was the only thing I owned that
might be turned into money. I walked to Davis Street and tried to
sell it to a filling-station man. He did not need a watch but he was
willing to lend me a penny for car fare.

My next stop was in the pawn-shop area on Elm Street. After
visits to several shops and some angry haggling I pawned the
watch for a dollar and a half. I went out on the street holding the
money in my hand, my hand in my pocket. That was all we had
between us and starvation until I could find a job.

There were only three immediate prospects: Butler Brothers, Sears Roebuck, and Kress. Knowing my chances were not good at the first two, I went along Elm Street to the Kress store. It was larger than the Paris store, but the counters were so much the same that I felt as if I were back on my old job. I was on my way to the back of the store, looking for the manager, when I heard someone calling me.

It was Miss Merz, coming toward me from another aisle, calling "Owens, Owens, wait."

She came toward me with both hands outstretched. She took my hand in both of hers and looked up at me, her cheeks flushed, her eyes full of welcome.

"Owens, I'm so glad to see you. What're doing in Dallas?"

I was too embarrassed to tell her that I needed a job.

"Nothing much. Just got here. I've been going to summer school."

Suddenly she was businesslike.

"Could you work for us some? We could sure use you. We're moving to a new store and everything is running behind time. You doing anything?"

I had to admit that I had come in hoping for a job.

"Good," she said. "I'll take you to Mr. Gingerich and tell him to put you on. You remember Mr. Brown? The district manager? He's here in the store today. I'll tell him you're here. He always did want you to be a learner." She held my arm and guided me along an aisle. "All of us hated it when you decided to quit."

Within fifteen minutes Mr. Gingerich had hired me at three dollars a day and Mr. Brown had talked to me about the Paris store. In another fifteen minutes I was at work in the stockroom, checking in shipments of new merchandise and getting them ready for the new store, grateful for the chance to keep us off the streets.

That night Mr. Gingerich paid me in cash and gave me another dollar for supper money. He was a stern man, a hard-driving man, not at all like Mr. Watkins. For him, time and mind belonged to S. H. Kress and Company.

By quitting time, at ten o'clock, I could hardly remember that I had been a teacher at Pin Hook, or that in the middle of October

I would open school at Forest Hill. All that mattered was getting the new store open on time.

58

When I knew that I could not leave my mother in Dallas I rented an apartment for her and Roy in Paris. She was as eager as ever to move back to Pin Hook but willing to stay in Paris, at least till Roy could finish high school. It would be his fourth year and fourth high school, but I could see no other way. Even that was more than the rest of us had had.

On a Saturday night after work I rode a truck loaded with our belongings to Paris and got them set up in an apartment. On a Sunday afternoon I took the bus from Paris to Petty and from there, carrying my suitcase, I started walking to Forest Hill and the Halliburton home, where I was to board. It was a warm, dry afternoon and the black earth was like concrete in the automobile tracks. Walking was easy and I took my time, glad to be in the country again, glad to be going back to teaching. There was a sense of being at home. I passed cotton fields with rows of bare stalks. Most of the picking was done, just in time for the children to start school.

When I had walked about a mile out of the four a car came on the road behind me. The driver, a young boy, pulled up beside me and leaned out.

"Want a ride?"

"I sure do."

I put my suitcase on the back seat and got in beside him. His face was friendly, his eyes curious.

"Where you going?"

"Mr. Halliburton's."

He turned to me with a puzzled smile.

"You the new teacher?"

"I am."

"I never thought a teacher would be walking."

I knew what he meant. Teachers did not make much money but more than most of the people in the community, enough to afford a car of some kind. He was Morty Laird and he would be in my room at school the next morning. He did not know what to make of a teacher who had to come walking in.

He went out of his way to take me to the Halliburton house, a house with a front porch and two rooms and a hall across the front. It looked deserted and lonesome. Morty let me out at the paling gate and drove on. I put my hand on the gate and called hello. Mrs. Halliburton came to the door.

"It's Mr. Owens, Will," she called back into the house, and to me she said, "Come on in."

She met me at the steps, a woman as old as my mother, or older, a woman with a kind face and a touch of humor in her gray-blue eyes. He came and stood beside her, a man strong of mouth and chin, not a man to be tangled with, a man awkward in starched white shirt and dark Sunday suit. They both shook hands and I knew they were glad to see me.

"Take his suitcase, Will. I'll go light a light."

I followed him through a dark hall and into the west room. She came in with a coal-oil lamp and set it on the table. I glanced quickly at the bed and chairs.

"Don't expect too much," he said. "We're just country folks here."

The room looked comfortable and I felt at home in it. There were nails in the corner where I could hang my clothes and I could put the suitcase under the bed.

"Tonight's prayer meeting," Mrs. Halliburton said. "You want to go with us?"

It was a way to get acquainted with the people and I was glad to go.

"We'll go toreckly after supper," she continued. "Supper's on the table, waiting. I just left it cold."

We ate at the kitchen table in the dim light of a coal-oil lamp, with him at the end of the table, her to his left, me to his right. The wood stove at one end of the room was cold, the firebox dark. The safe, the tin doors punched in designs, was a dark shadow against a dark wall. The furniture, like the people, was plain, well worn.

"I want me a zinc in that corner," she said. She laughed without bitterness. "I been wanting it a long time."

After supper, he got the model-T out of the barn and drove us slowly over dirt roads to a white-frame church to the south of the school. People were already gathering and there were coal-oil lights inside.

"We'll go on in," Mrs. Halliburton said. "You come in when you feel like it. They'll get the singing started soon."

A group of boys stood at one side, talking. Morty came over to me and the others followed. There were no introductions but I knew they were my pupils and they knew I was the teacher. Morty struck a match and held it so they could see my face. I could see theirs, young, earnest, reddened by the light. The match went out. I could hear their voices and their names: Arthur, Ray, Floyd, Harlan. Some would be in school the next day, some in the cotton patch.

The singing—singing school songs—started and we went inside. I did not know the songs and the book someone passed me did not help. It was easier to sit at one side and wonder about the people and what parts of their lives would touch mine.

The tunes were lively; their voices were not. Not enough could sing harmony to fill in the parts. Many did not sing at all. The prayers, made up at the moment, were long and solemn. Then it was over and we were on our way home.

Alone in my room, I took the lamp and held it close to a framed newspaper clipping on the wall. It was a poem to Myrtle Halliburton, who had died young of smallpox. She would have been their daughter, I thought, and wondered how her death had helped mold them. The poem was the only printed thing in the room.

59

We were up before daylight. Breakfast was by lamplight. When the sun was just beginning to show I took my lunch in a sack and cut across pastures and woods to the schoolhouse. Again I was my own janitor and had to be there before the pupils. The floors were clean and freshly-oiled, the blackboards washed in all three rooms. The rooms needed only airing and they were ready for school to start.

The book closet had to be opened and books laid out for all the grades. While I was still working with the books Miss Mildred Hinshaw, the intermediate teacher and Miss Ruby Brecheen, the primary teacher, came in. Miss Mildred had a tinge of red in her hair and a straightforward manner. Miss Ruby was quiet and shy. They were about my age but both more experienced in teaching. They let me know that I was the principal but not their boss. Discipline they would leave to me but I was not to interfere in their rooms.

Boys and girls came in their new fall clothes. The older ones gathered in the sun on the south side of the building. Younger ones chased each other around the yard in a game of tag.

At eight o'clock I rang the bell and the pupils formed three lines for marching in. Mine came quietly and took their desks by grades —seventh, eighth, ninth—with a row left over for the tenth, though at the time there were no pupils in the tenth. Then I began to learn the names I would live with for seven months: Arthur and Ruby Lee Halliburton, Mildred McClure, Vada Hightower, Ray and Harlan White, Floyd Tucker, Jennie Linn and Josie Phine Staton, and a dozen more. Their names I soon knew, and some of their dispositions: the eager, the sullen, the shy, the silent.

Rolls had to be made out, books distributed and covered with brown paper covers. Seventh- and eighth-grade books were for the most part the ones I had used at Pin Hook. In the ninth they were new: second-year algebra, modern European history, physical geography, Spanish. A language was expected for them and the Spanish I had learned that summer was the best I could do.

By the noon recess I was overwhelmed at the amount of studying and teaching expected of me, and reminded again of my own poor preparation. I would do the best I could, just as thousands of teachers like me were doing the best they could in schools like Forest Hall all over Texas.

For me it became a day of exploring, to find their outer boundaries, their upper limits. Geographically, their boundaries reached to Honey Grove—for a few to Paris. Their intellectual limits seemed no broader. Few had books in their homes. Most of them looked forward to getting through the ninth grade at Forest Hill, if they could go that far, and settling down for life in Forest Hill.

With the Halliburtons, to enter their home was to enter their lives. That night after supper they sat in cane-bottomed chairs on the front porch. I sat on the floor, in a rectangle of moonlight, and leaned against the wall. It was a time for getting acquainted. They had taken me into their home and made me one of their family. Now they wanted to search me out, to let me talk and to talk themselves.

We talked first about school. I named the boys and girls in my room; they named others who should be in school but were not, in spite of the compulsory school law. Some were troublemakers and I was better off if they never darkened the schoolhouse door. Some were too no account to go to school.

I told them about Pin Hook and why I had come to Forest Hill, and why I was glad I had come. I was starting out all on my own. No one knew anything about my past. All day long everyone had called me mister.

Gradually I learned about them. He had lived out his life on this same place and had never traveled far from it. She had married him when she was a young girl and had lived there ever since. In ways they were alike; in tastes they were different. She liked to go; he was content to stay where he was. At times she would burst into laughter; there were long stretches when he sat in pipe-smoking silence.

Both were lonesome. They had taken me in because they were lonesome and needed somebody to talk to or to join them in a game of dominoes. They had no radio and no way of reaching outside Forest Hill except for an occasional trip to Petty or Honey Grove. There had been four children, two boys and two girls. One daughter was dead, I knew. So was one son, they told me. In a way, they seemed to be asking me to take the place of the lost son.

Quietly but insistently, as if no other way would do, they laid on me the privilege and the burden of being one of the family.

My first Saturday in Forest Hill I was in the cotton patch with a cotton sack, pulling bolls. It was back-breaking work but I did not mind. Many of the boys and girls in my room were also in the fields, picking or pulling. I wanted them to know that I was willing to do the kinds of work they did and to share in the lives they lived.

Another reason was there: impending hard times. Prices were down for cotton and corn and cattle on the hoof. Money was tight. Banks were foreclosing or threatening to foreclose. Farmers who borrowed at planting time and paid back at gathering worried that there would be no money to borrow. Money panic, they began to say. It could be another money panic. Things were bad in the fall. They would be worse after Christmas.

60

On the night after Christmas I was back at Forest Hill, a week earlier than I had to be, to go to a play-party with the boys and girls in my room. The party was at a house about three miles from the Hilliburtons', on the black land toward Honey Grove. The road too muddy for a car, all of us had to walk.

I started soon after dark through damp woods, walking in mud that clung lightly to my shoes. By the time I passed the schoolhouse I could hear someone up the road blowing on his fists. There were answers from boys and girls coming across fields. I answered and walked faster. Soon the sounds of talking and laughing were clear on the night air and I came up to half a dozen boys and girls already gathered.

There was some pairing off but most of us walked in a group, and there was low, quiet excitement in their voices. On the black waxy, mud balled on my heels and soles. No matter how often I stopped and scraped, mud piled up till I could feel it heavy around my ankles.

Half an hour of walking and we came to a small house close to the road. There was a lamp in the front room and a lantern in the shed room—the two rooms in the house. On the porch the girls took off boots and put on Sunday shoes; the boys swept mud from their shoes with a broom. Then we went inside, some straight to the water bucket and tin dipper on the kitchen table.

The man and woman giving the party were in their early twenties, not much older than the boys and girls in my room.

"Come in if you c'n git in," the young man said. "We took down the bed to give us more room." The only furniture left was a dresser with a lamp on it. Chairs and benches had been moved to the kitchen. "You git tired a-standing, you c'n set on your fist and lean back on your thumb."

It was an old joke that still brought laughter.

There was a time of quiet talking, of boys and girls pairing off. Then there was talk of the games they would play. Suddenly one of the boys in my room at school called out, "Get your partners and clear the floor."

They cleared the floor by standing with their backs to the walls, two deep.

"The Girl I Left Behind Me," the leader called. "Get your partners. Let's go."

It was a play-party game, an old-fashioned ring game. I found myself in a circle with one of my pupils a partner to my right, but I did not know the game.

"You'll catch on," the leader said. "Just follow everybody else."

He danced out into the ring, singing:

241

First young gent across the hall
And swing her by the right hand;

He danced across and swung the girl opposite around once.

Swing your partner by the left

He swung his partner around once. So did the other boys.

And promenade the girl behind you.

The girl to my left reached out her hands and caught mine, and guided me in a promenade around the ring, with all of us singing:

> *Oh, that girl that pretty little girl,*
> *The girl I left behind me*
> *With rosy cheeks and yellow curls*
> *The girl I left behind me.*

I now had a new partner and it was my turn to be "first young gent." There was some awkwardness and a great deal of laughter as I danced across the ring to swing my "opposite lady" and then back to my partner. They were teaching the teacher. A part of the lesson seemed to be: sing loud and move fast. By the time the game was over, by the time each young gent had had his turn, I knew the game, and felt that I knew the boys and girls in my class better than I had ever known them at school.

It was lively and beautiful and innocent, even to a Southern Baptist who looked on dancing as a sin. The difference was that they had no fiddle, only the music of their fresh young voices. In their thinking and mine, though the game we had gone through was the same as a square-dance set, it was not dancing. A church member would not be called before the church for joining in play-party games.

Next they were choosing partners for "Going to Boston." There was no chance for me to wait one out. I was their teacher and they wanted me to take part. With a girl in the eighth grade as my partner, I joined in singing:

> *Come on, boys, let's go to Boston,*
> *Come on, boys, let's go to Boston,*

Come on, boys, let's go to Boston
To see this couple marry.

We formed two lines, the boys facing the girls. The head couple, the girl from the eighth grade, the boy from the ninth, promenaded down the back between the lines while we sang:

Ha-ha, Arthur, I'll tell your papa,
Ha-ha, Arthur, I'll tell your papa,
Ha-ha, Arthur, I'll tell your papa
That you're going to marry.

It was Arthur Halliburton, with a flush in his face, a laugh on his lips, a tenderness in his hand for the girl at his side. He left her at the head of the line and led the boys around the girls. Then it was Jennie Linn's turn to promenade with him, as we sang:

Ha-ha, Jennie Linn, I'll tell your mama . . .

She let us know by the pride in her step, the flash in her eye, that she cared only for Arthur. She led the line of girls around the boys and, when she came back to Arthur, they grasped hands and he guided her to the foot of the line, where they stood hand in hand while we sang:

Now they're married and living in Boston,
Now they're married and living in Boston,
Now they're married and living in Boston,
Living on chicken pie.

They had paired off. They were glad for the others to see that they had paired off.

When my turn came they stumbled over my name and then sang, "Ha-ha, *Mister* Owens, I'll tell your mama . . .." No matter how they tried, they could not squeeze or stretch my name to fit the rhythm.

Someone called for "Buffalo Girls" and there was quick choosing of partners. Boys and girls along the wall joined in the singing and stomped to the rhythm:

Buffalo girls, won't you come out tonight?
Won't you come out tonight?

Won't you come out tonight?
Buffalo girls, won't you come out tonight
And dance by the light of the moon?

It was a fast game with a dos-à-dos and a grand right and left. The floor swayed and buckled a little at the center but they kept right on. They rhythm became faster, the stomping harder. There was laughter above the singing:

Oh, I danced with a girl with a hole in her stocking,
And her toe kept a rocking and her heel kept a knocking:
Oh, I danced with a girl with a hole in her stocking,
The prettiest girl in the room.

At one side the floor separated from the wall, and a crack opened to the earth underneath. Still they danced to the end, and then fell on each other with arms on shoulders and eyes squeezed with the tears of laughter. They had almost danced the house down.

By eleven o'clock the party was over and couples began pairing off for the walk home. Walking with one of my students was forbidden, and there was only one other girl. Shyly I asked her; shyly she accepted. We walked together, with a group around us, couples stretched along the road ahead of us, couples trailing behind, and now and then a voice or a whistle on the tune of "Buffalo Girls."

From the school house on walking alone, I was glad they had made me a part of their singing and dancing.

Every night through New Year's there was a party, but not all were play-parties. Some of the homes did not have enough room; some of the women did not want their floor tracked up with mud.

Then we were back in school and the weather was too wet and cold for anyone to stay outside for anything longer than a quick trip to the privy. Some of the boys and girls came to me during the noon recess. They wanted to play "The Girl I Left Behind Me" in the hall. I could see no harm that could be done, or any objection, unless it came from the county superintendant or county supervisor. They were not likely to come. Roads were too muddy. Soon there was the sound of singing and of heavy-shod feet on the hall floor. Before books took up, I was joining in the games, but not the other teachers.

There were new words, new tunes for me to learn, new country humor for me to laugh at. There was "acting out" for the boys in "Old Dan Tucker":

> *Old Dan Tucker's back in town*
> *Swinging the ladies all around;*
> *First to the right and then to the left,*
> *And then to the girl that he loves best.*
> *Get out of the way for Old Dan Tucker;*
> *He's too late to get his supper;*
> *Supper's over and dinner's cooking*
> *Left Old Dan standing looking*
> *Old Dan Tucker, big and fat,*
> *Washed his face in my straw hat,*
> *Dried his face on a wagon wheel,*
> *Died with a toothache in his heel.*
> *Old Dan Tucker's mother-in-law*
> *Was the ugliest thing I ever saw;*
> *Her eyes stuck out and her nose stuck in,*
> *Her upper lip hung over her chin.*

The game started with a boy alone in a ring, waiting for a chance to steal a partner while the others marched around him singing. His part was to dance and clown up to the words "Get out of the way . . ." In the quick exchange of partners he had to grab one if he was faster than the other boys, or if some girl wanted it known that she liked him.

They could laugh over and over again at one of the stanzas in "Weevilly Wheat":

> *Take her by the lily-white hand*
> *And lead her like a pigeon;*
> *Make her dance to "Weevilly Wheat"*
> *And scatter her religion.*

And at the refrain of this remembrance of Bonnie Prince Charlie:

> *Charlie's here and Charlie's there,*
> *And Charlie's over the ocean;*

Charlie won't come home again
Until he takes a notion.

They did not know who Charlie was, nor were they interested in how far back in time the song reached.

They liked the words of these songs and the tunes. During books, I at times heard in a breathy whisper:

Green coffee grows on white-oak trees;
The rivers flow with brandy-o;
Go choose you one to roam with you,
As sweet as striped candy-o.

For almost a month we were caught up in these songs and games and I felt very close to the boys and girls. Then at the end of January the weather was good and we were outside playing basketball.

When the roads were dry enough for cars to pass we got ready for the supervisory visits. We washed blackboards and kept windows open the required number of inches top and bottom. With a hoe I scraped mud from the floors and cleaned them with a new coat of oil. We warned the boys and girls that they might have to recite for a stranger.

The county superintendent never came. Miss Mattie Epperson did. In the middle of the morning she stopped her car off the road and came across the school ground, looking young and pretty, a woman from town who had chosen to work in the country. For me it was a visit from a friend. My supervisor in practice teaching, she knew as well as anyone the problems of the country school. She was as firm as anyone in the belief that country schools all over the county had to be made more alike and better, and more like town schools, if Texas boys and girls were to be better educated. Two hours later, after talks to the teachers about changes to come, after hearing a few recitations, she went on toward Tigertown and we were glad she had come.

61

School rules—rules set by the teachers—were broken almost daily. At times a word with a boy or girl was enough. At times I looked the other way. Overcontrol could be as bad as no control. Then I knew that a trustees' rule was being broken. Some of the boys were smoking at school. There was a lingering smell of tobacco in the privy and cigarette ash on the dirt floor. When I could no longer ignore the signs, I went to the trustees for advice.

"Find out who it is and whup'm," they said.

"What if it's a trustee's boy?"

"It don't make no difference. You've got to treat'em all alike."

Catching them was not easy. They went to the privy during books. At recess they stayed away. Gradually I narrowed the suspects to two: Ray White, the son of a trustee, and Floyd Tucker. I told them I had found tobacco crumbs in the privy and asked them who was smoking, They claimed not to know.

One afternoon when I was keeping pupils after school for extra work I suddenly realized that Ray and Floyd had not left the schoolground with the others. Telling the pupils to remain in their seats, I went as fast as I could to the privy. There was no door, only a board blind. I went past the blind and there they were, one with a lighted cigarette, the other licking one he had just rolled. They saw me and a look of fright came into their faces. They had no escape.

"You smoking?" I demanded.

"Yes, sir."

"You know it's against the rules?"

"Yes, sir."

"What's the punishment for smoking at school?"

"A whupping?"

"Yes. You expect me to whip you?"

"I reckon."

I could not whip them right then. I had no switches and the nearest woods were too far for me to go at once. I still was not certain about the whipping. Ray's father was a trustee and I felt I had to talk to him.

"Go home and tell your parents what I caught you doing," I told them. "It won't hurt you to think about it tonight."

Sheepishly they said "Yessir" and went their separate ways.

I finished with the others, dismissed them, swept the floors, and went to see Mr. White. It was dusk but he was still working at the barn.

"Ray tell you?"

"He told me you caught him and Floyd smoking."

"He admits it?"

"Nothing else for him to do. You caught him."

"What do you think I should do?"

"Whup'em. They broke the rules. Ain't nothing to do but whup-'em. If you let them get away with this, they'll take advantage of you agin. They'll lead the others to take advantage."

"On the legs or in the palm of the hand?"

"It don't make no difference to us where you whup'em. Just go ahead. We'll back you up."

It was dark when I went home through the woods— too dark to look for switches but not too dark for me to worry about what I had to do the next day. I could whip them all right, but what after that? For me and for them. What would be our way together? I had teamed up with them both in basketball games and danced shoulder to shoulder with them at play-parties. Would they keep on liking me as well or would they turn sullen and look for ways to revenge?

At supper I told the Halliburtons what had happened and what I had to do. They were sympathetic with me but they knew I had to give the punishment. They did agree with me on one thing: whipping never corrected anything. Next year, I told myself, I would convince the trustees to abolish corporal punishment.

On my way to school I saw switches on peach trees in the orchard and on elm trees in the woods but I did not cut any.

Without switches, I could put off the whippings another day, unless I sent Ray and Floyd to cut their own.

On the schoolground a group of boys had surrounded Ray and Floyd and I could hear teasing laughter. I could also feel a change in them toward me. For the first time since I had come to Forest Hill I was the enemy. I wanted to call Ray and Floyd in, talk to them, and put them on their good behavior, but I knew the trustees would not agree.

As the day moved from recess to recess I could feel the pupils watching me and knew they were taking sides—some for whipping, some not. Before the last recess bell a boy stopped me.

"You gonna whup'em ?" he asked.

"I caught them smoking."

That was not an answer and he knew it. I worried through the last class period, knowing the punishment had to be that day, or be of no effect at all.

I rang the bell for them to rise for dismissal.

"Ray, Floyd," I said, "stay in your seats."

The others eyed them with sidewise glances as they marched out. When I had dismissed them from line I watched them grouping by the roads they traveled home. Then I went back to face the two boys who had only friendliness in their eyes.

"I've got to whip you," I said.

"We ain't a-blaming you none. You caught us."

I took a wood ruler from my desk and went to Ray.

"Put out your right hand, palm up."

He put out his hand and I felt worse than ever. It was a hand that had held mine in friendship, that had passed me food at his father's table, that had milked a cow early to give us warm milk for supper. But I could not turn back. I supported his hand with mine.

"Ready?"

"Yessir."

I gave a hard whack across the fleshy palm and watched the red rise under the skin. He said nothing—only looked at me as if he could not understand what I was doing. Unnerved by his look, I went through the ten licks as fast as I could.

"Sit down."

He sat down and stared at his hand.

"Come on, Floyd."

Floyd stood up and giggled as he put out his hand. That made the whipping easier for me, but not much. I gave him ten licks without pausing.

"Sit down."

They sat and I stood in front of them.

"You going to try it again?"

They looked at each other and then at me.

"Not on the schoolground."

"If you do, it'll be worse next time. Understand?"

"Yessir."

I dismissed them and they went on their ways, one west, the other south, each with time, if he wanted, for a smoke before coming in sight of his home.

With them out of the way, I had to go to my next job: emptying the pails in the girls' privy. I could see myself as they, looking back, could see me, a lone figure bent over with the weight of two buckets moving slowly into a field where I had dug a hole. It was a job I hated, but less than I hated whipping.

62

The letter from my mother was short and sad. Roy had quit school and joined the army. With only a few weeks till graduation he had thrown it all away for fifteen dollars a month in pay, his keep, and whatever satisfactions army life could offer him. It was a blow to me. I had great hopes for him. He had a good mind and a strong body. With help he could go far, and I was willing to help him. It was a worse blow for my mother. She was at last all alone—fifty years old and all alone.

Friday afternoon I went home for a gloomy weekend, to hear my mother repeat the story again and again. He had made up his mind and there was no stopping him. He was eighteen and did not have to have her consent. All she knew was that he had gone to San Antonio and she had no address for him. She cried more than I had ever known her to cry before. Something, she thought, she had not done for him but she did not know what. Neither did I. Nor in what way I had failed him. Three years would have to pass before he could begin again. Three wasted years, as I saw them, no matter how much he saw in them the freedom of being on his own.

My mother fretted about her uselessness and the waste of keeping an apartment in town just for her. As long as he was in school she was willing to adjust to almost anything—anything that would keep him in school. Now he was gone and with him that way of life.

She talked to me about her mother and her grandmother. At fifty, her mother plowed fields and raised crops. So did her grandmother. So did other women in her family. They did not have to spend their lives shut up in three rooms.

"I could keep house for you," she said. "You wouldn't have to rent the apartment and pay board at the same time. I could do something to help."

It was too late in the school year for an immediate change, but plans did begin to take shape in my mind. I could stay in the apartment and go to college in the summer. By fall, I could have a place for both of us in the country. She seemed satisfied, and in the middle of the afternoon, went to sleep sitting in a chair.

When I asked her about sleeping so much she said, "I get so worn out worrying that I just have to sleep."

Back at Forest Hill I heard of a farm for sale, a small farm with a small house on the road toward Honey Grove. I would have to take out a mortgage to buy it and then go into debt for a team and tools. I would have to work before and after school and on Saturdays to make it pay, but I was willing to try. More than any other place I had been, Forest Hill seemed right for me, as a teacher, as a part of a community.

63

On a Monday morning the trustees were waiting for me on the schoolground. I knew they had been to Paris on Saturday to see the county superintendent, but I did not expect what they had to tell me.

"We've got to cut the school short," one of them said.

"How much?"

"A month. We sure hate it."

A month for them. For me, a hundred and fifty dollars.

"How come?"

"We've run out of money. People're behind paying taxes, and it don't look like they're going to be able to pay any more this year. Prices are down and everything."

The effect of the stock-market crash was beginning to be felt in Forest Hill. Cotton was down. Corn was down. Butter and eggs brought next to nothing.

"How about pay for the teachers?"

"You'll have to get paid a month short. We've done the best we can."

They showed some sympathy for us, but not much. They were having their own money troubles, and at least one had not been able to pay his taxes. It was spring of the year and they had nothing left to sell. Quietly they went to their plowing, leaving me to tell the other teachers and the pupils. They were glad that a trustee election was coming up. Somebody else could take on the burden.

Miss Mildred and Miss Ruby took the news quietly. Country schools had been cut short before and people had got along. They would have less money but they could get back to their homes early. Quietly they went to their rooms to tell their pupils and to begin readjusting work plans.

Some of the boys in my room were glad to get out early. They had had more than enough of school for one year. Most of the others were unhappy. With school out, they would become regular hands in the fields. They would not see each other often and life would be dull.

A few of them worried about the teachers.

"I'll bet you wish you had stayed at Pin Hook," one of the girls said.

I tried to reassure them. My certificate was good for another year. I could get a summer job and skip summer school. By fall everything would be all right again.

Only one did I tell of my plan to buy the farm. His eyes brightened and he leaned toward me.

"I never thought we might live as neighbors," he said.

"Don't count on it till fall. This leaves me short of money."

Other decisions had to be made that day. There had to be a program at the close of school and time was short. With no time to order a new play, I had to fall back on the one I had used at Pin Hook. It had been good there; it ought to be good at Forest Hill. I went to the other teachers and asked them to assign songs and readings.

After school I emptied the buckets from the girls' privy and shoveled on dirt. At least that job would have to be done only one more time. When I went back to the schoolground a trustee was waiting at the road.

"We always paid the principal extra for that job," he said, "but we ain't got no money left and we ain't gonna have none till taxes comes in next fall." He smiled and there was some craftiness in his eyes. "I talked to the other trustees about it. They said you ain't complained before. It's too late for you to complain now."

It was late when I got back to the house. Mr. Halliburton had come in from the field and they were waiting supper for me.

"They told me about school," Mrs. Halliburton said. "I think it's a shame it had to close early."

Mr. Halliburton was silent for a time. Then he said, "Times is hard."

"We sure will miss you," Mrs. Halliburton said. "We never had anybody so much one of the family."

"I'll come back in the fall, if you want me."

They wanted me.

That settled, we talked of what I would do through the summer. I would take some kind of job, a farm job if I had to, but there were no farm jobs at Forest Hill. I would try in Paris. I might have to go on to Dallas.

In my anxiety I did what I had never done before in school: I lost control of my temper. Night after night boys who had quit school came to play practice. With nothing else to do they sat in the gloom of coal oil light talking together and laughing at muffed lines and awkward actions. At first I asked them to leave and wait for the night of the play. They did not. They stayed in their seats and stared at me sullenly. When practice began again they talked and laughed and let me know they were laughing at me.

They kept their voices low but the disturbance was just as great. At last I turned on them.

"Get out!"

They stared at me till I repeated "Get out!" Then they shuffled out, but they did not leave. From time to time I heard noises outside the windows as we went through an almost useless practice.

They did not come back but they took their revenge. Just before the end of school I decided to have a picnic for the boys and girls in the play as a reward for their work. We met in a pasture at sundown and by dusk had a fire going and weenies roasting. Suddenly there was a blow on the ground and a rock rolled toward us. Then there was a sound of laughter from a fringe of growth at the edge of the pasture. We were being tormented and there was nothing we could do but go on with our picnic.

No matter how hard we tried to have fun, the picnic was spoiled. As darkness came on we could see shadowy figures creeping nearer or running away after a rock fell, not close enough to hurt but close enough to hinder.

"It's them," the boys and girls said.

They did not have to tell me.

Hurriedly we finished our picnic and went on to practice.

64

School ended on a Friday and the play came that night. Rehearsals were not going well. There was not enough time for memorizing lines or for individual coaching. Nothing seemed to be going well. The trustees' election had created tension and I was worried about the next year. Contracts had not been signed. The new trustees had not mentioned contracts, even up to the last day of school.

Still the program had to go on. We did not have a stage. The best we could do was to string sheets on a wire across one end of the big room. Players would have to pass through the audience for entrances and exits.

By dark, people were coming in cars or walking along the roads, carrying lanterns, families together, boys and girls walking as couples. It was their one play of the year and they wanted to see it.

When the big room was filled I went to the middle room to check out final details with the cast. I was both actor and prompter, with most of their lines in my head. On my way through the hall a new trustee stopped me.

"We voted not to renew your contract," he said, and there was a deep flush under his dark skin.

"Why?"

"Folks just ain't satisfied."

"With what?"

"You just ask any o' them. They'll tell you they ain't satisfied."

The other two trustees came in, set-jawed, embarrassed.

"I just told him he ain't coming back,' " the first one said.

"That's right. We voted."

I asked about the other teachers.

"One's coming back. One ain't. Everybody's satisfied with the teaching in the little room."

"You could have told me before," I said angrily. "There won't by any jobs open this late."

"We waited till tonight so they wouldn't be no more trouble in school than they had to be."

It was time for the play to start. I left the trustees and went to the middle room, where the boys and girls, in costume, their faces made up with rouge and lipstick, waited, almost huddled in a corner. I told them what had happened, that this was our last time to work together, and begged them to do their very best for themselves and for me. Some looked surprised; some looked as if it was no more than they had expected.

With a taste of wet cotton in my mouth I went through my welcoming speech. After the songs and poems we went through the play as well as we could but there was no heart, no excitement in the performance. I could feel the flush in my face and hear the trembling in my voice. Players stumbled over lines; between acts all I could do was beg them to hold together to the end.

At last it was over and the people went out quietly. They knew what the trustees had done. They knew that taking sides would soon begin.

A few stopped to talk to me, one with his own explanation: "I seen it coming when you whupped Ray and Floyd. People wouldn't a been agin you if you'd a whupped them with a switch where they ought to be whupped. They don't like whupping on the hand. You might a hurt one, whupping him on the hand." Another said I made a mistake not letting the big boys come to play practice. Still another took me aside to whisper: "It ain't none o' your fault. The ones they're talking to to take the job is got kinfolks here."

One of the trustees waited after the people had gone to lock up and take the keys, and to tell me he was not "agin" me. Some things had gone wrong but he was not "agin" me. He'd as lief I was coming back.

Mr. and Mrs. Halliburton were waiting up for me, both in quiet anger at the trustees and at the people who had complained. They knew more than I did. One of the new trustees did not like me because I did not favor singing school music in school.

"What're you gonna do now?" Mr. Halliburton asked.

I had asked myself this question all the way through the woods.

My life as a country schoolteacher was over, I knew. It was too late to get another job, even if I could with the kind of recommendation they would give me. Gone also was my dream of buying a farm. I could not keep it going without money from teaching.

"I don't know."

Honestly I didn't. Nor could see then that the country school was on the way out and with it the country teacher, that roads I had mudded over would soon be graveled or paved, that school buses—chrome yellow against the sky—would end forever the American belief that school should be maintained within walking distance of every child.

65

I left Forest Hill, not on foot as I had come, but in a wagon driven by Mr. Halliburton, who wanted to take me to the highway near Honey Grove. By then it was a relief to go, relief from the friends who had lingered with me, trying to find ways to keep me on; relief from going over in my own mind the mistakes, the failures I had made. It was a sad leave-taking from Mrs. Halliburton.

"They needn't come to me to board another teacher," she said. "I won't take nobody else in my home. It hurts too much to have them go."

On the dirt road the mules crept slowly and we rode in silence. I had looked enough into the past. Now I had to look into the future. I had to find a way to tell my mother that I had lost my job and that our plans for a farm had ended before they began.

When we were coming close to Honey Grove, to a place on the highway where I could flag a ride, I looked at Mr. Halliburton, sitting motionless, grim, pulling hard on a pipe.

"If you were in my place," I asked, "what would you do?"

"Go on to school. You can work some, borrow some, and make it through somehow."

Someday, if I went all the way to the top in school, no trustee would be big enough to fire me. Whatever I did, I should leave the country, the farm at once, if I did not want to starve to death. Times were hard. They would be worse by gathering time.

He left me at the side of the road and went on across the prairie until I could see only the shape of a man, a wagon, a team antlike in motion. Only then could I finally turn my back on Forest Hill, with the knowledge that a part of my life was over. I had worked hard as a country schoolteacher and failed. I knew that at last I was finished with the country. Whatever I came to next had to be in town.

When I told my mother what had happened, she could only sit and cry and wait to be even more alone and of no help to anyone but herself, and very little of that. Three boys gone, and I would have to go. For her sake I tried for a job in Paris, but there was nothing—only talk of hard times and of grown men with families who could not find a job.

With a kind of desperation I said goodbye to my mother and walked out South Main Street, past the vinegar works, the railroad station, the cemetery—to flag a ride to Dallas. After an hour or more in the hot sun I watched a car slow to a stop and heard my name called. It was the George Graves family, who had lived at Pin Hook long ago. They had moved to the blackland and had, they told me, done well. They had a house, a car, a living to show for their work. I had nothing. They were friendly and offered to crowd up a little to give me a ride, but I did not take it. They were only going to their farm in Glory, and for me that was off the main road.